THE COMPLETE
Interior Decorator

THE COMPLETE
Interior Decorator

Mike Lawrence

Macdonald

A **Macdonald** BOOK

Copyright © Quarto Publishing Ltd 1986

First published in Great Britain in 1986
by Macdonald & Co (Publishers) Ltd
London & Sydney
A member of BPCC plc

British Library Cataloguing in Publication Data

Lawrence, Mike, 1947-
   The complete interior decorator.
   1. Interior decoration — Amateurs'
manuals
   I. Title
   643'.7   TH8026

ISBN 0-356-12390-1

This book was designed and produced by
Quarto Publishing Ltd
The Old Brewery, 6 Blundell Street
London N7 9BH

Senior editor: Stephen Paul
Editor: Peter Brooke-Ball
Art editor: Anne Sharples
Designer: Phil Chidlow
Illustrator: David Ashby
Photographer: Rose Jones
Art director: Pete Laws
Editorial director: Jim Miles

Typeset by Dimension Typesetting, London
Manufactured in Hong Kong by
Regent Publishing Services Limited
Printed by Lee Fung Asco Printers Ltd, Hong Kong

Macdonald & Co (Publishers) Ltd
Greater London House
Hampstead Road
London NW1 7QX

CONTENTS

MATERIALS
FOR EVERY SURFACE

Decorating is all about making decisions: get them right to begin with, and the job will be off to a smooth start. Once you've made up your mind to do some decorating, decision number one is what material to use — probably the hardest decision of all, since every other stage of the job will depend on it. Have you ever finished a job and wished you had done it differently? Looked at a painted ceiling or a papered wall, and felt that the other colour would have looked better after all? Picked — and laid — a new floor-covering that really doesn't quite go with the new curtains and upholstery? It happens to the best of us, and the trouble is that nowadays mistakes are expensive to rectify — few of us can afford to tear everything up and start again, even if we had the heart to after all the hard work that has already gone into the job. That's why this chapter is so important. It will help you to realize the advantages and disadvantages of choosing particular decorating products for particular jobs, and enable you to start the redecoration work you plan to carry out with confidence in your judgment.

We all view our homes — and the rooms within them — as a series of individual surfaces when it comes to decorating. What colour will the ceiling be? Will we paint or paper the walls? What about the woodwork? Which floorcovering will look right (and wear the best)? Not only do the results have to be right for each surface: they must all look right together as well. Chapter 2 comes into its own at this point, with simple-to-follow advice on colour scheming; read the two chapters together, and you will find the whole selection process far easier than you ever imagined. But first, let's have a look at some of the individual surfaces mentioned earlier, and see what the home decorator of the 1980s can use to decorate them.

Materials for walls

The way in which you decide to decorate your walls can make or break your colour schemes. They can be the back-cloth against which everything else is displayed, or the dominant feature in the room. For most of us, they are fea-tureless expanses of smooth (or fairly smooth) plaster, so there is virtually no restriction on how they can be treated from the decoration point of view.

Paint is the number 1 bestseller for decorating walls. It's cheap, simple and quick to apply, available in hundreds of colours and is easy to cover up when it's time to change the colour scheme again. The major paint manufacturers have poured money into new technological developments and packaging concepts in recent years — solid emulsion paint, paint in boxes instead of in tins and so on — and have fought tooth and nail for their share of the market by keeping prices astonishingly low. It's small wonder that wallcover-ings have seen such a slump in sales by comparison.

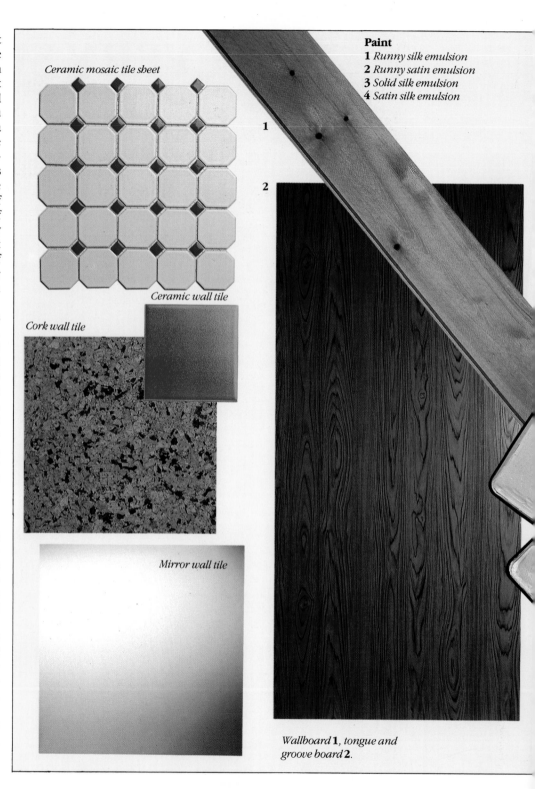

Ceramic mosaic tile sheet

Ceramic wall tile

Cork wall tile

Mirror wall tile

Paint
1 *Runny silk emulsion*
2 *Runny satin emulsion*
3 *Solid silk emulsion*
4 *Satin silk emulsion*

1

2

Wallboard **1**, *tongue and groove board* **2**.

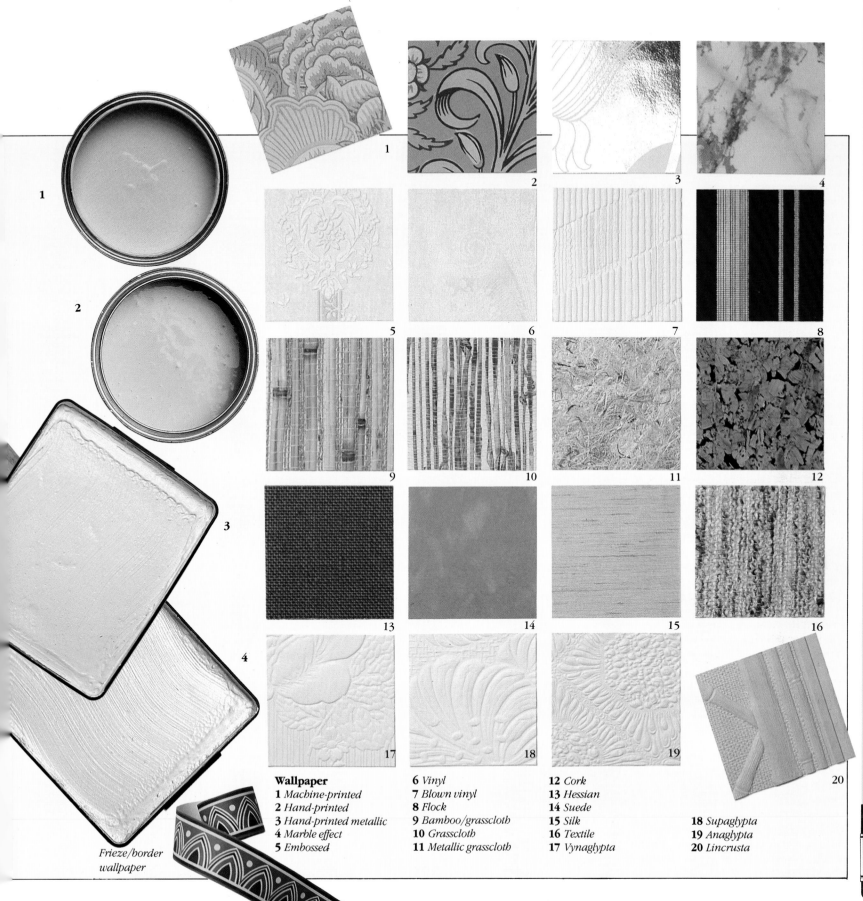

Frieze/border wallpaper

Wallpaper
1 *Machine-printed*
2 *Hand-printed*
3 *Hand-printed metallic*
4 *Marble effect*
5 *Embossed*

6 *Vinyl*
7 *Blown vinyl*
8 *Flock*
9 *Bamboo/grasscloth*
10 *Grasscloth*
11 *Metallic grasscloth*

12 *Cork*
13 *Hessian*
14 *Suede*
15 *Silk*
16 *Textile*
17 *Vynaglypta*

18 *Supaglypta*
19 *Anaglypta*
20 *Lincrusta*

Emulsion paint is by far the most widely used type of paint for plastered walls. It has come a long way from the distempers and colour washes used earlier this century, yet retains the most significant feature of those early decorating materials – it's water-based. From the paint chemist's point of view, emulsion is a complex mixture of ingredients that must be very carefully balanced if the paint is to flow and dry successfully. As far as the home decorator is concerned, a water-based paint is easy to apply, to wash out of decorating equipment – and to mop up if it lands up where it shouldn't!.

The most popular – and biggest-selling – type of emulsion paint is the non-drip type. This has been specially formulated so that in the tin it has the consistency of a rather sloppy jelly, yet as soon as it is taken onto the brush and spread on the wall it flows out smoothly just like ordinary non-modified paints. The action of brushing out the paint breaks down the jelly structure, but as soon as brushing ceases the paint regains it again. This property, known as thixotropy, stops the paint from running if it is applied thickly, helps it to smooth out brush marks and also makes it easier to load up the brush without the paint dripping everywhere. Both points are obviously helpful to the home decorator because they mean less mess and better covering power – one thick coat will often do the job where two coats would be needed of an ordinary 'runny' emulsion, so the job time is halved.

There is one other point to remember about non-drip paints: you shouldn't stir them immediately before use, because the 'beating' of the paint also breaks down the jelly structure, leaving it runny rather than non-drip. If you do have to stir emulsion paint of this type, for example to blend in any liquid that has separated out when you first open the tin, leave it for a while afterwards to regain its jelly-like consistency before you start decorating with it.

Ordinary 'runny' emulsions are still available, and are widely used by professional decorators. They are a little cheaper than non-drip paints, and there is no reason why you shouldn't use them if you wish, especially if you're not worried by the increased risk of a few drips.

At the other extreme, 'solid' emulsion is the latest development from the paint manufacturers to catch the headlines. It's not literally solid, of course – more the consistency of tub margarine – and has the same thixotropic properties that non-drip paint exhibits, of becoming runny as soon as it is disturbed. It's sold packaged in a tray rather than in a tin, and is meant to be applied with a paint roller rather than a brush. It's even less prone to drips than a non-drip paint, and the tray in which it comes can be resealed with a clip-on plastic lid if the paint is not finished when the job is. Naturally, it is more expensive than runny or non-drip emulsion, and is available only in white and a restricted range of subdued pastel shades. However, its obvious ease of use makes it an ideal choice for jobs where you cannot afford any mess and you are perhaps not able to clear the room or cover everything in it while you are decorating.

Emulsion paints, with the exception of solid emulsions,

are available in a huge range of colours, although probably three-quarters of sales are taken by brilliant white paint. Every manufacturer offers a range of pre-mixed shades which are detailed on a shade card; in addition, a few manufacturers also offer in-store colour mixing facilities, allowing you to choose a wider range of shades within individual colour groupings and so making it easier to get an exact colour match for, say, wallcoverings or upholstery materials (or existing paintwork).

In the last few years, the trend has been for paint manufacturers to offer a range of off-whites to complement their brilliant whites. These paints have a hint of a second colour – green, orange, pink and so on – that can give a surface a subtle colour sheen less strong than the effect a pale version of the tint itself would give.

The other factor you need to take into account when you are choosing emulsion paint is finish. Early emulsions always dried to a matt finish, but now every manufacturer offers a 'silk' or 'satin' finish as well. Which you choose is largely a matter of personal preference, although it should be borne in mind that matt finishes can show scuff marks quite readily, while a slight sheen can show up any irregularities in the surface more than a matt surface would.

Most manufacturers still sell emulsion paint in metal tins, though several have now gone over to plastic 'cans'. These don't dent or rust, so they are better for long-term storage – you don't get the problem of rusty dried bits falling into the tin when you reopen it. Sizes are wholly metric now – common sizes are 1, $2\frac{1}{2}$ and 5 litres.

A particularly useful innovation of recent years is the introduction of small 'sample' pots of emulsion paint containing enough to decorate a square metre (square yard) or so of wall surface – the perfect way to test out a new colour in your home and see how well it blends with existing items such as curatins, upholstery and carpets. They allow you to try out two or three similar shades without having to go to the expense of buying larger tins, and there is usually the offer of a refund on the price of the sample if you then buy a larger quantity of the same colour.

There is, of course, nothing to stop you from using other types of paint on your walls. Until modern emulsions were developed, many people used gloss and eggshell paints – traditional 'oil' paints – on their walls if they wanted a durable, wipe-clean surface; distemper couldn't be wetted without the colour coming off, and ordinary wallpapers were by no stretch of the imagination washable. You quite often find such a finish in older homes, often concealed underneath subsequent layers of wallpaper. Modern solvent-based paints – gloss or eggshell (often called satin gloss nowadays) – can be applied just like emulsion paints, although a plaster primer (see page 45) must be used if the paint is being applied to bare plaster or plaster that has previously been decorated with emulsion paint. For more details about solvent-based paints, see the section on Materials for woodwork on page 22.

Wallpaper is still number 2 in the charts for decorating walls, and held the number 1 spot until the paint revolution

Emulsion paint is without doubt the most popular decorating material around. It's inexpensive, easy to apply (and to cover up), and comes in an enormous range of colours. White and off-white **far left** are safe choices, setting off any combination of furnishings and accessories. Blue **left** creates a cool atmosphere in keeping with formal room settings. Pink **below left** adds a warmer, more feminine touch, while strong red **below** dominates any room in which it is used. Note the effect of random brush strokes over a paler background colour here — just one of the many special paint effects you can create with emulsion paint.

See page 192 for further information on the Dulux paints used **left** and **below left**.

MATERIALS FOR EVERY SURFACE

of the 1960s and 1970s. The term 'wallpaper' is still used by most people to describe any wallcovering on a roll, although strictly speaking it should be reserved for the basic type – **printed paper.** This has been around for centuries – the earliest known sample has been dated to the early 16th century – and is still made today. When mass-produced, it is generally the cheapest type of decorative wallcovering available, and is made in literally thousands of different patterns, designs and colours with both smooth and embossed surface finishes (hand-printed wallpaper, on the other hand, can be extremely expensive). The obvious drawbacks of printed wallpapers are that they are comparatively fragile (both during hanging and in use) and cannot generally be cleaned easily if they become marked. However, on walls not liable to wear and tear they are the most economical way of bringing pattern to your walls, and they are easy to strip off and replace when it's time to change the colour scheme.

Washable wallpapers are an improvement over ordinary printed papers on two counts: they are tougher, and therefore more resistant to knocks, and you can clean most marks off them comparatively easily. This is because the paper is coated with a thin, transparent plastic film after the pattern has been printed – not thick enough to withstand repeated scrubbing, but capable of being washed down fairly vigorously if needs be. However, they have one serious drawback; once hung, they are not easy to strip by the conventional soak-and-scrape method because the washable surface coating keeps water away from the paste very effectively. However, they cost little more than ordinary printed papers and so are an economical way of decorating areas that are subject to moderate wear, splashes and condensation.

Vinyl wallcoverings are a cut above washable wallpapers in both durability and convenience terms. The wallcovering design is actually printed on a layer of vinyl rather than on paper; this vinyl layer is then bonded to a paper backing to allow it to be hung using conventional paper-hanging techniques. The surface is therefore much tougher than that on a washable wallpaper, so you can actually scrub the surface quite vigorously without damaging it. Furthermore, the twin-layer construction means that when you want to strip a vinyl for redecoration, you can actually peel the vinyl layer off in one piece, leaving the paper backing on the wall ready to be removed by the usual soak-and-scrape method. Vinyls are more expensive than washable wallcoverings, but are available in all sorts of embossed and textured finishes as well as smooth ones – many are an extremely realistic imitation of far more expensive wallcoverings made from natural materials such as cork and grasscloth. The thicker 'blown' types, so called because the vinyl layer is expanded in thickness by the inclusion of tiny air bubbles, also offer a roll wallcovering that very successfully mimics ceramic tiling at far less expense and with the added advantage of being warmer to the touch – a distinct advantage in rooms prone to condensation.

Foil wallcoverings are a combination of the washable and vinyl types, consisting of a layer of metallized plastic backed with paper and protected by a clear 'wear' layer. The metallic surface is usually overprinted with designs of various sorts, giving a reflective effect that can be quite dramatic when used in moderation, especially in otherwise dark areas. However, you shouldn't hang them on walls that receive direct sunlight, since the resulting glare could be rather unpleasant to live with.

Coordinated wallcoverings and fabrics **left** are a popular way of creating a unified colour scheme. Foil wallcoverings **far left** combine pattern with a reflective surface that can help bring more light to small, dark rooms. Plain fabrics **below left** bring a touch of luxury, and suit the scale of this hallway perfectly. Patterned papers **below** can be cleverly matched to existing features such as carpets and even stained glass.

Novamura is a unique wallcovering material which, unlike all the other types mentioned so far, contains no paper. It's a printed sheet of foamed polythene, which is extremely light and warm to the touch, and comes in a wide range of traditional and modern designs and colours. It's hung by pasting the wall and brushing the wallcovering into place, so there's need for pasting tables, and the surface is completely washable once the paste has dried. Its one drawback is that it is rather fragile, and will tear easily if knocked or scraped. For this reason it is best avoided in areas of heavy wear – kids' bedrooms, for example, or staircases.

Flock wallcoverings are made by bonding very short lengths of fibre to carefully outlined parts of the surface of the wallcovering, which is first printed with a ground colour and sometimes a pattern. The result is a luxurious looking wallcovering that is ideal for less-than-perfect walls and which gives a feeling of warmth to any room in which it is hung. Traditional floral-style patterns are still widely available; some manufacturers also offer more modern geometric patterns. Originally, flocks were made with natural fibres such as silk on a paper backing, and these are fairly fragile in use; however, modern vinyl flocks have synthetic fibres bonded into a vinyl backing, and are as durable and scrubbable as any vinyl wallcovering.

It's worth remembering that any wallcovering with a surface that is impervious to water should be hung with a wallpaper paste containing a fungicide. This is because the paste takes longer than usual to dry out behind wallcoverings of this type, so mould could develop behind the material, discolouring it and spoiling its appearance.

All the wallcovering types discussed so far are widely available in ready-pasted form as well as in ordinary unpasted versions. Ready-pasted papers avoid the need for pasting tables, buckets and paste brushes; you simply immerse the cut length in a tray of cold water positioned at the foot of the wall, leave it to soak for the recommended time and then draw it up out of the tray and on to the wall.

Not all wallcoverings are 'decorative' in their own right; they have to be painted over once they have been hung. This group, known generally as **relief wallcoverings** and referred to in the trade as 'whites', includes embossed papers such as Anaglypta and Supaglypta and also woodchip wallpaper. Anaglypta comes in a wide range of embossed patterns and is made from wood pulp; Supaglypta is more expensive, made from cotton fibres that allow it to be given a deeper and more pronounced embossing. Woodchip paper is made by mixing small wood chips in with the pulp from which it is made – the resulting paper has the texture of thinly-spread oatmeal, and once painted gives walls a pleasing overall texture. All three types are good at disguising lumps and bumps in the wall surface, and once hung can be readily overpainted if a change of colour scheme is required (although once painted they are much more difficult to remove completely – the same drawback as washable wallpapers – since water cannot easily penetrate the painted surface). Woodchip is the

*Decorating fabric can be used on walls **above** for a warm, sumptuous effect; here split bamboo is used to conceal the edges and to complement the style of the furnishings. Coarse grasscloth **left** provides a dramatic backdrop for pictures and furniture alike, and can effectively conceal wall surfaces in poor condition too. Cork tiles **opposite** provide a warm (and sound-absorbing) wall surface that's especially popular in bathrooms.*

cheapest type, costing less than the cheapest printed wall-paper; Anaglypta can cost two or three times as much; Supaglypta is roughly twice the price of Anaglypta. For all three, you have to remember to add the cost of the paint needed to decorate them once they have been hung; they will need at least two coats.

Vynaglypta is a plain white paper-backed vinyl wallcovering with a heavily embossed surface – similar in relief to an Anaglypta. It can be overpainted if you want another colour, and since it can be dry-stripped like any other vinyl wallcovering it is much easier to remove if you want a change of decor.

Lincrusta is another relief wallcovering, made from fillers mixed with linseed oil and embossed with a range of designs. It too is designed for overpainting. You have to hang it with a special adhesive, and once hung it can be very difficult to remove. However, it is extremely hardwearing – it is said that the walls of many a pre-war house are still held up by the Lincrusta – and it deserves to be more popular nowadays than it actually is.

The third major group of wallcoverings is the **fabric type** - a huge range of rough and smooth, woven and laid fabrics bonded to a paper backing. The group includes materials such as hessian, silk, felt, corduroy and woolstrand, and also speciality products such as grasscloth, suede and thin decorative cork veneers. With the exception of hessian, all are considerably more expensive than most other wall-coverings, but once hung do tend to keep their looks for longer, especially if they have been treated to resist dirt and dust. They can act as quite effective heat and sound insulators, and the coarser fabrics are extremely good at covering up defects in poor wall surfaces. They do require extra care during hanging, since paste will stain the fabric, but since most are hung by pasting the wall it is generally easier to keep the paste off the surface than when hanging paste-the-roll types.

Most wallcoverings, including all the popular machine-made, printed, washable, vinyl and relief types, are sold in standard-sized rolls 10.05m (33ft) long and 530mm (21in) wide, so it's fairly easy to calculate how many rolls you need to cover a given area (see the estimator table on page 102, although the figures given there can only be a rough guide). Some of the 'blown' tile-effect vinyls come in half-length (5m/16ft) rolls because they are comparatively bulky. Speciality wallcoverings, including fabrics and hand-printed types, come in a range of widths and roll lengths; some are sold by the metre or yard. Because of their comparatively high price you should in any case measure up the area to be decorated very carefully, and then check your figures against the material sizes available.

Tiles for walls are number 3 in the wall decoration league table, and are getting more popular every year. They are made in a number of different materials, and offer an attractive and hard-wearing alternative to paint and wall-coverings. They also have the advantage that they are far easier to 'hang' than roll wallcoverings, since the individual tiles are relatively small and manageable – a boon when

you're decorating awkwardly-shaped areas. Set against that is the fact that they are generally comparatively expensive, and also pretty permanent; you can't remove them and decorate with something else very easily – a point worth thinking about when you're considering using them.

Ceramic tiles are the most popular and widely-used type. They come in an enormous range of plain colours and designs, and you can mix tiles of different styles to create your own unique wall patterns. They offer the home decorator a surface that is extremely hard-wearing and easy to keep clean, and for this reason ceramic tiles are used most in bathrooms and kitchens, although there is no reason why they should not be used in other areas of the house as well. Fixing them is very simple, using ready-mixed tile adhesive which you spread straight on the wall; even the once-tricky job of cutting tiles accurately is now far easier with modern tile cutters, and you can finish the job off quickly with a range of ready-mixed (and often coloured) grout. The hardest part is setting the tiles out accurately so that awkward cut pieces are avoided and the rows are laid to a true horizontal (this is particularly important where you are tiling adjacent walls, or tiling all the way round the room). As you might expect, they make an excellent cover-up for less-than-perfect wall surfaces, since any lumps and bumps are taken up by the bed of tile adhesive. However, the surface must be sound or the weight of the tiles may simply pull the loose plaster away from the masonry behind. You shouldn't tile over old wallcoverings, but painted plaster is perfectly satisfactory; you can even tile directly over old ceramic tiles so long as they are fixed securely to the wall.

The commonest sizes for ceramic tiles are 150mm (6in) squares and 200 x 100mm (8 x 4in) rectangles – the smaller 108mm (4in) squares so popular in the 1960s are not as widely available nowadays. Most are sold in packs of 25, so you have to check carefully the precise area a pack will cover when you are working out quantities; for example, a pack of 25 150mm-square tiles will cover just over half a square metre (about 6 sq ft). Most stores will also sell tiles singly, so if you find that your calculations (or a higher-than-foreseen breakage rate!) have left you half-a-dozen tiles short, you won't have to buy a whole new pack to make up the numbers.

These days, most tiles are manufactured without spacer lugs, so spacing them as you fix them calls for some care. They should not be butted tightly together, since any slight movement in the wall surface could result in cracking of the tiles or even in a whole area of tiling bursting off the wall surface. You can either use home-made spacers (the cardboard boxes the tiles come in is ideal if cut into narrow strips) or buy small cross-shaped plastic spacers that can be removed and reused. The other recent change in manufacturing practice involves the tile edges. You used to be able to buy plain tiles (called field tiles) and also tiles with one or two adjacent edges rounded and glazed (they were called RE and REX tiles) so you could finish off tiled areas with a neat, fully-glazed edge. Now most manufacturers make all their tiles with two adjacent edges glazed, and you

position them with glazed edges outermost at the edge of tiled areas. The trouble is that with many cheaper tiles the edge glazing is often imperfect or incomplete, so it pays to examine the tiles carefully if you want a perfect glazed edge on show. Alternatively, you can edge the area with a pre-formed plastic edging trim that is bedded in the tile adhesive before the last row of tiles is fixed.

Mosaics are an alternative to ceramic tiles for wall surfaces, especially for small or awkwardly shaped areas where their small size makes cutting to fit that much easier. They come in a range of interlocking shapes as well as in small squares and rectangles, and are generally sold in sheets on a mesh backing to make installation quicker – you 'hang' the sheet as if it were a flexible tile, then grout the gaps between the individual mosaic pieces. Most mosaics are plain or mottled rather than patterned, so they can look rather dull and bitty if used over large areas.

Cork wall tiles are made by slicing up compressed 'logs' of cork bark into thin squares or rectangles. The colour of the natural material varies from a light honey to a dark brown; it can also be dyed in various colours, and may even have designs printed on the surface for extra effect. As a wallcovering it looks attractive and is an excellent insulator, both of heat and sound – used on cold walls it can cut out condensation; fixed to walls behind TV and hi-fi sets it can soak up high sound levels and make life for your neighbours less unpleasant. A cork wall or smaller tiled area can also do double duty as a pinboard – particularly useful in children's bedrooms, allowing drawings, cuttings and posters to be displayed and changed with ease. You can even use them in 'wet' areas such as kitchens and bathrooms, as long as you seal the surface first with a varnish to stop the cork absorbing water.

The only drawback with cork tiles and panels as a wallcovering is that, since you have to stick them up with a contact adhesive, they're up for good – it's almost impossible to remove them or the adhesive without seriously damaging the wall plaster. For this reason, many people fix them to hardboard or plywood panels first, and then screw these to the wall. The panels can then be removed with ease if you want a change of decor in the future.

Cork tiles are commonly 305mm (12in) square and about 3mm ($\frac{1}{8}$in) thick, although other sizes are available, especially in stained or overprinted panel types. You usually buy them in packs that will cover a particular area, so it's essential to measure up the area you want to cover accurately and to check the pack contents in the store when you buy.

Two other tile types you could consider for small areas are **metallic tiles** and **mirror tiles.** The former are usually made from aluminium and are often embossed or have a pattern printed on them. The surface is protected by a plastic coating, so they can be washed down if necessary, but they do tend to show marks easily. They are also comparatively expensive. Mirror tiles come in plain, tinted and patterned varieties, and are both cheaper and easier to handle than large mirrors. However, you do tend to get a

Ceramic tiles **top right** *are the perfect surface to choose for areas where hygiene and water-resistance are important factors. Plain tiles can be coordinated with patterned ones, while colour can be a subtle outline to each tile or a strong overall effect.*

Mirror tiles **centre right** *help to create an illusion of light and space, and in mosaic form can cope with curved surfaces too. You can mix them quite happily with other tile types.*

Natural timber **below right** *offers a warmth and richness few other wallcoverings can match, and can be given a natural finish or a variety of stains. Panelling can bring a traditional period look to walls and ceilings.*

MATERIALS FOR EVERY SURFACE

'broken' image unless great care is taken with the fixing of each tile, so they are best used as a decorative aid – for example, to show off ornaments or to bring light to a dark corner – rather than for their ability to provide an accurate reflection. Both types are generally square – 100 and 150mm (4 and 6in) squares are the commonest – and they are sold in packs. Fixing is usually by means of small self-adhesive foam pads stuck to the back of the tile.

Rigid sheet materials – usually hardboard or plywood with a decorative facing that simulates effects such as timber cladding or ceramic tiles – are useful products for decorating walls that are in really bad condition, or where you want the visual effect they provide without the expense of buying and fitting the real thing. They're known collectively as wallboards, and come in a wide range of designs and colours. You can either stick them to the wall surface with panel adhesive (but if you use this method, remember that they will be quite hard to remove in the future) or pin them to a framework of timber battens mounted on the wall. Using the latter method means you can incorporate insulation behind the cladding – a useful way of killing two birds with one stone by insulating as well as decorating the wall. Standard sheet sizes are 2440 x 1220m (8 x 4ft), although smaller panels are also generally available.

Natural timber can also be used as a wall cladding. Perhaps the commonest type is tongued-and-grooved softwood ('knotty pine'), which is usually installed by pinning successive lengths to a framework of timber battens on the wall. The surface is then varnished or painted to give a durable and attractive finish. As with wallboards, natural timber cladding is an excellent cover-up for poor walls that would otherwise have to be replastered before they could be decorated.

Textured finishes are generally more widely used on ceilings (see page 93) than on walls, but there is no reason why they should not be used there too, either as whole-wall treatments or for feature panels, alcoves and the like. Most of the products on the market are now sold ready-mixed in tubs: you simply brush them thickly onto the wall and then use tools such as combs or special rollers to create the surface texture you want. White is often the only colour available, although some brands come in a restricted range of pastel shades; they can, however, be overpainted easily if you want a particular colour as well as a textured finish. They are excellent cover-ups for poor-quality wall surfaces, but tend to collect dirt and dust in the surface irregularities and are difficult to clean effectively. They are also difficult to remove if you want to change the decor, although special liquid strippers are now available to make the job a little easier (page 58).

Friezes and borders come into the category of wallcoverings, but have been left until the end of this section because they are not wallcoverings in their own right, merely decorative additions to a painted or wallpapered wall. Friezes are hung at picture-rail level or just below the ceiling, while borders are used to form decorative panels on the wall surface.

*Friezes and borders are perfect for defining breaks between wall areas such as dado and picture rails **above**, where the two areas are given different decorative treatments. They can also be used with an otherwise plain colour scheme to accentuate features such a a dormer window opening **left**.*

Materials for ceilings

When it comes to decorating ceilings, many people treat them as a rather unimportant fifth wall of the room – and a horizontal one at that! However, the way you treat your ceilings can have a major effect on the success of your overall colour scheme, and there is no reason why they should be treated as the poor relations when you are redecorating. There is certainly little restriction on your choice of decorative treatments.

Paint and **wallcoverings** of the types used on walls can also be used to good effect on your ceilings. Since the ceiling surface is usually of plaster or plasterboard, you treat it exactly as if it were a wall, brushing on the paint of your choice or hanging whatever wallcovering you have selected. The actual techniques you use may differ slightly from those used to decorate walls – see Chapters 4 and 5 – but the principle remains exactly the same.

Of the other materials mentioned earlier for use on walls, the only ones you are likely to consider using on ceilings are fabrics, wallboards and natural timber. Again, only the fixing techniques differ; the actual materials are used in very much the same way.

There are also a number of materials on the market specifically for use on ceilings, and you may wish to consider using these as an alternative to the 'wall' decorations already mentioned.

Ceiling tiles are the most obvious contender in this area, and several types are available. The commonest (and cheapest) is the plastic tile – a square of expanded polystyrene with a white plain or patterned surface which is stuck to the existing ceiling with a special adhesive. The tiles are usually 300 or 450mm (12 or 18in) square and between 3 and 6mm ($\frac{1}{8}$ to $\frac{1}{4}$in) thick – not thick enough to provide any worthwhile thermal insulation in a cold room, but certainly helpful in reducing the incidence of condensation. A wide range of regular and random patterns is available and since the tiles are so light and easy to cut the job of fixing them in place is very straightforward. They are a quick and relatively inexpensive way of redecorating a ceiling, especially if its condition is too poor for paint or a wallcovering to give satisfactory results, but two points have to be kept in mind if you are thinking of using these tiles. The first is that once they're up, they are very difficult to remove if you decide you want a change of finish at any time in the future. The second is that they are inflammable, and can cause a very rapid spread of flame across the ceiling if they catch fire. For this reason they should never be used in a kitchen – the most likely site in the house for a fire to start. In addition, they should never be decorated with solvent-based paint; only emulsion should be used if you want to give such a ceiling a coloured finish. The tiles are usually sold in packs – either in tens or containing enough tiles to cover a certain area. The special ready-mixed adhesive is sold in tubs; the instructions will tell you what area the contents will cover, so you can work out how many tubs you will need to buy for your ceiling.

Fibre tiles are made from compressed mineral or wood

2

1

1 Cornices
2 Ceiling rose
3 Prismatic ceiling lenses
4 Fibre acoustic/insulating tile
5 Fabric-covered acoustic tile
6 Needlepoint acoustic tile
7 Mineral fibre acoustic tile
8 Louvred lighting tile
9 Mineral fibre acoustic tile
10 Mineral fibre acoustic tile
11 Polystyrene tile
12 Cork Tile
13 Ceiling rose

fibres. Not only are they less flammable than the plastic types (the mineral fibre ones are completely non-combustible, while the wood fibre types are usually treated with a fire-retardant chemical); they also have much better thermal and sound insulation properties, and are often referred to as acoustic tiles for this reason. Common sizes for both types are 305 and 610mm (12 and 24in) square, although some manufacturers offer larger squares and even rectangles in their ranges; thicknesses are a standard 12 or 18mm ($\frac{1}{2}$ or $\frac{3}{4}$in). The tile surface may be smooth, textured or perforated – the last two types offer the best sound insulation properties – and the edges are usually tongued and grooved so that they interlock as they are put up. You can stick the tiles to the ceiling surface with a contact or panel adhesive, but this method has the same drawback as polystyrene tiles: changing the ceiling finish in the future can be difficult. An alternative fixing method is to staple them through their tongues to a network of slim battens fixed to the ceiling surface – the fixing in each tongue is concealed by the groove of the next tile placed. Some tiles of this type are designed to be installed as a suspended ceiling system on a network of supporting channels –see page 142. They are all usually sold with a white finish which can be decorated with emulsion paint if another colour is preferred.

Other less common materials used for ceiling tiles include vermiculite (the same mineral is used as a loose-fill loft insulation and an additive for insulating concrete), glass fibre, reinforced gypsum (like small plasterboard panels) and metal. Most are fitted as suspended ceilings, and are generally available only from specialist contractors.

You can, of course, use wall tiles of various types as ceiling decorations, although cork and lightweight metal ones are the only realistic candidates – you could hardly stick ceramic tiles to a ceiling and expect them to stay put. If you want the effect of ceramic tiles on a ceiling, you would do better to use either a wallboard or a blown vinyl wallcovering with a tile-effect finish. Similarly, if you want a mirrored ceiling, mirror tiles are not really a safe proposition; mirrors fixed directly to the ceiling joists would be the best bet.

Illuminated ceilings are a variation on the tiled ceiling theme. The tiles are made from translucent plastic (usually PVC) in white and a range of colours, either plain or with a variety of surface textures and embossed patterns, and are suspended from a lightweight metal grid that is fixed across the room some distance below the existing ceiling. Fluorescent light fittings above the suspended ceiling illuminate it, providing a soft overall light that can be effective in rooms such as kitchens and bathrooms. Some ranges include opaque tiles, so you can arrange for only part of the ceiling surface to be illuminated by, for example, fitting opaque ones round the perimeter of the room. You usually buy ceilings of this sort as a complete kit, by specifying to the supplier the room dimensions and the tile type you want; installation involves cutting and fitting the grid components and dropping either whole or cut tiles into the gaps to complete the ceiling.

Cornices and **coving** are decorative 'trims' used to finish off the angle between walls and ceilings. Strictly speaking, coving is a quadrant-shaped moulding only; the term cornice is used for the wide range of intricately detailed mouldings often used in this situation. Until recent years, cornices were usually formed in situ by skilled plasterers using moulds and special plaster. Nowadays they are prefabricated and are fixed in position either during building (in new homes) or as a decorative addition otherwise. Plain coving is either made in the same way as plasterboard, with a shaped paper sheath enclosing a plaster core, or else from expanded polystyrene. The first comes in depths of 100 and 150mm (4 and 6in), usually in 2m (6ft 6in) lengths, and is stuck in place with a plaster-based adhesive that is spread along the back of each section. Internal and external angles are cut as required before installation, and the surface is decorated with emulsion or solvent-based paint as desired, just like a plasterboard wall or ceiling surface. The polystyrene type is also made in several depths, and is stuck in place with special adhesive – the same type as is used for fixing polystyrene ceiling tiles. Corners can be formed by cutting the coving with a fine-toothed saw, but the foamed plastic is difficult to cut cleanly and better results can be obtained by using pre-formed internal and external mitres. If painting is required, only emulsion paints should be used.

Decorative cornices are made from rigid plastic foam, glass fibre or reinforced plasterwork, in a huge range of sizes and profiles, many of them authentic copies of traditional cornice styles. The first two mentioned are very light in weight, and so are easy to cut and fit using appropriate adhesives. The plaster types, by contrast, are very heavy, and will need some additional means of support to hold them in position. All are usually sold in standard lengths of around 2m (6ft 6in), and corners are formed as required by cutting mitres at the end of the piece. You can decorate them after installation using emulsion or gloss paint, but care must be taken to avoid filling in the detail of the moulding.

Apart from decorative cornices, ceilings in many older homes were finished off with a variety of plaster decorations – ceiling centres, panel mouldings and ornaments, scrolls and so on. Modern reproductions of these are available in both plaster and rigid plastic foams, and are designed to be stuck in place with the appropriate type of adhesive. They are generally white, but can be coloured by painting them with emulsion paint.

Materials for woodwork

The inside of your home may well contain a surprisingly large amount of exposed woodwork — doors and door frames, windows and window frames, skirtings, architraves, staircases, possibly even areas of wood panelling on walls and ceilings. You could leave them all bare, but almost everyone prefers to decorate them in some way, so they become part of an overall decorating scheme, and also to make them resistant to dirt and surface damage and easy to keep clean. For this there are several options

Paint is by far the most popular choice for decorating

*Wallcoverings can be used on both walls and ceilings **top left, top centre**; the effect can be dramatic if natural breaks such a door frames are used to outline the decorated surfaces.*

*Stencils **top right, centre left** allow rooms to be given an individual touch that can be subdued or dramatic, and can help to disguise a wealth of awkward details into the bargain.*

*Suspended ceilings **centre, centre right** can help correct the proportions in rooms with high ceilings, and allow concealed lighting to be installed. The effect can be warm and intimate or light and airy, depending on the materials and colours chosen.*

*Ceiling features can be made a part of any decorative scheme: beams can be painted a different colour to the rest of the ceiling; natural timber can be stained to match the furniture; and original coving **bottom right** can be given an 'antique' look by clever use of colour washes.*

woodwork, for exactly the same reasons that make it everyone's favourite wall decoration - it's cheap, easy to apply, available in hundreds of colours and provides both excellent protection for the wood and a surface that's hard-wearing, easy to keep clean and easy to redecorate when you want a change of colour scheme. It will also cover up a multitude of sins — patches of wood that have been filled, for example, or unsightly knots.

While you *can* use emulsion paints on woodwork, it's more usual to use solvent-based types. These paints are a complex mixture of ingredients — a pigment to give them their colour, a binder to form the paint film itself, a solvent to allow the paint to be brushed out, a catalyst or hardener to help convert the paint from liquid to solid form and other additives to improve performance in the tin and on the wood. The binder in modern solvent-based paint is a synthetic resin (you may see names like alkyd and polyurethane on the tin), but before the development of petrochemicals the binder was usually a drying oil such as linseed oil — hence the old-fashioned name 'oil paint'. The solvent, commonly white spirit, evaporates as the paint dries, and it is this in particular that gives solvent-based paints their special smell. The paint may dry to give a high gloss finish, one that has a definite sheen (often called satin or silk finish) or an almost matt one called eggshell.

As with emulsion paint, solvent-based paints are available in non-drip (thixotropic) or ordinary 'runny' forms; the former has the same time- and labour-saving advantages of better covering power and less messy application, but does cost a little more than the latter. There is, as yet, no solvent-based equivalent of the new 'solid' emulsions, but no doubt paint chemists are at work on this development.

The range of colours available is, if anything, even greater than for emulsions; it includes both standard 'off-the-shelf' colours and those mixed by in-store tinting machines. Most manufacturers coordinate colours, so you can expect to be able to buy the same shade by the same name in both emulsion and gloss paint — useful for colour-coordinated decorating schemes.

Solvent-based paints are usually still sold in the traditional tin, although plastic containers that don't rust and are easier to reseal are now becoming more widely available. Sizes are wholly metric; you can expect to find 500ml tins in most ranges in addition to the standard 1 and 2½ litre sizes, and some manufacturers make even smaller sizes that are extremely useful for decorating small areas in a particular colour. You can also buy aerosol cans of gloss paint — useful for painting awkward objects like wicker chairs where using a brush would be extremely tricky — but they are expensive when compared with an ordinary tin.

Varnish is just paint without any pigment, and so offers the same level of protection to the wood surface while allowing the colour and grain pattern of the wood to show through the surface film. In fact, it actually improves the appearance of the wood by strengthening any natural colour it may have and enhancing the contrast between the lighter and darker areas of the surface. However, because it

is transparent, the wood beneath a varnish must be reasonably attractive — defects such as patches of white filler or blowlamp scorch marks from previous paint stripping activities tend to look pretty unsightly.

Most modern varnishes are based on synthetic resins — polyurethane is the most common — but you can still buy varnishes based on oil binders such as copal. The oil types tend to give a deeper, richer finish than the modern resin versions, but the latter are harder-wearing and more resistant to scratching. You can have high gloss, satin gloss or matt finishes, as with solvent-based paint; it's generally best to avoid a high gloss finish on less-than-perfect surfaces, since the gloss will highlight the imperfections.

Varnish is available in tins and bottles, in quantities from as little as 250ml up to 2½ and 5 litre containers for large jobs. There is no equivalent type to non-drip paint, but it is possible to obtain gloss varnish in an aerosol dispenser — again ideal for decorating surfaces that are difficult to coat by other means.

If you want to keep the wood grain visible but would like to colour it — either to a different wood colour or to a bright primary colour such as red or blue — you have two choices. You can either stain the wood first to the colour you want and then finish it off with clear varnish, or you can use a tinted varnish.

Wood stains are concentrated pigments dispersed either in water or in a solvent such as white spirit. They are available in a wide range of colours, and you can dilute them (with the appropriate thinner) or intermix them (only with others of the same type) to produce exactly the shade you want. However, it is worth remembering that changing the colour at any time in the future will be a lot harder than if you were simply repainting the surface, so it's important to make the right choice first time around. It *is*

Paint for woodwork **top right** *can have a satin or a high gloss finish, although the former is kinder to less-than-perfect surfaces and brushwork. Wood stains and varnish* **centre right** *bring out the natural sheen and grain pattern of timber features such as ceilings and fireplaces. You can add the finishing touches with techniques such as stencilling* **below right** *or create your own work of art* **below.**

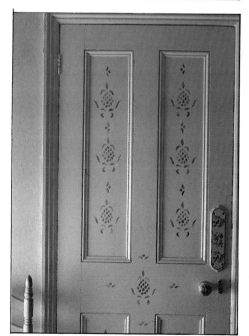

possible to bleach out an old stain once its protective varnish has been stripped, but results can be hard to predict. The spirit-based types penetrate more quickly and more deeply than the water-based types, and dry more quickly. The water-based types have a tendency to raise the grain of the wood, so careful light sanding is needed after the stain has been applied to leave a smooth surface, ready for varnishing. Both are sold in small jars or tins, usually containing around 125ml (about a quarter of a pint); a little goes a long way. Larger tins are also available if required.

Varnish stains speed up the decorating job by combining the staining and varnishing stages into one operation. As with ordinary wood stains, a range of wood shades and bright colours is available, but you cannot achieve the same depth of colour as you can get with the separate stains, even if you apply several coats. However, there is the advantage that you can change the colour of the wood simply by stripping off the varnish layer, since the colour has not actually penetrated the wood grain. Most varnish stains are the polyurethane type, and are generally available only in a gloss finish. If you want a satin or matt finish, you should use the appropriate type of clear varnish for the last coat.

Stencils and **transfers** can both be used to apply motifs to wood surfaces (and, for that matter, to walls and ceilings). A stencil is a piece of stiff card with parts cut away to form a simple design motif that can be used on its own or repeatedly to build up a complete pattern. It is taped in position on the surface to be decorated, and then paint is stippled on to the surface through the cut-away parts of the stencil. This is then lifted and repositioned to allow the next pattern repeat to be painted. The effect can be applied to painted or varnished wood using ordinary solvent-based paints. Transfers are thin self-adhesive films printed with designs of all sorts, mounted on a backing paper from which they can be removed by soaking or peeling. They are mainly used for decorating surfaces in children's rooms, and can be removed from the surface when they are no longer wanted.

Plastic laminates are familiar in the kitchen, where they are used to provide a hard-wearing and attractive decorative surface for worktops and cupboards. They are made by bonding together layers of resin-impregnated paper (the top layer bears the pattern or design), into a thin, hard board which can then be stuck to timber surfaces with a contact adhesive. They are very durable and easy to keep clean, and so can be considered for all sorts of surfaces elsewhere in the house — doors, windowsills, splashbacks and so on — where the extra expense compared with other decorative finishes can be justified. There is a huge range of colours and designs available, including many wood and stone effects and abstract patterns, and also a growing range of textured finishes resembling materials such as linen, slate and leather. Various standard sheet sizes are available, the commonest ones being 2440 x 1220mm (8 x 4ft) and fractions of this standard sheet — halves and quarters measuring 1220mm (4ft) square and 1220 x 610mm (4 x 2ft) respectively.

Materials for floors

Floor surfaces can be a decorative feature in their own right if the material from which they are constructed is attractive. Timber boards, many natural stones and even composite finishes such as terrazzo and granolithic concrete are examples. For most of us, however, floors are just another surface in the home to be covered up in some way with a decorative finish which is both attractive and hard-wearing. That's where floorcoverings come in.

Making the right choice of floorcovering is more important than selecting materials to decorate your walls, ceilings or woodwork. There are two reasons for this: your floors have to put up with a great deal more wear than the other surfaces mentioned; they also cost a lot more per unit area to decorate in the first place. It's therefore important to ask yourself some specific questions about what you expect your floorcoverings to do for you before you make that final choice.

Durability is one of the most important factors. Obviously, different areas of your home will have to put up with different degrees of wear, and you will want to tailor your choice of floorcovering to reflect this. Living rooms and stairs are likely to get the heaviest wear, so a really durable floorcovering should be chosen here, while bedrooms and other comparatively seldom-used areas will be well served by something less hard-wearing (or expensive). Generally speaking, hard floorcoverings wear better than soft ones, but that's not the whole story; floorcoverings in particular areas of the house will have to put up with individual 'attacks'. For example, a kitchen floor will have to cope with spillages of oil, fat and other foodstuffs, while a hall will be trampled by muddy feet and a bathroom treated to copious splashing – especially if there are young children in the family.

This raises the question of surface texture too. Smooth surfaces are generally easier to clean than textured ones such as carpet, but you have to set against that the need for a floorcovering that feels warm underfoot, especially in rooms such as bedrooms, bathrooms, nurseries and playrooms.

Next, think about noise, and whether the floorcovering you choose should help to muffle it – again, probably more important in a household with children. Hard floorcoverings not only absorb less noise than soft ones, they can actually help to amplify noisy footfalls.

There are two other points to consider when you are choosing a new floorcovering. First, is home safety important? If so, you should avoid smooth, potentially slippery floorcoverings, especially in areas such as kitchens, bathrooms and hallways, and most importantly of all, on stairs. Remember that loose rugs can be a hazard too. Secondly, should the new floorcovering be continuous – wall-to-wall carpet or sheet vinyl, for example – or can it be laid in sections such as tiles? Most people prefer the former, but the latter can be easier to handle in small or irregularly-shaped rooms.

Now let's have a look at some of the individual floor-

1 *Parquet panels*
2 *Cork tile*
3 *Vinyl tile*
4 *Sheet vinyl*
5 *Ceramic tile*
6 *Carpet samples*
7 *Wilton (tufted) carpet*
8 *Carpet tiles*
9 *Axminster (bonded) carpet*

covering types in more detail.

Carpet probably covers a greater floor area in most homes than any other floorcovering. The reason why it is so popular has a great deal to do with the feeling of warmth and luxury that it generates; it can also be surprisingly hard-wearing provided that the correct type is chosen for the area concerned. It therefore helps to know a little about how carpets are made.

Traditional carpets are woven by one of two methods, Axminster and Wilton (these terms are not brand names, though they are commonly thought of as such). The backing is woven at the same time as the pile itself. The main difference between the two is that Axminsters are usually patterned, while Wiltons are usually plain (although tonal effects and simple patterns are also available). Modern carpet technology has also produced tufted and bonded carpets. Tufted carpets are made by bonding the pile tufts into a fabric backing using synthetic latex or a similar material to anchor the tufts in place. Bonded carpets are made by stitching the pile through two layers or woven backing which are then sliced apart to make two separate carpets. Both types are often backed with a latex foam underlay, bonded to the carpet backing itself.

The pile can be left as individual tufts or loops, sometimes woven tightly to the backing (as in cords), twisted or left long (as in shag pile carpets). It can also be cut – to one height, or to several different heights to create a sculptured surface effect.

Several different fibres are used to make carpets, either singly or in well-tried combinations. One of the most popular is a mixture of 20 per cent nylon and 80 per cent wool; the nylon adds extra wear resistance, while the wool offers excellent warmth and resilience to soiling. Acrylic fibres have similar wear characteristics, and also resemble wool in softness and warmth. Nylon fibres are usually used as mixtures, as are the cheaper rayons. Polypropylene is also used to improve wear resistance in wool and acrylic mixtures; it's rather harsh when used on its own.

The vast majority of carpets are made in what is called 'broadloom' widths – again, not a brand name, just a description of the carpet width, which is at least 1.8m (6ft) wide. Narrower widths are called 'body' widths; they are usually around 900mm (3ft) wide, and are intended for use on stairs and in corridors, although they can also be seamed together to cover larger areas. Most broadloom carpet is nowadays made in metric 4 and 5m (13ft and 16½ft) widths, allowing all but the largest rooms to be carpeted without seams.

Carpets are classified according to the amount of wear they are designed to withstand. The actual classification usually grades the carpets using terms such as light, medium and heavy domestic, and light/medium/heavy contract; the latter group is intended to withstand heavier use than the former. For example, a light domestic grade carpet will soon wear out on a staircase, while a heavy domestic (or its equivalent medium contract) grade would be wasted on a bedroom floor.

Obviously, most people choose their carpets in a colour or pattern to suit the colour scheme they have or want to achieve. It's essential when shopping for a new carpet to keep in mind the other points mentioned – weave, backing, pile type, fibre content and wear classification. You can then be sure of getting a carpet that precisely suits your home's requirements.

Carpet tiles are exactly what their name implies: small squares of carpet laid edge to edge to give the appearance of a continuous floorcovering. They have the obvious advantage of ease of laying and ease of maintenance – a dirty or damaged tile can be readily lifted for cleaning or replacement. Various types are available in woven and tufted varieties, and also in several hardwearing (and rather course) cord and fibre types – the sort often found in offices. The more expensive types are often foam-backed. Sizes range from 225mm (9in) up to 500 or 600mm (20 or 24in); some are sold singly, others in packs to cover a particular area (for example, eight 500mm squares to cover 2sq m). Their main disadvantage is that they can creep or ruck up under mobile furniture such as armchairs.

Sheet vinyl floorcoverings have almost completely replaced linoleum as the first choice floorcovering in rooms where a smooth, hygienic and easy-to-clean surface is required – for example, in bathrooms, kitchens and hallways. They are made in several different types. The cheapest have a clear vinyl wear layer over the pattern, while more expensive types may be coloured right through. The surface layer is often embossed to simulate effects such as ceramic floor tiles, cork or natural timber. Cushioned types have a foam layer sandwiched between the patterned/coloured surface layers and the backing, and are warmer to the touch and more resilient to walk on than the 'solid' types. The main advantage that sheet vinyl has over old-fashioned linoleum is that it is more flexible, so it's easier to cut and fit, and it comes in an enormous range of patterns and colours. It's sold by the metre or yard from rolls up to 4m (13ft) wide, so in many cases it is possible to floor a room without any seams – an obvious advantage in bathrooms, for example.

Sheet rubber is a relative of the sheet vinyl family; it started life as a commercial floorcovering, but has become popular in the domestic sector too because of its striking looks and excellent wear characteristics. It comes in plain colours, but the surface is usually ribbed or embossed in some way to provide an interesting and virtually non-slip floor surface. Roll widths are the same as those for sheet vinyl.

Vinyl floor tiles are made from pvc resins, with fillers and pigments added. They are thinner and more rigid than sheet vinyl floorcoverings, and so feel colder (and sound noisier) underfoot, and can even be prone to condensation in cold, damp rooms. Some types have printed patterns; others have plain colours or marbled effects that continue right through the thickness of the tile. In both types the surface may be smooth, textured or embossed; some of the more expensive types are excellent imitations of luxury

Plain carpets **top** *look equally at home with modern or traditional furnishings, and provide the background setting for all sorts of decorative details. Shag pile* **centre left** *has an unmistakeably luxurious feel about it, while a patterned carpet* **centre** *can be the centrepiece of the room — and can move house easily when you do if it's not fitted. Sailcloth* **centre right** *is an unusual floorcovering, but it can produce a dramatic effect. Rush matting* **below left.** *and coarse cord carpet* **below centre, below right** *are economical and hard-wearing cover-ups for bathrooms, stairs and even bedrooms.*

floor surfaces such as terrazzo and marble. The commonest tile sizes are 225 and 300mm (9 and 12in) squares, although more expensive types are also sold in rectangles too. The tiles are designed to be stuck down to the sub-floor, and many are self-adhesive to make this operation easier to carry out. They are usually sold in packs containing enough tiles to cover 1sq m or 1sq yd, according to the size of the individual tiles. Their big advantage over sheet materials is that they are very easy to lay in awkwardly-shaped areas and around obstacles such as bathroom fittings, since there will be less wastage involved in trimming them to fit than with sheet materials.

Cork floor tiles are made in the same way as their wall tile relatives, by slicing compressed cork bark up into squares and rectangles. The main differences between the two types are that cork floor tiles have a higher density and a greater thickness, in order to provide better wear resistance, and they they have to be sealed before or after laying to protect the surface from spillages and soiling. The cheaper types are given two or three coats of a clear polyurethane floor sealer after they have been laid; more expensive types are pre-coated with a transparent vinyl wear layer, and so do not need any further sealing treatment. As a floorcovering, cork is warm to the touch and also quiet and fairly resilient in use; it offers an ideal compromise between comfort underfoot and easy of cleaning in rooms where the two qualities are essential. Apart from being available in a range of natural shades, it is also possible to obtain tiles with printed patterns overlaid on the natural cork texture – an extremely striking combination. Tile sizes are commonly 225 and 300mm (9 and 12in) square, but rectangles are also made, especially in the pre-coated ranges.

Ceramic floor tiles are also similar to their wall-hung cousins, being available in a huge range of colours, designs and shapes. As with cork tiles, the floor types are thicker – usually 9 or 12mm ($\frac{3}{8}$ or $\frac{1}{2}$in) thick compared with 4 or 6mm (up to $\frac{1}{4}$in) for wall tiles – and they offer a floor surface that is more hardwearing than anything else except natural stone. However, there is a price to pay: ceramic tiled floors are very cold underfoot, and also rather noisy in use. The tiles are bedded in special tile adhesive, and are generally best laid on a solid sub-floor, although they can be laid on a suspended timber floor so long as a layer of waterproof plywood is fixed first to provide a firm bed for the tiles and to guard against movement in the floor cracking the tiles. It's also wise in such a case to check that the floor structure is strong enough to bear the extra weight. Common sizes are 150mm (6in) squares and 200 x 100mm (8 x 4in) rectangles, but interlocking shapes in various styles are also available.

Quarry tiles are unpatterned, unglazed ceramic tiles made in pleasing natural red, brown and buff tones. They are laid in a mortar bed rather than in tile adhesive, and mortar is also used to fill the grout lines. The surface has to be sealed or polished to keep out stains and spills once the tiles have been laid. Tiles 100 and 150mm (4 and 6in)

square are the most common, although larger sizes are also available; all are generally thicker than ceramic floor tiles, and can be difficult to cut.

Mosaics for floors are also thicker than the type used on walls. They are usually supplied bonded to a net backing, or else with a paper overlay that is washed off once the mosaics have been bedded in the tile adhesive. the joints between the mosaic pieces are then grouted as for ceramic tiles. A range of mosaic shapes, colours and surface textures is available, and mosaics have the advantage of being easier than ceramic or quarry tiles to fit in awkward areas. They can, however, look rather bitty and fussy if used for large expanses of floor unless some element of pattern is introduced.

Natural timber floors come in two main types – as floorboards, or as a decorative cover-up for an existing floor surface. Softwood is generally used for boarded floors, although some period houses may boast floors in a hardwood such as oak and there is no reason why hardwoods should not be used if they are available and affordable. Laying new floorboards may be worth considering if the existing floor is badly damaged or decayed, and the opportunity can be taken to treat them so they can be left on show as a feature floorcovering. Decorative cover-ups can take the form of narrow planks of solid timber or veneered plywood, solid blocks, or made-up mosaic or parquet panels consisting of fingers of natural timber glued together, all of which are sanded and sealed ready for laying like floor tiles. Many of the strip types are tongued and grooved, so the fixing nails are concealed as they are fixed in place. Solid blocks and man-made panels are generally laid in a bed of adhesive; the surface may need sanding and finishing once the floor is complete. A range of woods is available in all types, and the resulting floor surface is both good-looking and hard-wearing; it is, however, rather noisy underfoot, and can be slippery if over-polished. Strips are generally about 75mm (3in) wide, and are sold in random lengths. Solid blocks generally measure about 150 x 50mm (6 x 2in), although any other convenient size can of course be cut. Panels are usually either 305 or 455mm (12 or 18in) square.

Paint, varnish and stain can all be used on timber floors, whether they are of natural timber or a man-made board such as chipboard or plywood. Clear finishes are the most popular, used over wood stains if extra depth of colour is required; ordinary wood varnish can be used, or else specially-formulated floor sealers. Paint offers a cheap and cheerful cover-up for a timber floor in poor condition, but does tend to chip in use.

Natural stone is the oldest known floorcovering. It may not be widely used in the home nowadays, but is worth considering in small areas such as an entrance hall, or where the age and character of the building warrants it. The type of stone chosen could range from slate or marble to a local sandstone or limestone; the choice is enormous, but the advice of a local stonemason is worth seeking out before any final decisions are taken.

Sheet vinyl **top left** *comes in a wide range of patterns and effects, and is easy to lay and to maintain. Plain vinyl tiles* **top centre** *are immensely hard-wearing, and can be laid in a wide variety of patterns as an alternative to plain colour. Sealed cork tiles* **top right** *are warm and resilient underfoot, and can be plain or patterned.*

Ceramic tiles **centre** *come in an enormous variety of plain colours and patterns, and provide perhaps the most durable of all floorcoverings; however, they do amplify every noisy footfall.*

Quarry tiles and mosaics **bottom left** *come in a range of natural buffs and reds, but need sealing if they are not to become stained with dirt. Brick* **bottom centre** *and natural stone* **bottom right** *can suit either traditional or modern settings, but can be expensive to lay and are distinctly cold and noisy in use.*

Floorboards in good condition can be stripped and sealed to create a floor that's hardwearing and naturally beautiful **right**. *Wood blocks and strips, either plain or stained, can be laid as a floorcovering in a wide range of individual designs* **far right**. *You can add decorative details with techniques such as stencilling* **below left**, *or simply gloss-paint the entire floor* **below right** *to cover up all the blemishes and create a surface that's cheap and easy to redecorate.*

BASIC
COLOUR SCHEMING

The art of colour scheming has long had the reputation of being something of an arcane mystery – a kind of alchemy somewhere between art and science into which only the chosen few, the interior designers, have been initiated. While a certain amount of flair and talent obviously helps, anyone can come up with a perfectly satisfactory colour scheme. It's simply a matter of following a few basic rules, which you can bend as required to bring your own personality and imagination into play.

Colours are, of course, the building blocks with which you have to work, and as there are so many – just take a quick look at some paint colour charts – it's convenient to divide them up into groups. Every colour is made up of a mixture of red, blue and yellow – the three so-called primary colours. Now imagine them set out as three equal segments of a circle, and imagine what happens when you mix adjacent pairs of colours together – red with blue, blue with yellow, yellow with red – to give the circle three more segments. Red and blue gives violet, blue and yellow makes green, while yellow and red equals orange. These are the three secondary colours. Finally mix all the adjacent colour pairs once again – in other words, each primary colour with its adjacent secondary colour – to produce the six tertiary colours – red/orange, orange/yellow, yellow/green, green/blue, blue/violet and violet/red. Add these to the imaginary circle to give twelve segments and you end up with an elementary 'colour wheel' which is the most fundamental of the interior designer's tools. The colours it contains (or those it would contain if the mixing was continued indefinitely), and their relationships with each other, form the basis on which all colour scheming decisions are made.

As a starting point, you will notice how the colours in the red/orange/yellow half of the wheel seem warmer and stand out more than those on the yellow/green/blue side. This ability of colours to advance or recede is something you can make use of when working out the colour scheme for a room. If you decorate the walls using colours from the advancing, warm side of the wheel, you know you'll make the room feel cosy and welcoming. You will, incidentally, also make it appear slightly smaller than it really is, which may or may not be an advantage. Conversely, using receding colours will make a room seem larger, but their coolness will create a chilly, rather uninviting atmosphere.

The next thing you will notice about the colour wheel is that, while adjacent pairs on the wheel seem to harmonize with each other, colours on opposite sides – red and green, or orange and blue, for example – provide a sharp contrast with each other. They are called 'complementary' colours. By using harmonious colours, you will produce a balanced, restful effect in which the qualities of advancing warmth or

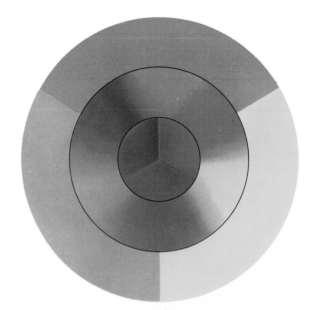

Successful colour scheming is based on choosing colours from the colour wheel **left** *which either harmonize or contrast with each other. In this room* **below**, *a variety of shades of brown have been used on the woodwork and walls to echo the colours in the carpet and furnishings. The overall effect is calm, soothing and unobtrusive.*

See page 192 for further information on the Dulux paints used **below**.

receding coolness are felt to the full, while contrasting colours tend to create something more lively and exciting. The trouble is that neither approach works particularly well if taken to extremes; a room containing nothing but contrasting colours will look fragmented and overpowering, and most people find that once the initial novelty has worn off, the effect of such excessive contrast is actually to jar the nerves rather than to excite the eye. Similarly, a scheme limited to the use of harmonious colours often appears so restful as to seem bland and boring.

For these reasons, the vast majority of successful colour schemes are the result of a carefully thought-out balancing act in which contrast and harmony are combined in just the right proportions to give the required degree of excitement or tranquility. This is where your own taste and personality can really make themselves felt. However, you do need to keep the purpose of individual rooms in mind. For example, in rooms where you spend comparatively little time – halls, bathrooms and so on – you can generally afford to be a little more adventurous in what you do, while in the living room it is probably better to play safe rather than risk a bold scheme you will very quickly tire of. Similarly, while a lively colour scheme may be just what you decide you need in a kitchen or workroom, most people prefer something quieter and less demanding in the bedroom to help them relax.

In this context there is another point about the various colours on the wheel that you need to take into account. Each one has a definite personality – most people associate certain colours with particular moods and emotions. Reds, for example, are usually regarded as hot, intense and vigorous; oranges are warm and vibrant, yet reminiscent of the soothing effect of an open fire. Either can therefore be used to create an atmosphere of intimacy or excitement, depending on the context. Yellows, not surprisingly, remind people of summer sunshine, making them an excellent choice for cold gloomily-lit areas that need cheering up, while greens tend to suggest the cool serenity of nature (perfect for rooms set aside for relaxation, and also for workrooms such as kitchens where their calming influence can stop you from boiling over when the dinner does!). Blues also have a cool and tranquil quality and are particularly good if you want to bring an airy, spacious feeling into your home – say in a small kitchen or bathroom. They should not be used in north-facing rooms, however, or that coolness soon becomes a distinct chill. Finally, there is the richness of the purples and violets – colours that somehow combine the warmth and excitement of the reds with the dignity of the blues. They are colours so overpowering that they must be used with restraint.

Of course, some reds are 'hotter' than others, just as some blues do not look especially cold. In fact, the degree to which a colour exhibits this sort of trait depends on its intensity – another factor to be taken into account when you are creating a colour scheme. As with contrast and harmony, it is possible to have too much of a good thing. A room in which intense colours have been used throughout

would quickly prove a strain for both your eyes and your nerves; it's far better to use such strong colours sparingly and deliberately to produce a calculated dramatic effect or to highlight a particular feature of the room. The snag is that none of the colours on the basic twelve-sector colour wheel could be described as subdued. The primary colours are particularly intense, and even the secondary and tertiary ones are fairly strong.

The answer to the problem is to choose from the ever more subtle intermediate shades that result from continuing the process of mixing adjacent colour pairs on the wheel. In addition, the intensity of a given colour can be altered simply by adding white to make it appear lighter, black to make it darker, or grey for something in between. The resulting colours are known as tones, and the change

Contrasting colours such as red and green combine to create a room that's much more stimulating to the eye than the complete harmony of the room setting opposite. The carpet contains elements of both colours, and so helps to unify the overall effect.

The effect of contrast can be played down by using softer shades of one of the colours concerned. Here a range of blues and mauves blend happily with strong orange highlights and a weaker biscuit colour on the walls.

See page 192 for further information on the Dulux paints used **above.**

that toning can bring to a colour's personality can be enormous. Red lightened to pink, for example, takes on a comforting warmth ideally suited to bedrooms and nurseries. However, do bear in mind that some tones, notably cream, beige and brown, can look rather lifeless unless they are given a lift by introducing small areas of more positive colour somewhere in the room.

Finally, don't forget the so-called 'neutral' colours – white, grey and black. White can be used to set off other colours, or on its own to give a light, airy atmosphere. Black tends to produce a more dramatic effect, but needs to be used with great care if you are to avoid funereal overtones.

Armed with this basic knowledge of colour theory you can start thinking about your own colour schemes – in other words, how to apply them to the decor of your own home using real paints, wallcoverings and floorcoverings. This raises the next question: what about pattern, and

when should it be used instead of (or as well as) plain colour? The answer depends to some extent on your own personal taste. Some people feel that plain colour is boring, while other find patterns distracting and cluttered. Your opinion may fall somewhere between the two, but the following pointers may assist you in making up your mind.

While it is true that patterns help to add interest to large plain areas of flat colour, not least by providing a relatively easy way of introducing some small amounts of intense contrasting colours into the overall scheme, there are alternatives. You can use texture, light, or a combination of the two to introduce the required contrast. You may be able to break the surface concerned up into smaller sections by using the room's architectural features, and treat each one separately when it comes to choosing colours. You can rely on accessories to break the monotony – pictures on the walls, rugs on the floors and the like. If it is

simply a matter of introducing contrasting, bright colours into the scheme, then bright cushions, ornaments and so on may well do the trick. In any case, remember that over a very large area, repeating patterns are only slightly less boring than plain colour.

As far as choosing patterns is concerned, the style of decor you have chosen must be the over-riding factor; you must simply try to avoid the obvious pitfalls. Patterns have individual charateristics just as colours do, and so need to be treated in a similar way. Avoid over-using any pattern that is very strong – either in colour or design. Be sure to 'lift' quieter designs by introducing stronger colours or motifs somewhere nearby. Try to strike a balance when combining different patterns that contrast or harmonize with each other. The size of the pattern motif is also important; as a rule of thumb, avoid using large motifs in small spaces and small motifs on large areas. Watch out too for

'novelty' designs, particularly in children's rooms. Thomas the Tank Engine may delight your child this month, but may not be so popular next month. Perhaps the answer here is to restrict such patterns to one feature wall that can easily be redecorated when a change has to be made.

Another factor you should take into account when applying basic colour scheming theory to real situations is that the rooms you are working in will probably not be ideal. Most have something visually awkward about them, and such problems can tend to increase when you introduce a style of decoration for which the room was not really designed. An example is in trying to decorate a Victorian room in a modern style. In such circumstances purists would argue that such alterations are doomed to failure from the start, because the visual contradictions are too great to be overcome. In practice, so long as the changes you have in mind aren't too extreme, conversions of this

Attention to detail can round off any colour scheme. Once the basic shades have been allowed to establish themselves, features like lampshades, cushions and pictures can be added to complement or contrast with the overall effect; finishing touches like the stencilling below the cornice complete the job.

*See page 192 for further information on the Dulux paints used **above**.*

sort can be very successful, even without resorting to structural alterations. In fact, whether you are changing styles or simply disguising visual faults the look of a room can often be radically changed using nothing more than a few simple tricks that exploit the effect of colour and pattern.

Take a high ceiling for example. To make it seem lower, all you have to do is paint it in a darker colour. Use a very light colour (or better still, white) to pick out any cornices, mouldings and so on associated with it, and the ceiling will appear lower still – the more noticeable things are, the closer they seem to be to the eye. You can enhance the effect still further if you wish by laying a floorcovering similar in colour and tone to the ceiling. The two dark surfaces will then appear to come together, creating the illusion of a very low ceiling indeed. Installing a picture rail or high-level frieze and then painting the area of wall above it in the same colour as the ceiling is another effective answer to the problem.

Pattern can also be pressed into service here. Choose a wallcovering or curtain fabric pattern with a strongly horizontal bias; this will make walls and windows seem wider and less tall.

All these tricks also work in reverse. For example, to raise the apparent ceiling height you should paint the ceiling in white (or in a light colour) and the walls dark, or else use a wallcovering and curtain fabric pattern with a strong vertical accent – bold stripes are best.

Sloping ceilings, such as those in loft conversions, present more of a problem. The difficulty is in deciding where the wall ends and the ceiling begins. The best advice, especially in small rooms, is to treat everything as wall (including flat areas of ceiling if these are relatively small) and to use the same colour paint or pattern of wallcovering throughout. Obviously a wallcovering must have a reversible pattern, and ideally a random pattern match and a small motif (or none at all) for ease of hanging and matching. If you prefer paint and feel that the overall look may lack interest, you could pick out any features such as beams in another colour, or else run a decorative frieze right round the room just below the sloping section.

This sort of visual trickery can also be used to alter the apparent size of a room, by pushing the walls back to make it seem larger, or drawing them in to make it smaller. As mentioned earlier, advancing and receding colours obviously help here, as do colours of high or low intensity. Advancing and high-intensity colours effectively draw the walls in; receding and low-intensity colours push them out. Pattern, too, can work wonders. Wallcoverings with a strongly horizontal design appear to make walls look wider than they really are, and those with a vertical emphasis make them appear less tall. Similarly, patterns containing large motifs make the walls seem closer to the observer; those with a small print make them recede.

By applying these techniques selectively to individual walls, you can even alter the apparent shape of the room. Decorating one pair of opposite walls to make them advance and the other pair to make them recede will give a

Simplicity is often the secret of successful colour scheming. Where a strong overall colour is chosen, too much clutter can be distracting; strong directional lighting makes the most of dominant features in this hallway **above** *At the other extreme, a restful background colour can be pepped up with splashes of contrasting colour from furniture and houseplants* **left, right**.

Cool blues and greens combined with a white ceiling create a room that's spacious and soothing to be in **above***; they work especially well with modern furnishings. Subdued patterns and colours allow displayed ornaments to hold their own in an alcove display* **above right***.*

square room an oblong appearance. Conversely drawing in or pushing out just one pair of opposite walls will help make a rectangular room appear more square.

Another way in which a deliberate optical illusion can help to improve the appearance of a room is when it comes to disguising unattractive features that you simply cannot remove. Central heating radiators, for example, can be camouflaged quite effectively by painting them the same colour as the walls, and door frames and other architectural features can be similarly subdued. Even something as massive as a chimney breast can be made to look far less noticeable by decorating it to match the alcoves on each side of it.

These same techniques will also prove invaluable where you want to simplify a room containing too much architectural detail. Alternatively, you can take the opposite tack and add interest to an otherwise featureless area – emphasizing features to provide a room with a focal point is particularly effective. Chimney breasts are a natural choice for this; decorate the side alcoves in receding (or contrasting) colours to thow the chimney breast into stark relief, or else treat it with a particularly striking decoration such as natural stone or brick. Alternatively, you might consider

converting a disused fireplace into a recess for ornaments or plants. Even a plain wall can be turned into an eye-catching feature given a little imagination. Try painting it in a really strong colour, or apply an unusual wallcovering; pictures, wall lights and so on can then complete the room's transformation.

There are all sorts of other tricks you can use, many of them far more subtle than the basic examples given here. Some homes pose more complex decorating problems too, often needing individual solutions. Unfortunately, no book can teach you to cope with them all, nor can it hope to encompass every aspect of interior design. Fashions change, and new ideas are born every day. So before you decide on how you are going to decorate your home, take the time to look around you. Pick up as many ideas as you can from other people's homes, from books and magazines, films and television programmes, and see if you can make use of them yourself. Remember that the rules of colour scheming and interior design were not handed down on tablets of stone: they are just guidelines to be referred to when they help. Ultimately, it's the look you and your family like that counts; after all, you are the ones who will have to live with the results!

PAINLESS PREPARATION

Ask anybody what they least like about decorating, and they will almost certainly tell you that it's the preparation. It can certainly be a hard, messy, and boring job, but it is important to do it thoroughly: skimp, and you run the risk of new decorations looking shabby. Thankfully modern materials, techniques and tools simplify the task and, although the traditional craftsman may frown on them they do make the job both quicker and easier.

So, where should you start? To begin with, you need room to work, and traditionally that means clearing the room of everything movable — ornaments, furniture and even carpets. In practice though, it is rarely necessary to go that far. A lot depends on the scale of the redecoration work, the materials you intend to use, and the amount of messy preparation required. Unless you are tackling a floor, you should be able to get away with merely protecting carpets and large items of furniture, in situ, using dustsheets or polythene sheeting (cotton sheets are better because plastic sheeting is slippery underfoot). Stack furniture in the centre of the room so you can work round it most of the time, thus minimizing the need to move it again. Remove wall lights, light shades, and similar minor obstacles, too, if you can; protect exposed electrical wiring with insulation tape (be sure to turn off the electricity supply at the mains before you remove light fittings). Strictly speaking, door and window furniture (knobs, latches and so on) that isn't to be painted should also be taken off at this stage, but for convenience and security you may prefer to leave this until the last minute and replace everything as soon as the paint has dried.

Preparing walls

Perhaps the simplest situation you are likely to face is an existing wall painted with emulsion. Generally all that is needed is to wash the surface down with detergent to remove dirt and grease, and then to fill obvious defects with a proprietary interior filler — sold either ready-mixed or, less expensively, as a powder to which you add water. Most cracks are easy enough to fill. Enlarge them slightly with the corner of a filling knife (this looks like a scraper, but is more flexible), aiming to undercut slightly the surrounding plaster, and press the filler into place, smoothing it off with the filling knife's blade. It's best to leave the filler just proud of the surrounding surface to allow for shrinkage during drying. The excess can be removed when hard using medium and fine grade glasspaper to leave a smooth finish — an orbital sander is a boon here. Incidentally, don't bother with hairline cracks. These will not show through the decorative finish.

Small holes can be treated in exactly the same way, but larger ones need a different approach. Those in solid walls are best tackled in stages to stop the wet filler 'slumping' under its own weight. With large holes (more than 50mm/2in across), use ordinary plaster for the initial filling — it's cheaper than filler when bought in 'handy packs' — but finish off with proprietary filler for a smooth finish. Level off the plaster infill by 'sawing' a timber batten across the surface, keeping it pressed against the adjacent plaster to leave the repair flush with the wall.

As for large holes in stud partition walls, the only satisfactory way to make a repair is to remove the damaged plasterboard, cutting it back until half the width of the adjacent supporting timber studs are exposed. Nail new horizontal timbers between the exposed studs, and use these, together with the studs themselves, to support a piece of new plasterboard cut to fit as a patch. The cracks around the edges can be made good by covering them with plasterboard joint filler and tape, but for a small repair, it is simpler to use just filler, having first chamfered the edges of the old and new boards with a sharp knife or file.

The only cracks and holes that may not respond to any of the above repairs, are those between masonry and woodwork such as door and window frames. Ordinary plaster-type filler simply falls out as the wood expands and contracts. The solution is to use a permanently flexible filler such as acrylic based caulk. Sold ready for use in cartridges, caulk is extruded into the gap, rather like toothpaste, with the aid of a special gun.

Cracks apart, there are just two other common faults you are likely to find in an emulsion painted wall. One is efflorescence — salts that have leached from the plaster. Scrape these off before washing down. The other is where the existing paint has begun to bubble or flake. Scrape off as much loose material as you can, and feather out the sharp edges of the remaining paintwork using wet and dry abrasive paper (used wet). The resulting shallow depressions in the surface can be 'filled' by retouching with two or three coats of emulsion before repainting in earnest. To complete the wall's preparation, if you intend hanging a wall covering, brush on a coat of size, or wallpaper paste diluted according to the manufacturer's instructions.

Gloss painted walls are treated in much the same way as emulsion painted ones; the only big difference being that you must take off the shine to provide a key for new decorations — most stick better to matt surfaces than to glossy ones. Do this by rubbing down with damp wet and dry paper — another job for an orbital sander — before washing the wall. Even so, you can still run into trouble if you don't repaint with gloss or some other resin/oil based paint. Emulsion tends not to adhere very well to non-porous surfaces, especially where there is a lot of moisture about, as in, say, a kitchen or bathroom. Similarly, if you plan to put up a

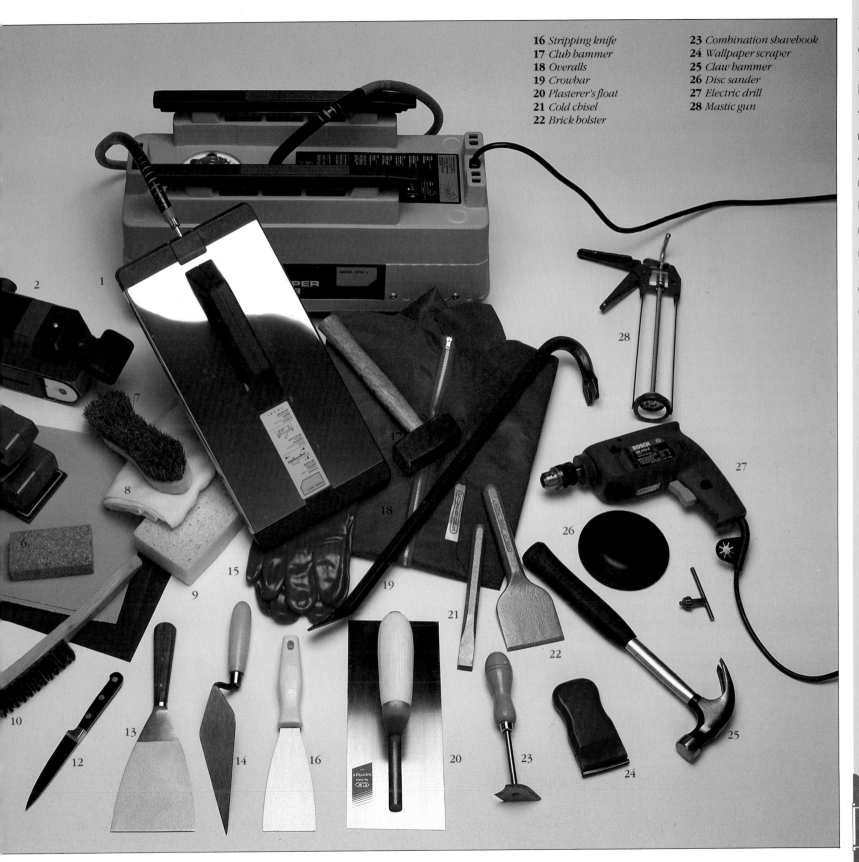

16 *Stripping knife*
17 *Club hammer*
18 *Overalls*
19 *Crowbar*
20 *Plasterer's float*
21 *Cold chisel*
22 *Brick bolster*

23 *Combination shavehook*
24 *Wallpaper scraper*
25 *Claw hammer*
26 *Disc sander*
27 *Electric drill*
28 *Mastic gun*

wall covering, it is best to cross-line the wall first. The resulting smooth, slightly porous surface helps the new wallcovering to stick.

And if you are dealing with a wall that has been papered over? The textbook method is to strip off the old paper and start again from scratch. To be on the safe side, this is still the best policy. Washables and vinyls must certainly be removed — in the case of 'easy strip' vinyls, all you have to do is remove the vinyl surface. With ordinary paper (and the backing paper of 'easy-strip' vinyls), so long as it is reasonably clean, in good condition, and still firmly stuck to the wall you may well get away with leaving it in place and decorating over the top. Try to arrange for the vertical joins in the old and new paper not to coincide, or the finish may be weakened. If this isn't possible, cross-line the wall before hanging the new wallcovering.

Painting over old wallpaper is another matter, especially if you intend using a water-based paint such as emulsion. Unless it has already been successfully painted (thus sealing the surface), there is a risk that the water in the paint will soften the wallpaper paste and cause the old paper to peel off. The older the paste, the greater the chances of this happening, which is why you can hang woodchip, or something similar, and safely paint over it straight away. There is also a risk of the inks in the old paper bleeding through the new paint — you can end up with the ghostly images of the original design dotted unevenly across the wall. Metallic inks are especially bad in this respect, though treatment with shellac knotting compound does help. There is also the possibility of dirt and grease embedded in the paper's surface stopping the paint sticking.

Assuming you have decided to remove the old paper, the first step is to soak it thoroughly with plenty of water in order to soften the paste holding it in place. It's best to use a wall brush or a sponge to slap the water on. Adding a proprietary wallpaper stripper to the water will also help speed things up by helping the water to penetrate, as will adding a few drops of washing up liquid. You must now allow the water time to do its work — say, for ten or fifteen minutes. If the paper is still difficult to peel off, repeat the soaking process and try again later. Since all this is rather time consuming, if you have a lot of paper to strip, it may be worth renting a steam stripper from a local tool hire shop. Rather like a giant steam iron, it brings the paper to a strippable state very quickly indeed.

Obviously, neither soaking nor steaming will have much effect on washable wallcoverings — the surface is designed to keep water out. With many, therefore, you have to score through the surface with either a special serrated scraper (called a Skarsten scraper), or a makeshift 'comb' made by driving panel pins through a piece of scrap timber until the points just protrude — with either tool, take care not to scratch the plaster while scoring. Fortunately, many modern vinyls offer a simpler way around the problem. If you pick at a corner, you should find that the vinyl surface simply peels off, leaving ordinary paper on the wall. This can usually be left as a lining for new decoration. Novamura

FILLING CRACKS

1 *Use a narrow-bladed scraper to rake out any unsound material from the crack, and undercut the edges slightly at each side so the filler can make a more positive bond.*

2 *Wet the crack before applying the filler, to help cut down on the suction; if this isn't done, the filler may dry out too quickly and could crack. You can use a small hand spray unit as shown, or simly brush water along the crack.*

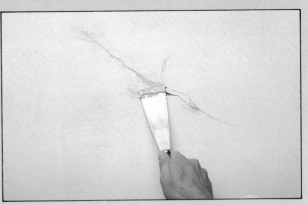

3 *Mix up the filler to a firm, workable consistency (if it's too wet, it will slump out of the crack) and press it into the crack. Draw the blade across the crack line first, then remove excess material by drawing it along the crack.*

4 *Leave the filler slightly proud of the surrounding wall surface. When it has dried hard, remove the excess using abrasive paper wrapped round a sanding block or a softwood offcut to leave a perfectly smooth surface ready for redecoration.*

wallcovering is still easier to remove because it contains no paper and is hung with a special adhesive: you merely work a corner free and pull the whole lot off the wall.

But back to ordinary paper. When the paste is soft enough, choose an easy starting point – there is usually one bit that is obviously liftable – and use a stiff, broad-bladed scraper to strip off the softened paper. Take care not to let the scraper blade dig into the wall, and don't worry about islands of paper that refuse to budge at this stage – further soaking will lift them off in time. You can ignore completely the little flecks of paper that inevitably cling to the wall. These will disappear during the preparation of the newly revealed bare plaster, which you should tackle in exactly the same way as the emulsion painted wall described earlier. There is just one additional point to watch. If the surface of the plaster leaves a chalky deposit on your hand when you brush over it, be sure to seal the surface with a stabilizing primer.

Of course, all this rather assumes that the surface of the wall is in reasonably good condition. If, when filling cracks and holes, you find you are virtually replastering, you need to think again. Cross-lining (or even double lining in extreme cases) should produce a sufficiently smooth surface for papering. You can also paint over lining paper, though a woodchip, or a more heavily embossed paintable wallcovering such as Anaglypta, tends to be more attractive and covers defects rather better. Or you could actually replaster.

Applying a skim coat of traditional finishing plaster to produce the necessary smooth, flat surface is, however, a rather skilled job, so consider using a synthetic plastering system designed for the amateur. This is a cross between very thick emulsion paint and filler. Once brushed on, you can take your time to smooth it out with a plasterer's float or with the special tool that is usually provided in the pack. Unfortunately, it is also rather expensive, and therefore best reserved for relatively small areas – those too small to make it worthwhile hiring a professional plasterer.

And what about preparing surfaces prior to redecoration with something other than paint and paper? For most the preparation is no different, though clearly, with something like cladding there is no need to be too fussy – it will happily cover quite major defects. If you are putting up ceramic tiles, though, make sure that the surface is not only smooth and clean, but also reasonably flat. Level off very bumpy walls by cladding them with plasterboard or tempered hardboard.

Preparing such miscellaneous finishes themselves for redecoration is a little more complicated. Cork tiles are so difficult to remove they are normally best left in place. Cross-line the walls if you want to paper; cover the tiles with lining paper, woodchip, or something similar if you want to paint. In both cases, apply plenty of size (or diluted wallpaper paste) to the tiles first, and if they have been sealed with a high gloss finish, rub down with wet and dry abrasive paper or wire wool to remove the shine.

Ceramic tiles are also usually worth leaving in place, so

REPAIRING CORNERS

1 *Where an external corner has been chipped or broken away, use a timber batten as a guide to replastering. Pin it to one face of the corner, flush with the other face. Leave the pins partly driven.*

2 *Press fairly dry filler into the gap between the batten and the edge of the damaged area using a filling knife or a small pointing trowel. If the gap is deeper than about 6mm ($\frac{1}{4}$ in), apply the filler in stages until it's just proud of the surface.*

3 *When the patch on one side of the corner has dried hard, prise the batten away carefully by pulling out the partly-driven fixing nails. Don't worry if a little of the patch is pulled away as the batten is removed; it can be filled afterwards.*

4 *Reposition the batten on the patched side of the corner so it's flush with the other face of the wall. Then repeat the filling process. Remove the batten, touch in any defects in the repaired area with more filler and finally sand it smooth.*

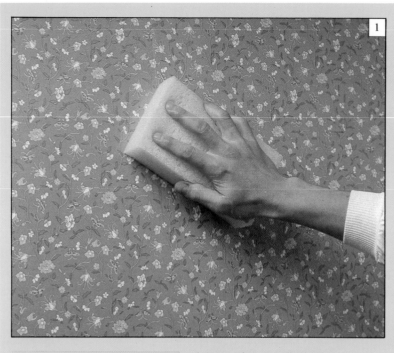

STRIPPING WALLPAPER

1 *Strip ordinary wallpaper by the soak-and-scrape method. Start by saturating the surface of the wallpaper with water from a sponge or a small garden sprayer.*

2 *Start scraping at a seam, keeping the blade of the scraper at a low angle to avoid gouging out the plaster surface.*

3 *Repeat the soaking as necessary to soften the paper and the paste holding it in place.*

4 *Continue scraping until the wall surface is bare, then wash down thoroughly to remove the remaining scraps and nibs and leave the surface clean, ready for redecoration.*

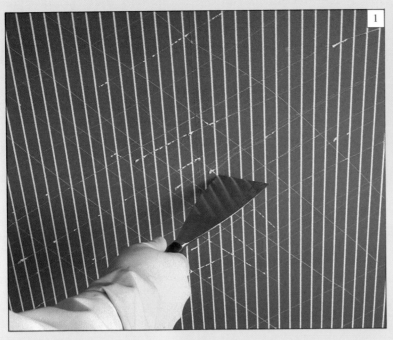

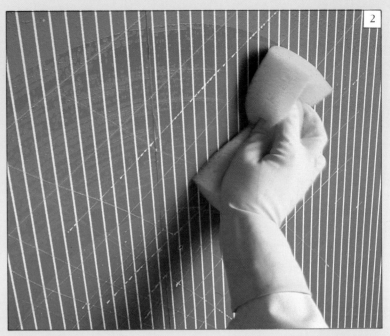

STRIPPING WASHABLE WALLPAPER

1 *Washable wallpapers are extremely difficult to strip because the water cannot penetrate and soften the paste.*

2 *The traditional method of removing them is to score the surface with the edge of a scraper (or with a special serrated tool), then to soak, scrape, soak and scrape until the paper is removed.*

3 *However, this can be very long and tedious process, and quicker results will be obtained by hiring a steam stripping machine.*

4 *This has a hand-held plate which forces steam into the paper, softening the paste and allowing it to be scraped off more easily.*

REMOVING FABRICS

1 Some paper-backed fabrics can be removed by soaking the fabric thoroughly with water using a sponge or garden sprayer, then lifting a corner and peeling the material off the wall.

2 Other types stuck direct to the wall with adhesive can generally be peeled off in continuous lengths. Start at a bottom corner seam, peel the full width away at skirting-board level and then pull the length steadily away from the wall.

long as they are in good condition and firmly fixed to the wall — potentially loose ones have a hollow sound when tapped. Removing them involves hacking away with a club hammer and bolster chisel and you will almost certainly have to replaster the exposed wall. So, consider a cover-up instead. New ceramic tiles can be stuck directly on top of the old ones, or you can apply a resin-based paint. If you decide to paint, give them a good wash, degrease with white spirit, and wait for a warm, very dry day — to reduce the risk of painting over condensation — before priming with an all-surface zinc chromate primer ready for the finishing coats. But don't regard painting as a permanent solution: it tends to flake easily, particularly in the humid environment of a kitchen or bathroom. Smartening up old, dirty grouting provides a more permanent facelift, and can be surprisingly effective. Either rake out and replace the old grout, or carefully paint it with emulsion paint. Better still, use a modern, purpose-made grout paint; any that strays on to the glazed surface can be polished off when dry. To complete the renovation, chip out any badly damaged tiles using a club hammer and cold chisel, and replace with a few new contrasting 'feature' tiles.

That just leaves one final aspect of wall preparation to be considered — making sure the surface is dry. This doesn't simply mean waiting for it to dry after a washing down, it

means making sure the masonry itself isn't inherently damp, because that sort of dampness will ruin almost any form of decoration and is quite likely to lead to more serious problems such as wood rot.

The condition of old decorations is a good indication of the extent of any problem. Badly flaking paint and peeling wallpaper could be due to poor workmanship, but when accompanied by soft, crumbling plaster, and possibly mould growth, damp is the more likely culprit. Before you do anything else, you must identify the source of the problem, and put it right. There are two main types of damp in walls — rising damp and penetrating damp.

Rising damp is due to masonry soaking up moisture from the ground. All walls do this, but in all modern homes a damp-proof course (dpc), built into the structure about 150mm (6in) above ground level, stops the dampness reaching anything that might be damaged by it. If your home doesn't have a dpc, most of the lower parts of ground floor walls may be damp, and you should have one installed by a specialist contractor whether rising damp is obviously present or not. For cheapness and simplicity, this is normally done by drilling holes into the wall at dpc level, and forcing in a silicone-based solution under pressure to saturate the masonry and render it waterproof. The holes are then made good with mortar.

Where your home has a dpc, rising damp tends to appear in patches near sections that have failed to do their job. This may be due to physical damage (either due to subsidence or old age) in which case you should call in a specialist contractor or a competent local builder to make repairs — a new chemical dpc may be required. It is more likely, though, that dampness has found a way round the dpc, perhaps using a flower-bed or the walls of an extension as a 'bridge'. In the former case, simply remove the offending heap; in the latter, call in a builder to put things right — preferably the one who built the extension because new work should not cause this sort of problem. There is one other way dampness can get past a dpc. If a path or patio finishes less than 150mm (6in) below dpc level, heavy rain can bounce off it on to the wall above.

Penetrating dampness is usually more straightforward, the most common causes being faulty pointing in brickwork, leaking gutters, and things of that sort. Making the necessary repairs should be all that is necessary, though in old houses the bricks themselves can become porous with age. In this case, protect them with paint, rendering, or clear silicone exterior sealant.

If dampness does not appear to be due to either of the above, suspect condensation. This appears independently of wet weather. Choosing a 'warm' finish such as cork for the affected surface may help, but it is better to tackle the problem at source by improving your home's heating and ventilation.

Whatever the cause of dampness, allow plenty of time for the masonry to dry out before decorating in earnest. To complete the cure, scrub off any mould growth and treat the wall with a proprietary fungicide to prevent regrowth.

REMOVING TEXTURED FINISHES

1 *Remove modern textured emulsion paints by brushing on a generous coat of special textured paint remover.*

2 *Traditional powder-based textured finishes such as Artex will not be shifted by the chemical. Instead, use a steam stripper to force steam into the surface and soften it.*

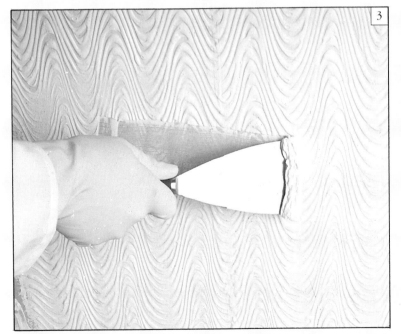

3 *When the solvent stripper has penetrated sufficiently to soften the paint, use a broad-bladed scraper to remove it from the wall. Have a metal container handy to take the scrapings.*

4 *When you have removed the bulk of the finish from the wall surface, use a medium grade abrasive wrapped round a sanding block to remove the remaining nibs.*

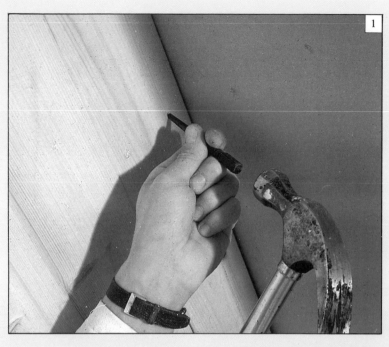

REMOVING CLADDING

1 *Free the last piece to be fitted to the clad area by punching in the fixing nails with a hammer and pin punch.*

2 *When you have punched all the fixing nails through into the battens beneath, prise up the length with a chisel or similar lever, lift it away from the wall and set it aside.*

3 *Work your way across the wall, prising away each length in turn. The fixing nails will have been driven through the tongues on each length; pull away any strips of wood that splinter off as you work.*

4 *Complete the job by removing the wall battens using a crowbar. Insert the end of the bar behind each batten and press down on the other end in a rolling motion.*

REPLACING BROKEN TILES

1 *Prise out the pieces of any broken tiles using a small cold chisel. Work from the centre towards the edges.*

2 *Chip away as much of the old, hard tile adhesive as possible. If you have damaged the plaster underneath, make good with filler. Then spread a* thin layer of tile adhesive in the recess.

3 *Wipe the surrounding tile surfaces with a damp sponge to remove excess filler or adhesive before it has a chance to set hard.*

4 *Press the replacement tile firmly into place, flush with its neighbours, and grout the edges all round it using a squeegee. Polish off excess grout when it has dried using a dry cloth.*

Preparing ceilings

Ceilings are prepared in much the same way as walls — the work is just a little more awkward, and you are likely to encounter a few new existing finishes which need special handling.

The most likely of these is the sort of textured finish created using a plaster-like texturing compound. Artex is probably the best known brand name in the UK, but there are others, some of which have slightly different properties. For example, whereas Artex and similar products need the protection of paint, other textured finishes are intrinsically waterproof. Then there are finishes which are essentially thickened emulsion paint — usually recognizable by the low relief of the texturing. Whichever applies in your particular case, so long as you want to do no more than repaint, the preparation is relatively simple. You just give the surface a good wash with warm water and detergent, taking care to flush out any grease and grime that may be trapped in the texturing's detail; then rinse off.

Your problems really begin when you decide that you want a change from a painted, textured ceiling. With the possible exception of a very low relief decoration where cross-lining or double lining may 'soak up' the texturing sufficiently to allow the ceiling to be papered or painted flat, the only sensible options are to have the ceiling replastered (and a DIY plastering system is ideal here), or to install an expensive cover-up such as a suspended ceiling. Stripping off the texturing compound itself is that difficult. With the non-washable types you have to use paint stripper to remove the paint, and then repeatedly soak the exposed texturing compound until it is soft enough to scrape off — both jobs that are far easier said than done. With washable and paint-like finishes, you are likely to have to use a special chemical stripper throughout, softening and scraping off the finish as if it were an extra-thick coat of paint.

Polystyrene ceiling tiles and mouldings form another potentially difficult surface to deal with. The choice is between washing them down in order to give them a new lease of life, or removing them. Never paint them. The paint film negates the effect of the fire-retardant chemicals used in modern tiles, and increases their flammability to the point where a fire can sweep across the room in seconds. In fact, if you are not sure that the tiles have been correctly put up, it is probably worth removing them in any case. The old practice of sticking them up on blobs of adhesive rather than on a continuous adhesive bed makes them especially dangerous in the event of a fire.

Unfortunately, although stripping off the tiles themselves is relatively simple — just prise them off with a scraper — quite a lot of adhesive gets left behind. Removing this is far from easy. Really all you can do is hack at it with a scraper, which, no matter how carefully you work, tends to leave the ceiling in need of a lot of repair. It is therefore best to leave the adhesive where it is and choose a decorative treatment that will cover it — a thickly embossed paper, some form of panelling or even new ceiling tiles. Or you might consider a high-relief textured finish.

MOVING CEILING LIGHTS

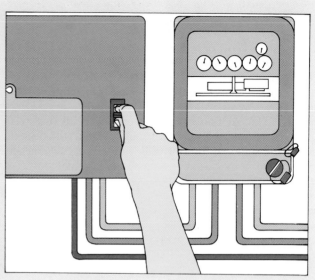

1 *You may need to take down a pendant light fitting to redecorate a ceiling; you may even want to remove it altogether and reposition it somewhere else. Start by turning off the electricity at the house's main on/off switch, and then either remove the appropriate lighting circuit fuse or switch off the miniature circuit breaker (MCB).*

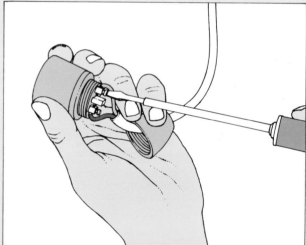

2 *With an ordinary pendant lamp, remove the lampshade. Then unscrew the lampholder cover to gain access to the terminals inside, and use a small screwdriver to disconnect the two flex cores. You can then pull the flex through the cover and set the complete lampholder aside.*

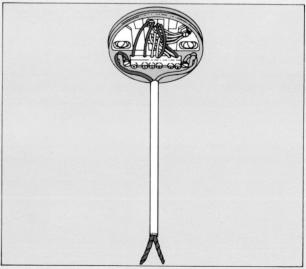

3 *Unscrew the cover on the ceiling rose, and slide it down the pendant flex to remove it. Then disconnect the other end of the pendant flex from the rose terminals and remove it. Replace the rose cover. If you want to remove the rose entirely, disconnect the cables from each terminal bank in turn and connect each group to a small connector block to maintain circuit continuity.*

Old acoustic ceiling tiles are another matter. Having been thoroughly cleaned, these can be painted using either resin-based or emulsion paint, provided you first seal the surface with a coat of stabilizing primer. Don't be tempted to remove them unless they are in very poor condition. Quite apart from the fact that taking them down can prove difficult, the chances are that they were originally put up to disguise an awful ceiling.

Finally, in old houses that haven't been all that well looked after, you may still find ceilings painted with distemper — the standard interior wall and ceiling paint before emulsion paint came along. There are two types — one washable, and one not. The former can be treated in exactly the same way as emulsion paint; the non-washable type — easily recognizable, because if you wipe it with a damp cloth it comes off — must be removed. Even if you succeeded in getting new decorations to stick to a powdery distemper, the material is so unstable that they will almost certainly peel off again in no time. Removal isn't difficult, but it is hard work. You have to scrub it off with a stiff brush and warm water. Once you have got back to clean plaster, treat the surface with a coat of stabilizing primer.

Don't be surprised if the ceiling revealed by the removal of these old finishes is riddled with cracks. Cracks are a problem even in modern plasterboard ceilings, though here they are usually confined to the joins between individual plasterboard sheets. The reason is that ceilings tend to flex in use due to people walking on the floor above, and to the natural movement of the supporting joists. Filling is therefore really something of a temporary solution. Textured finishes offer one way out because they are semi-flexible — hence their popularity for ceilings. But if they are not for you, consider papering instead.

Of course, the real difficulty in preparing a ceiling (and in decorating it, for that matter) is not so much the work itself as the fact that you are doing it off the ground and with your arms above your head, which makes it very tiring. There isn't, unfortunately, a great deal that can be done to alleviate this problem. But good access equipment undoubtedly helps. It's safer, too.

Most people normally work from a step ladder, but while that is certainly better than using chairs and tables, it is far from ideal. To begin with, the average step ladder allows you to reach only fairly low ceilings in comfort. If you find you have to work standing on the step's top platform, you should find some better means of access: on many ladders, the top platform isn't designed to take weight — its primary function is to provide a convenient place to stand paint pots and tools. The other main drawback with steps is that they allow you to work on only a relatively small area of ceiling at one time. This, of course, means that you tend to waste a lot of time and energy climbing up and down and moving the steps from one place to another, which in turn may tempt you to overstretch in order to reach that extra little patch. And that's how accidents happen.

The problem of reach is easiest to overcome. Team the step ladder up with a painter's trestle and span a scaffold

FILLING CRACKS

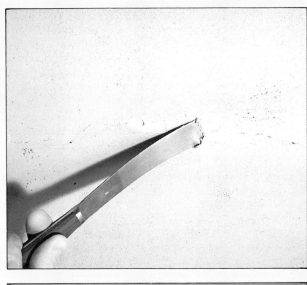

1 *Fill holes and cracks as for walls, drawing the knife across to remove excess filler from the area before leaving it to dry hard. Leave the filler just proud of the surrounding ceiling surface.*

2 *When the filler has set completely, sand over the repaired area with a sanding block to leave a perfectly smooth surface. Avoid standing directly underneath the patch, or you will get plaster dust in your eyes.*

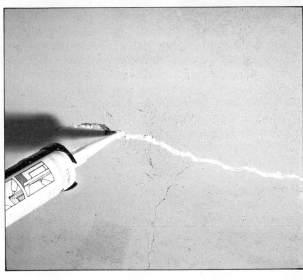

3 *Seal troublesome cracks between sheets of plasterboard or in the angle where the ceiling meets the walls using a flexible decorator's mastic. This comes in a cartridge, and is piped along the cracks like toothpaste. Run over it with a moistened finger for a neat finish.*

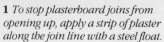

FILLING JOINS IN PLASTERBOARD

1 *To stop plasterboard joins from opening up, apply a strip of plaster along the join line with a steel float.*

2 *Next, bed a length of special joining scrim in the plaster, unrolling it with one hand while pressing it firmly into position with the edge of the float.*

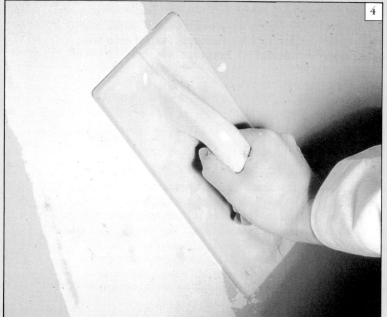

3 *Spread another layer of the plaster on top of the layer of scrim, drawing the float down the join line to remove excess material and leave a flat, smooth finish.*

4 *Polish the surface of the strip with a dampened float or a special sponge to feather out the edges, so the filled strip will be invisible when decorated over.*

board between the two. Both trestle and scaffold board can be rented quite cheaply from a good tool hire shop, and you will find that because you can walk the length of the board in comparative freedom, the work will progress far more quickly. You will certainly appreciate the benefits of the set-up when you come to paper the ceiling, and it is equally useful for cross-lining walls. If you are not very good with heights, tie a rope or long timber batten between trestle and ladder to provide a comforting handrail.

The alternative is to work from a small scaffold tower — undoubtedly the safest option if you have to work a long way off the ground to reach a very high ceiling. Again you can hire one suitable for use indoors quite easily, and they are really very simply to use. You should be given detailed assembly instructions by the hire shop, but basically you just slot the component parts together, tighten up a few bolts, and slide in enough short scaffold boards to provide a safe secure working platform complete with safety rail. The area you can cover from one of these is quite sizeable, and in any case, since most models are fitted with heavy-duty castors, moving the tower is no problem. But, for safety's sake you must remember to lock the wheels with the brake provided before climbing the tower to resume work.

Preparing woodwork

Although new, bare, smoothly planed timber may not look as if it needs much in the way of preparation, there is, in fact, a fair amount to do if you want the best results from a paint or varnish finish.

The first job is to fill any cracks, holes, and dents. Traditionally, ready-mixed stopping compound in a colour that matches the timber is used for this, and it is still best if you intend to give the wood a clear finish. If you plan to stain the wood before varnishing, choose a stopping or wood filler designed to take the stain — not all will. Under paint, however, you can use almost any filler you like. Ordinary plaster-type interior filler is certainly suitable for small cracks and holes. For making good larger defects, a modern, two part epoxy resin based wood filler (usually marketed as part of a wood rot repair system) will give more durable results.

The minute holes formed by the wood grain may also need attention. On some timbers, notably those used to face the plywood cladding on the cheaper flush doors, the grain is so open that no amount of sanding will produce a satisfactory finish. The trick is to fill them with a slurry made from interior filler — the sort that comes as a powder. Mix this with water in the usual way, then keep adding water until the mix has the consistency of thick cream. Pour this on to the wood and then scrape it off again with the edge of a steel rule, scraper blade, or something similar, holding this hard against the surface so that you carry the slurry across the entire surface of the wood at the same time. Given the amount of slurry that comes off, this may seem a pointless exercise, but, in fact, enough filler gets left in the grain pores to to the job.

The next step is to get the surface really smooth, and that

WASHING AND SANDING WOODWORK

1 *Always wash woodwork down before repainting, even if the surface seems to be in perfect condition, to remove dirt, grease and so on from the surface. Use detergent or sugar soap, then rinse down with clean water.*

2 *Next, key the surface of the paintwork with abrasive paper or a proprietary sanding block to ensure that subsequent coats will bond well to it. Silicon carbide abrasive (known as 'wet-and-dry' paper) used wet gives the best results.*

3 *When the grain of the abrasive becomes clogged with a fine slurry of paint, rinse it out in clean water. Use an old scrubbing brush to clean the surface if it won't rinse off easily.*

PAINLESS PREPARATION

TOUCHING IN CHIPS

1 *To touch in a damaged area of paintwork, sand the surface round the blemish lightly first of all to provide a good key for the new paint.*

2 *Use a small paintbrush to work paint into the blemish. If bare wood is exposed, wood primer should be used rather than undercoat or gloss. A second application may be necessary to give good coverage.*

3 *When the touched-in paint has dried completely, brush on second and third coats and feather the edges with light brushstrokes away from the blemish onto the surrounding paintwork.*

means sanding. A light hand sanding will do the trick in most cases. Wrap a sheet of medium grade glasspaper (or dry, wet and dry paper) around a cork sanding block, and work it to and fro across the surface, taking care to keep your movements in line with the timber's grain. Working across the grain tends to produce unsightly scratches which can be difficult to remove — that is, unless you are sanding endgrain in which case it is best to work the sanding block in a circular scrubbing motion. Having got the surface as smooth as you can, switch to a fine grade abrasive paper and sand it all over again to leave it smoother still. If sanding complicated mouldings, sand using wire wool instead of abrasive paper to reach right into nooks and crannies.

Obviously, all this requires a fair amount of elbow grease, but over small, often fiddly surfaces there is very little you can do to mechanize the job. There are, of course, a fair number of sanding gadgets that you can fit on to an electric drill, but in this situation the only one likely to produce a finish comparable to that achieved by hand is the sanding drum — basically a foam plastic cylinder wrapped in abrasive paper (normally medium grade garnet paper, a tougher version of glasspaper). Relatively large flat surfaces, however, can be sanded very successfully using an orbital sander — available either as an integral power tool, or as a drill attachment. In theory, given its scrubbing action, there is a risk of scratching the surface, but in practice this shouldn't occur. Disc sanding drill attachments, incidentally, are not to be recommended for this sort of work. They are difficult to control, and will almost certainly scratch the work, if not gouge chunks from it. They are far better reserved for rough shaping.

Having smoothed the wood, you must now seal it. If you are going to varnish it, the usual method of sealing is to dilute a little of the varnish itself using white spirit, and to rub this firmly into the grain using a soft, lint-free cloth. If you will be painting, brush on a thin coat of ordinary wood primer, all-surface primer, or primer-undercoat (which should be thinned enough for the grain to show through). In all cases, once the priming coat has dried, lightly sand the surface once again ready for the finishing coats. This removes any roughness caused by the surface wood fibres absorbing liquid from the primer and swelling up, and gets rid of any dust that may have stuck to the surface while the primer coat was wet.

The primer will stop the wood soaking up too much expensive finish, but it won't stop any resin in the timber from oozing out, and resin will damage paintwork. On ordinary softwoods, this harmful resin is to be found in the timber knots. If you carefully warm a knot with a blowlamp or hot air paint stripper, it will actually seep out in sufficient quantities for you to scrap it off, and this is a worthwhile procedure on very new wood. In most cases, though, it is sufficient merely to seal the knots with shellac knotting compound before priming. The exception is where you are dealing with a particularly resinous wood. Here, a special primer is needed — aluminium wood primer. It is also advis-

STRIPPING PAINTWORK

1 *Play the flame onto the paint surface until it begins to blister. Then scrape it off with a shavehook.*

2 *Where there are several layers of paint to be stripped, you may have to go back over the area you've just stripped and burn off the earlier coats.*

3 *Continue burning and scraping the surface until you are back to bare wood. Don't keep the flame on any one area for too long or you risk charring the wood. Use a combination* *shavehook to strip intricate mouldings.*

4 *Take care on windows not to crack the glass. A hot air stripper with a deflector shield may be more effective here.*

USING A LIQUID STRIPPER

1 *Brush liquid stripper liberally onto the painted surface using an old brush.*

2 *As soon as the paint surface begins to blister, start scraping off the paint. Deposit the scrapings in a metal container as you remove them. Apply more stripper if necessary to remove* *earlier layers of paint.*

USING A PASTE STRIPPER

1 *Spread paste stripper thickly onto intricately-moulded surfaces and leave to penetrate thoroughly.*

2 *After leaving the stripper to penetrate for the recommended time, use a scraper to start peeling it away from the wood. Follow the maker's instructions about neutralizing the* *surface afterwards.*

able to use this on hardwoods.

Of course, in practice, you will rarely begin work faced with brand new wood. It is far more likely that you will be dealing with wood that has already been painted or varnished, and the big question here is: should you strip the old finish off, or decorate over the top of it? The answer is that it all depends on the condition of the existing finish. In general, if it looks reasonable, and shows no overall signs of peeling, flaking, or blistering it can be left, though stripping may still be desirable if, for example, the paint film has built up to such a thickness over the years that doors no longer close properly.

If stripping isn't necessary, preparing the surface for redecoration is quite simple. Wash it down with warm water and detergent (or you could use traditional sugar soap), then give it a light sanding to provide a key for the new finish. In this instance it is best to use wet and dry abrasive, and to use it wet. It gives a faster, more even cut than glasspaper and is less likely to clog.

Don't worry if, on closer examination, small areas of old paintwork prove to be unsound. Simply scrape or sand off the loose material, lightly feathering the edges of the surrounding paintwork, then smooth out the resulting hollows with filler, or, if they are sufficiently shallow, by retouching them with a few extra coats of new paint. Such minor defects are more of a problem where varnish is involved, particularly if the old varnish is tinted. In theory, you could scrape off the damaged areas, and retouch them before revarnishing the surface as a whole, but in practice, you will find it extremely difficult to obtain an 'invisible' repair, and would be advised to strip the old finish completely and start from scratch.

So how do you strip off old paint and varnish? Starting with paint, there are two basic approaches: you can burn it off, or you can remove it using a chemical paint stripper.

Where you intend to repaint, the former is best — it's quicker, cheaper, and a lot less work. You need a blowlamp (preferably a modern gas-operated model), a flat scraper for dealing with flat areas, and a combination shavehook for fiddly bits. All you do is play the flame lightly and evenly over the surface of the paint until you see it start to bubble. You then take the flame away, and scrape off the softened paint with the shavehook or scraper. And that's it!

There are, however, a few points to watch. If you find another layer of paint beneath the one you have stripped you can repeat the softening process to remove it, but take care when using the flame to soften isolated patches of stubborn paint or pockets of paint trapped in mouldings, or you will scorch the surrounding bare wood. Any paint you cannot easily remove with the blowlamp can be sanded off later. Always remember to keep safety firmly in mind: keep children, pets, and similar distractions out of the room in which you are working, and be careful where you point the flame when not directing it on to the paintwork. Wear thick gloves as protection against burns from the very hot, softened paint, and sweep up what you scrape off at regular intervals before it builds up to the point where it presents a

FILLING KNOT HOLES

1 *Dead knots eventually shrink and fall out of the wood, leaving a rounded hole — especially at edges. Use a proprietary wood stopper to fill them (match the wood colour if the surface is to be varnished); cellulose fillers may crack and drop out.*

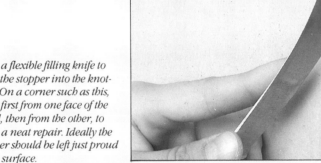

2 *Use a flexible filling knife to force the stopper into the knothole. On a corner such as this, work first from one face of the wood, then from the other, to leave a neat repair. Ideally the stopper should be left just proud of the surface.*

3 *When the stopper has dried hard, sand it down flush with the surrounding surface using fine-grade abrasive wrapped round a sanding block. Treat any sound knots by applying a coat of shellac knotting compound to stop resin bleeding through and spoiling the finish.*

BLEACHING STAINS

1 *To change the colour of stained wood, apply a special wood bleach to the surface using a sponge or brush. Wear gloves to protect your hands. Leave the bleach in contact with the wood as recommended by the manufacturer.*

2 *When the bleach has worked, rinse the surface thoroughly to remove all traces of the liquid. If any areas have been bleached unevenly, apply more bleach until the overall colour is uniform.*

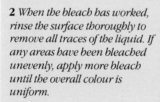

3 *Fresh stain can then be applied to the surface with a brush or cloth pad. It's a good idea to dilute the first coat; a second coat can easily be applied if the depth of colour achieved is not sufficient after one application.*

fire hazard — although it shouldn't happen, fragments of paint can catch light, and could start a fire if they fell into a pile of old paint peelings. Finally, always turn the blowlamp off when you are not using it, and follow the manufacturer's instructions to the letter if you have to change a gas cartridge. Follow their advice on the disposal of old cartridges, too.

Stick to the rules, and you will soon find that you can operate the blowlamp to strip paint quickly, efficiently, and in complete safety. But the tool does bother some people, so you might consider using an electric hot air stripper instead. It's a bit like a high powered hair dryer. The technique for using it is exactly the same for a blowlamp, except that there is considerably less risk of scorching the woodwork and virtually no chance at all of the paint catching light. If you are careful, you could, therefore, use a hot air stripper to strip paint prior to varnishing. However, the more usual method of stripping paint in this situation is to employ a chemical stripper.

For large areas, a traditional liquid stripper is best. Those neutralized with water are more convenient than the sort neutralized using white spirit. Decant a little of the thick liquid into an old saucer or something similar, and then, using an old paint brush, apply it thickly to the surface using a stippling action. The paint may start to bubble immediately but leave the stripper to work for at least fifteen minutes (longer if the paint film is very thick) before scraping off softened paint with a scraper or shavehook. If any paint remains, repeat the process until you are left with bare wood, then wash the surface down with plenty of clean water (or white spirit). You'll probably find that some paint will remain in the crevices of moulding. This can be scrubbed out with wire wool dipped in stripper, but for this sort of fiddly work it is far easier to use a different type of stripper.

This comes as a powder that you mix with water to form a thick paste. This is then spread on to the paintwork with a filling knife, and left to work. It's slower than liquid stripper, taking an hour or two (longer for thick paint layers) to do the job, but at the end of that time the paste poultice should come away fairly easily taking the paint with it. Any that remains is usually a sludge that will come off if washed down with plenty of water. You have to wash the surface anyway to neutralize any stripper left in the wood. This type of stripper will, of course, work on straightforward surfaces, too. However, it works out too expensive to be viable for anything more than small jobs.

Whichever chemical stripper you use, take care and always follow the manufacturer's safety instructions to the letter. With the latter type, take care not to inhale the powder when mixing, and don't let it get on your skin or in your eyes. Wear rubber gloves, too, when applying and removing the paste. You also need rubber gloves when using a liquid stripper. It really is very strong stuff and will react with skin, synthetic fabrics, and plastics as well as paint, so avoid splashes, wear sensible protective clothing (with long sleeves), and protect vulnerable floorings with

REPAIRING WOODWORM AND ROT DAMAGE

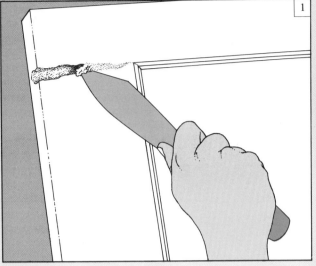

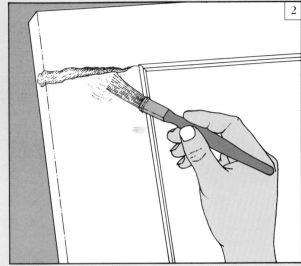

1 & 2 *One of the quickest ways of repairing small areas of rotten wood — on doors and windows for example — is to use a proprietary rot repair system. First cut away the rotten wood cleanly with a knife or chisel; then brush on special wood hardener to stabilize the surrounding woodwork.*

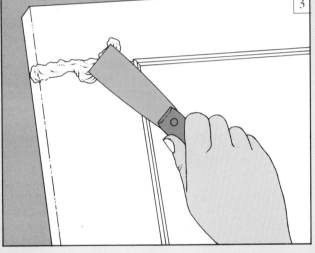

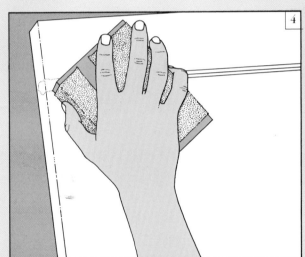

3 & 4 *Build up the cut-away areas using the special resin-based wood filler, applying it with a filling knife and building the repair up in stages. Finish the patch slightly proud of the surrounding surface and leave it to harden thoroughly. Then sand off the excess filler to leave a smooth, almost invisible repair.*

5 & 6 *To discourage fresh outbreaks of wood rot from occurring in vulnerable areas such as these, drill a series of small holes in the wood on either side of the repaired area and insert small pellets of wood preservative, hiding the holes with more filler. These gradually release the preservative into the wood.*

At the beginning of the job, the sheer amount of preparatory work necessary can look extremely daunting. However, the end result always makes thorough preparation worth the effort.

newspaper. If you do get any on your skin, wash it off quickly with plenty of water. You should also ensure ample ventilation, and turn off anything that will heat the fumes. Smoking is particularly dangerous. The fumes aren't explosive — they just turn into a poisonous gas when heated.

And what about stripping varnish? A chemical paint stripper is the best bet, and the only option if you intend to revarnish. But a lot depends on the type of varnish used. Some respond to a fairly mild stripper, others need something far stronger.

Once you have stripped off the old finish, prepare the surface in the same way as new wood. The only complication likely is where the wood has been stained. If you want to varnish but don't like the stain, either restain the wood with a darker shade (bearing in mind that the combination of tones can produce unpredictable results) or bleach out the stain using a proprietary wood lightener.

Preparing Floors

Different floorings differ very little in their needs as far as preparation is concerned. You have to try to ensure that the surface on which they are laid is clean, dry, sound, and reasonably flat. The last is especially important, because a bumpy floor will not only make the new flooring look bad, but also tends to make it wear unevenly, so that its appearance deteriorates with use far more rapidly than is normal. Because levelling directly affects what you do about the rest of the preparation, it's best to make it the first job, and how you set about it depends on whether the floor is made up of floorboards or solid concrete.

In the case of a timber floor, start by attending to any boards in particularly bad condition. There is rarely any need to replace a board entirely as cutting out and replacing a damaged section is sufficient. To do this, lever up board at one end (with tongued and grooved boards, you must saw through the tongues at each side first), and using a couple of stout old chisels or something similar, work along freeing it from the joists until you have lifted a little more than the obviously damaged portion. Now, saw through the board immediately above a suitably placed joist so that when you let it fall back into place, only half of the joist is covered. The exposed half can then be used to support the replacement board which can be screwed or nailed in place — use special flooring brads if you decide to nail.

While you are lifting floorboards, take the opportunity to inspect for signs of wood rot and insect attack in both the boards themselves and the supporting joists. A mirror and a torch will help you make a thorough visual check, and it is also worth prodding suspect timbers with a screwdriver to test their soundness. If you find any suspect timbers or fungal growth, call in a specialist contractor to assess the situation and make the necessary repairs.

Having ensured that the floor is structurally sound, refix any loose floorboards — screws are better than nails here, particularly if the boards are slightly warped — and assess how uneven the floor is as a whole. If things aren't too bad,

LIFTING CARPETS

To lift a fitted carpet, raise one corner and pull it steadily away from the gripper strip. Then prise up the strips all round the room unless carpet will be re-laid.

LIFTING SHEET VINYL

Peel up sheet vinyl that has been stuck to the floor. Then use a hot-air stripper to soften the old adhesive so it can be scraped off the floor surface.

LIFTING WOOD MOSAICS

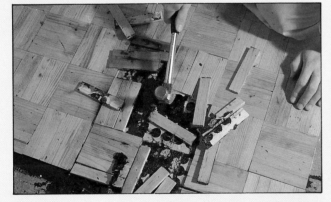

Use a claw hammer or similar lever to claw up wood mosaic blocks. Then play a blowlamp flame over the old bitumen adhesive to soften it so you can scrape it away with an old broad-bladed chisel or similar tool.

LIFTING CERAMIC TILES

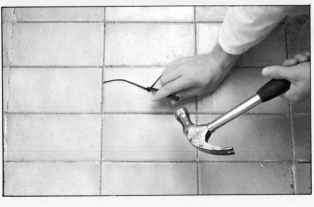

Use a small cold chisel and a hammer to crack and break up old ceramic floor tiles. Then prise them up one by one and chisel away the adhesive bed underneath them as much as possible.

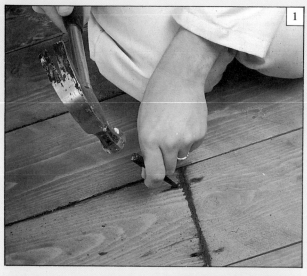

FIXING LOOSE BOARDS

1 & 2 *Before laying a new floorcovering, punch in the heads of any nails protruding above the surface of the boards. If any boards are warped and nails won't hold them, drive in screws instead.*

3 & 4 *To replace a damaged board, check whether it is tongued and grooved by pushing a knife down the crack. If it is, saw through the tongues with a flooring saw. Then prise up the boards at one end using two bolsters or floorboard chisels.*

5 & 6 *If the board passes under a partition wall, cut through it above the centre of the last joist using the curved section of a floorboard saw (or a circular saw if you have one). Then cut the new board to length and nail it into place.*

PATCHING SOLID FLOORS

1 & 2 *Use a cold chisel or brick bolster to chop away crumbling concrete from around holes and cracks in a concrete floor. Then moisten the concrete with water to cut down on the suction and prevent the fresh mortar from drying too quickly.*

3 & 4 *To improve the adhesion of the repair (and to bind together the concrete surface if it is dusty), brush on a diluted solution of PVA building adhesive and leave it to dry. Then mix up a small quantity of ready-mix mortar, adding some PVA adhesive to the mix.*

5 & 6 *Trowel the mortar firmly into the hole, pressing it down to ensure that all voids are filled. Finish off by trowelling the surface smooth and level with the surrounding concrete, and leave it to harden for at least three days before allowing traffic over it.*

P A I N L E S S   P R E P A R A T I O N

it should be all right to carpet over provided you use an underlay. However, other types of flooring — sheet vinyl, and the various tiled finishes — tend to be less tolerant, and so unless the floor is in immaculate condition, it is best to smooth it off by covering it with a layer of hardboard.

Buy this as full sized 2440 x 1220mm (8 x 4ft) sheets and saw it into manageable pieces 1220mm (4ft) square. Brush or spray a liberal, but not excessive, amount of water into the rough side of each sheet, then leave the sheets stacked back to back in the room in which they will be used for at least a couple of days; preferably longer. This conditioning process ensures that when laid, the hardboard will neither absorb moisture from the air and buckle, nor dry out and curl up, so it is important to heat the room normally throughout. To actually lay the hardboard, start putting down a row of sheets along the longest, straightest wall in the room, cutting the last in the row to fit as necessary. Use the off-cut to start the next row. This not only cuts down on waste, but also helps ensure that the joins between individual sheets are staggered brick fashion — vital if the hardboard is to be strong enough to smooth out major undulations in the floor. Fix each sheet into place as you go, starting in the centre and working outwards, using 25mm (1in) annular nails (also known as screw nails). These should be roughly 300mm (12in) apart across the surface of the board, and about 150mm (6in) apart around the edges. Don't worry about cutting in round chimney breasts and so on. Small gaps can be filled later using odd scraps of hardboard.

Solid floors are a little easier to level. Again start by putting right major defects such as deep cracks and holes. Clean them up using a club hammer and cold chisel, aiming to slightly undercut the surrounding material in order to provide a key for the repair. Sweep out any dust using a wet brush and paint the damaged area with a PVA building adhesive. Once this has become tacky, mix up some mortar (for such small repairs it's convenient to buy this dry mixed in small bags) adding PVA to the mixing water according to the manufacturer's instructions. Press the wet mortar into the crack or hole with a trowel, smooth it off level with the surrounding floor, and leave it to set.

Whether or not the floor needs further levelling depends on the flooring you intend to use. Carpeting and quarry tiles bedded in mortar will accommodate a fair amount of roughness, but sheet vinyls, and tiles laid on thin beds of adhesive need an almost completely smooth surface. To obtain this, use a self-smoothing flooring compound. Sold as a powder, you mix it with water, following the manufacturer's instructions, to produce a sort of runny plaster. Pour this on to the floor and roughly smooth it out with a steel float, aiming for an even layer no more than 3mm ($\frac{1}{8}$in) thick, then leave it to set. It will settle out of its own accord to leave a perfectly smooth finish, and if a 3mm ($\frac{1}{8}$in) layer isn't thick enough to cover the ridges in the floor, just apply a second coat as soon as the first is really hard.

Having levelled the floor, whether it is solid or timber, you can be sure it is also sufficiently sound and clean to

SANDING FLOORS

1 *Strip old finishes from floorboards with a power sander — either a belt type for small areas, or else a full-size floor sander. Fit the abrasive belt to the machine.*

2 *Start with a coarse abrasive, and sand at an angle of 45° to the direction of the boards to remove the damaged and discoloured surface of the wood. Fit new belts as they become worn.*

3 *Change to a medium-grade abrasive belt, and sand the surface once again, this time working parallel with the board direction to remove scratch marks left by the initial sanding.*

4 *Finish the job by using a fine abrasive, again working parallel with the board direcion. You will need a small belt sander to reach the edges of the floor if you have used a large floor sander for the bulk of the work.*

receive the new flooring – though it is a good idea to give it a final run over with a broom or vacuum cleaner. But what if you are dealing with a floor that already has some sort of flooring? In most cases it is best to lift it and prepare the bare floor as described above. The main exceptions are permanently-fixed floorings such as old quarry tiles, lino tiles, and so on. So long as they are in sufficiently good condition to provide the new flooring with a sound base, they can be left. Re-stick loose lino tiles. Remove loose or damaged quarry tiles with a cold chisel and club hammer, then fill the resulting hole with mortar, before finally levelling off the entire floor with a self-smoothing flooring compound.

However, if you are covering up old quarry tiles, take care. It is highly likely that rising damp is present, and even if this isn't evident at the moment (quarry tiles usually let the moisture evaporate as fast as it rises through the floor) it could build up into a significant problem once the new flooring is down, destroying any adhesive and possibly the flooring itself. In fact, rising damp is a possibility in any concrete ground floor, so it is always worth testing for it (ideally in winter). The simplest way to do this is to stand a tumbler upside down on the floor, bedding the rim in a ring of putty to form an air-tight seal. If after two or three days, condensation appears *inside* the glass, rising damp is present.

The textbook cure is to dig up the floor, removing at least the top 50mm (2in) or so, and continuing down to a level below that of the damp-proof course in the wall. The floor is then smoothed off with fresh concrete so that a damp-proof membrane can be laid – usually heavy gauge polythene sheets taped together. Having been carried up the wall beyond the level of the dpc, the membrane is finally covered with a 50mm (2in) thick mortar screed. Quite a job, and one most people would prefer to leave to a professional. But it really is the only way to guarantee a cure. Alternatives, such as brushing a couple of coats of bitumen emulsion out over the surface of the concrete, and then covering up with the self-smoothing flooring compound used for levelling floors will, it's true, provide sufficient damp-proofing to protect the new flooring. However, there is a risk that the build-up of moisture beneath the bitumen will simply transfer the dampness to the wall. If you really can't face having the floor dug up, you would be well advised to stick with quarry tiles or some other flooring/adhesive system that doesn't mind getting wet.

Of course, you need not necessarily cover wooden floors. Bare boards, suitably polished, are a very attractive, durable flooring in their own right. If they haven't been polished before, though, you must be prepared for a fair amount of preparation work, because the entire floor must first be sanded smooth.

Start with the normal preparation for wooden floors – repairing damaged boards, and refixing loose ones – then, using a hammer and nail punch, knock every single nail head well below the surface of the boards. You should now turn your attention to any gaps between the floorboards.

To improve the look of the finished floor and prevent draughts, these must be filled. This is simplest using papier maché. Tear newspaper into small squares, soak it in water for about a week, then knead it into a mush, strain off the excess water, and mix with wallpaper paste (one containing a fungicide) to produce a smooth dough that can be pressed into the gaps and neatly smoothed off. The trouble is that papier maché obviously doesn't look like wood when varnished, although the effect can be quite attractive provided the gaps are relatively small and reasonably even. The alternative is to fill the gap with slivers of real timber, carefully planed to fit tightly in between the boards. Drive these slivers firmly into place – protect the edges with scrap wood if you are using a hammer rather than a mallet – leaving them just proud of the surface, then plane off the excess timber.

Of course, you may find that, even after all this careful preparation, the existing boards are not really in a fit state to be sanded and sealed – on an old floor it is quite likely that they are patchily stained and badly dented. In this case, you have two options. The first is to lift every single board and relay it with what was the underside on top, closing up the gaps between boards in the process. The trouble with that is that the underside of the floor may be in little better condition. The second option is to abandon the idea of using the existing boards altogether, and to cover them with a superimposed wooden floor. Normally made from a superior sort of plywood with a thick hardwood veneer, you can choose between parquet effect tiles, or floorboard-like planks. Both are usually tongued-and-grooved for easy fixing, and need the same sort of preparation as a tiled flooring.

Assuming the floor is fit for sanding, you will have to hire two types of floor sander. The first, looking rather like a lawnmower, is a powerful electric belt sander, and is used to tackle the bulk of the floor. The second, is a heavy duty disc sander, and is needed to smooth those areas the main sander cannot reach. Hire a face mask at the same time to keep the dust out of your lungs. Everything you need can be got from a good tool hire shop, who will also sell you the necessary abrasive paper and give you instruction in the tools' use. However, basically what you do is this.

Fit the main sander with a coarse abrasive, and work it diagonally back and forth over any warped boards until they are flush with the rest of the floor. Now, position the sander in a corner of the room pointing in the same direction as the floorboards' grain (ideally next to a long, straight wall), switch on and let it carry you forward, sanding the band of floor next to the wall as it goes. When you have reached the far side of the room, without switching off, pull the sander back over the same strip to its starting point. You will find dragging the sander backwards hard work, but the entire process, and in particular the change of direction at the far wall, must be carried out as smoothly as possible. If the sander is allowed to linger in one spot, it will gouge into the floor and leave a dip that will prove almost impossible to remove. Continue sanding the strip in this way until it is

PAINLESS PREPARATION

as smooth as you can get it.

You can now switch off, move the sander along a little, and tackle the next strip of floor in the same way. Carry on like this, with each strip slightly overlapping its predecessor, until you have smoothed as much of the floor as you can reach with the main sander. Now, change the paper on the sander to a medium-grade abrasive, go back to the beginning, and sand the whole floor over again. Finish off by sanding the entire floor for the third time using a fine-grade abrasive. To complete the sanding, smooth the edges and corners of the floor left untouched by the main sander. Working through coarse, medium, and fine grades of abrasive as before, simply stroke the disc sander over the surface of the wood, keeping the abrasive as far as possible in line with the timber grain. Any corners that the disc sander cannot work into must be sanded by hand.

All that remains is to clean up before working a priming coat of varnish diluted with white spirit into the wood with a lint-free cloth. The sanding will have produced a lot of dust, so a vacuum cleaner is best for the job. Go over the floor two or three times, allowing sufficient time to elapse between cleaning sessions for any dust to settle.

Preparing details

As well as preparing the obvious parts of the room — the floors, walls, ceilings, and woodwork — there are usually quite a few odds and ends that need attention before you can decorate and many of them may be metal.

In many ways, preparing metal for painting is no different to preparing wood. Faced with bare metal, you simply wash the surface to remove any dirt (and use white spirit to remove grease), then rub it down thoroughly using dry wet-and-dry abrasive paper. You do need to be rather more thorough here, though. The idea is not only to provide a key for the new paintwork, but also to remove any surface rust and other deposits that might stop the new paint adhering.

Once the metal is as bright as new, the final job is to prime it. Do this as soon as you have finished rubbing down — many metals tarnish very quickly – and do use the right primer. For iron and steel, a zinc chromate primer is best indoors, unless the metal has been galvanized, in which case you should use a calcium plumbate primer. Zinc chromate is also the primer to use on aluminium — though anodized aluminium doesn't really need painting. In fact, by painting aluminium you actually make work for yourself in the future, because, although the aluminium won't need any maintenance, other than the occasional wash, the paint film will have to be replaced at regular intervals in the usual way. Brass and copper do not need priming at all. You can apply the top coats of paint directly to the shiny bare metal.

And if the metal has already been painted? As with painted wood, if the existing paint film is in generally sound condition you can merely rub it down with wet, wet-and-dry abrasive, wash off any dirt and grease, then apply new finishing coats directly on top of the old. If, however, it proves necessary to strip off the old finish, use a chemical paint stripper. The heat of a blowlamp (or hot air stripper)

STRIPPING AND REPAIRING CORNICES

1 *Old decorative plasterwork such as cornices and ceiling centres are often so clogged up with distemper that much of the detail is lost. Spray water onto the surface to soften the old paint.*

2 *Use a narrow scraper (or even clay modelling tools or similar implements) to pick the softened distemper out of the recesses in the plaster. Keep spraying on water as you work, and keep a small brush handy to brush away the debris as you loosen it.*

3 *Use a hard interior filler or plaster of Paris to patch small parts of the moulding that are cracked or missing. Build up the repair in stages, allowing each layer to dry fully before adding more filler and shaping the repair to match its surroundings.*

could cause some metal items to twist and buckle, and with metal window frames, there is the additional risk of the heat being transferred to the glass, causing that to crack.

There is another important difference between the preparation of metal and that of wood. Metal − or, more specifically, iron and steel − can rust. And quite apart from the fact that rust will ruin your new decorations, if left unchecked it will continue consuming sound metal until nothing else remains. If you find any trace of rust − and bear in mind that it may be concealed beneath blisters in the paintwork − you must deal with it before continuing with the rest of the preparation. Provided it is not so advanced as to warrant the replacement of the affected metalwork, this isn't too difficult.

Start by removing as much loose rust and flaking paint as possible with a stiff wire brush. You can buy wire brush drill attachments for the purpose, but for such small jobs it's not generally worth it. At the same time, cut away any rusty metal that is so obviously weak as to be useless, then carefully rub down the entire area with dry wet-and-dry abrasive and/or wire wool. When you have finished, you should be left with clean, bright metal without any trace of rust at all, and this must now be treated with a proprietary rust inhibitor. That done, you can set about repairing the damage, and in most situations you will find that a car body repair kit contains everything you need. In fact, all of the materials needed to deal with rust tend to be most readily available from car accessory shops. With the damage taken care of, finish off by treating the exposed metal and filler with the appropriate primer. As with sound metal, it is vital you prime as soon as possible − before rust reappears on the surface.

Ornate plasterwork is another detail that will need careful preparation. The general principles involved are the same as for plain plaster walls, but the very intricacy of some plaster detailing poses special problems. To begin with, although it is perfectly possible to merely wash down the surface and repaint (indeed, it's the easiest option), there comes a point when the paint layer on the moulding is so thick that it completely masks the finer details of the ornament. In this situation, you may feel it is worth going to the trouble of stripping back to bare plaster before repainting, but that is easier said than done. You will certainly have to use a chemical paint stripper, but which?

Both the liquid and paste varieties have their advantages and disadvantages in this situation. The paste type, for example, should prove easiest in terms of removing paint from the intricacies of the moulding without the need to resort to a scraper, but it can work out expensive over a large area, and if you allow the stuff to dry out to the point where you have to use a scraper to remove it, there is a chance that you will get plaster and stripper poultice confused − they look similar. A liquid stripper, on the other hand, will be cheaper, but isn't very good at removing old paint from tiny crevices unless you scrub it out with wire wool dipped in the chemical. If the plaster is at all fragile, it could be damaged in the process. The choice is therefore

PREPARING METALWORK

1 *To prepare metalwork for redecoration, start by washing the surface down thoroughly and then sand it over with fine-grade silicon carbide (wet-and-dry) abrasive paper to remove any surface roughness and provide a good key for subsequent coats of primer, undercoat and topcoat.*

2 *If the surface is rusty or pitted in places, use a wire brush to remove the deposits and leave a bright metallic surface. A cup or wheel-pattern wire brush fitted in an electric drill will be quicker than hand-brushing if large areas have to be tackled.*

3 *Alternatively, rust can be removed with a proprietary rust remover. This is brushed onto the metal surface and usually left to dry, by which time it has converted the rust into a hard, inert surface that needs no further preparation before primer and paint coats are applied. Follow the manufacturer's instructions carefully, and take care to avoid splashing the chemical on your hands or in your eyes.*

P A I N L E S S   P R E P A R A T I O N

REPLACING GLASS

1 & 2 *The simplest way of removing a cracked pane of glass to to stick adhesive tape over it and break it with a hammer. Wear gloves for protection as you lift out the broken pieces.*

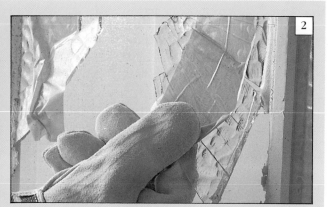

3 & 4 *Use an old chisel or a glazier's hacking knife to remove the old putty from the rebate. Prime any bare wood you expose, then thumb in a layer of bedding putty all the way round the rebate.*

5 & 6 *Offer up the replacement pane to the bottom edge of the rebate, align it carefully and then press it into place. Use firm hand pressure at the edges of the pane, not in the centre.*

7 & 8 *Secure the pane with glazing sprigs along each edge, then thumb in the facing putty all the way round. Smooth it off neatly with a putty knife, forming neat mitres at the corners.*

largely a matter of personal preference, but whichever you choose, you will have to work very carefully, and you can expect the job to take a considerable period of time.

Repairing ornate plasterwork can also be a problem. Minor dents, holes and cracks can be tackled using interior filler in the same way as those in a flat wall. Chipped and missing decoration is another matter. Interior filler is again the thing to use, but shaping it in order to replace lost moulding takes time, patience, and not a little skill. You will almost certainly be able to manage small repairs of this sort — few visitors will inspect the results close enough to notice mistakes — but where the moulding is in generally poor condition, complete replacement is a better option.

What you replace old moulding with depends largely on how much you are prepared to pay, and on how keen you are to retain the original design. If the existing moulding is so attractive that you are determined to keep it at all costs, investigate as many firms specializing in reproduction period plasterwork as possible to see if any have your particular moulding (or something so like it as to make no difference) in stock. Failing that, you may be able to find a local specialist willing to produce lengths of replacement moulding from casts taken of the original — but that is expensive. If a plaster replacement is out of your price range, look at glass fibre as an alternative. Most are faithful reproductions of original period mouldings, but are rather cheaper and a lot easier to put up — they usually snap on to clips fixed to the wall. At the very bottom of the price range, come mouldings in expanded polystyrene. These tend to come in a smaller range of simpler designs (including plain modern ones), and should be left unpainted for the same reasons that you shouldn't paint polystyrene ceiling tiles. However, they are better than nothing in a room proportioned to have some sort of cornice, and putting them up is simply a matter of gluing them in place with a special adhesive. Both glass fibre and polystyrene covings and cornices, incidentally, are widely available with ready mitred corner sections to make installation easier still.

If you are planning to completely revamp the room, you may have decided to alter the fireplace and surround, and since this is a fairly major job it should be taken care of before tackling anything else. You may, for example, wish to block off a fireplace that you no longer use, or open up one previously closed up in order to put in an open fire. Or you may simply wish to change the existing fire surround for something more to your taste.

Changing an existing surround is usually the easiest of the three. To remove the old surround, hack away the plaster at each side using a club hammer and bolster chisel, and you should find one or more pairs of lugs through which the surround is fixed to the wall with screws or nails. If these won't come away easily, chop through them with the cold chisel. You can now lever the fire surround from the wall with a crowbar, garden spade, or something equally robust, and cart it away. But do get some able-bodied help for this stage of the operation — fire surrounds can be very heavy. The superimposed hearth in front of the fireplace

REPAIRING STAINED GLASS

1 *Remove the damaged panel and lay it flat on a board. Then cut through the outer section of the lead came with a sharp knife.*

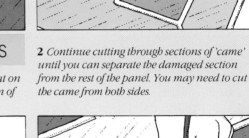

2 *Continue cutting through sections of 'came' until you can separate the damaged section from the rest of the panel. You may need to cut the came from both sides.*

3 *Scrape out the old putty and any splinters of broken glass bedded in it using an old knife. Then brush out the cames with a fine wire brush.*

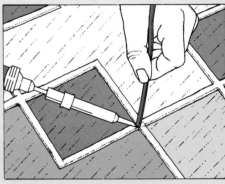

4 *Fit the new piece of glass in position, and reassemble the panel sections carefully. Then apply flex to the joints and solder them together.*

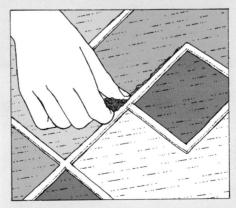

5 *Use your thumb to press putty into the cames all round the new piece of glass, and trim off any excess with an old knife. Then repeat on the underside.*

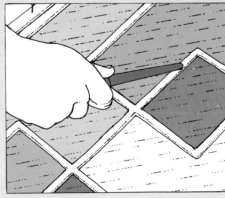

6 *Finish off by pressing the came back flat with knife strokes. Then polish up the came surfaces by running the wire brush over them.*

should also lever up relatively easily, leaving the opening ready for whatever new surround you have in mind. There are quite a few to choose from including models made from stone, brick, decorative concrete blocks, wood, and even cast iron. They are most widely available from specialist firms as kits, and come complete with detailed installation instructions.

The old surround and hearth must also be removed if you intend to block up the fireplace. Once they are out of the way, clean up the resulting opening, and block it off with a small brick or concrete block wall — you may have to break up and shovel out the old fireback to make room for this. Be sure to build an air-brick into this wall a few inches above the floor; without this to provide ventilation, condensation is likely to form within the disused flue, leading to a nasty outbreak of damp. Finally, plaster over the new masonry and surrounding area to leave a smooth, flat surface flush with the surrounding wall. You can do this yourself using a DIY plastering system. After decorating, neaten the airbrick opening by fitting a metal or plastic grille if desired.

Re-opening a fireplace is a little more complicated, although, basically, you just hack off the plaster, knock down the brickwork sealing it off, and have the chimney swept. But whether or not that leaves you with a usable fireplace depends on a great many other factors – whether the old fireback was removed, the condition of the flue lining, the state of the chimney stack, and so on. Unless you are absolutely sure that everything is in good working order, it is generally best to seek expert advice. Any good supplier of fires and fire surrounds should be able to help.

Finally, don't forget any glass in the room — glass in windows, doors, partitions, and so on. Any broken panes should be replaced before the new decorations go up. Unlike the replacement of external panes, replacing an interior pane of glass is very straightforward. In most cases, the old pane will be simply set into a bed of putty or flexible mastic (probably a silicone based mastic similar to that used to seal gaps around baths), and held in position by lengths of quadrant wooden beading, mitred at the corners and fixed in place with small panel pins. To replace the pane, start by smashing it with a hammer, and pick out as much of the broken glass as possible by hand, wearing gloves for protection. It's a good idea to lay strips of masking tape over the pane before you set to with the hammer: the tape will bind the shards together so they don't scatter all over the floor. Any small pieces that remain embedded in the putty can be extracted with pliers.

Next, carefully lever off the wooden beading using an old blunt chisel or something similar. Scrape out the remains of the old putty, and clean up both the beading and the rebate in which the glass sat with glasspaper, before protecting the exposed timber with a coat of primer. While this is drying, measure up the opening for the new glass. Take two or three readings in different positions to allow for the fact that the frame may be out of true, and working to the smallest height and width, deduct 3mm ($\frac{1}{8}$in) from each dimension to find the size of the replacement pane. Have this cut at the shop where you buy it. The supplier should also be able to advise you on the thickness and type of glass you need. If the original pane used an obscured glass, you might like to choose something more in keeping with the new decor as a replacement. In any case, if the pane is in a door, or some other position where there is a risk of someone accidentally bumping into it or falling through it, choose some form of safety glass — wired glass if you want an obscured pane; toughened glass if you want a clear one. The latter may have to be ordered specially in the size you want.

Having got the glass home, start by running a thick bed of mastic around the rebate. Like caulking, suitable mastic is widely available in cartridges from which you can extrude it using a specially designed gun. Offer the glass up to the opening, centring it within the rebate, and press it into place around the edges using the palms of your hands. Any excess mastic that oozes out can be wiped off with a wet cloth. Run a second bead of mastic around the perimeter of the opening on the face of the glass, ready to receive the beading — you can use the original beading if it is in good condition. Press this on to the mastic, then settle it down into the rebate, and fix it in place with at least two panel pins per side. Again, use a wet cloth to wipe off any mastic that oozes out, and finish by punching the pin heads fractionally below the surface of the wood, so you can hide them beneath filler or stopping ready for painting.

THE COMPLETE PAINTER

Painting with a brush 74

Painting with a roller 82

Painting with a pad 86

Spray painting 89

Special techniques 93

Fifty years ago, applying any sort of paint – and gloss in particular – was a real craft. Paints in those days were simply so thin that you had to know what you were doing in order to achieve even coverage and avoid such faults as brushmarks, sags and runs. Today, things are different. Some modern paints are so designed that a child could obtain a near perfect finish. You don't even have to use a brush anymore. You can roll the paint on, spread it on with a pad, or use a spray gun, if you wish. But some of the traditional skills are worth knowing. They make the paint go farther. And they enable you to achieve good results using the cheaper, more traditional varieties of paint and varnish.

Painting with a brush

The brush is, of course, the traditional tool for applying paint, and in many ways, it remains the most versatile. You will need a selection to do the job properly. For gloss painting, varnishing, and other small scale work, use what's called a varnish brush – the ordinary flat paint brush. These come in a range of sizes, but a 50mm (2in) model is probably the best general purpose tool, while a 25mm (1in) one will enable you to cope with a certain amount of intricate work. For painting walls, a larger, coarser brush is used – called, not surprisingly, a wall brush. These too come in a range of sizes, and when choosing you should bear in mind that, although a large brush will allow you to cover the wall more quickly than a small one, when loaded with paint it may prove too heavy to use for long periods, thus losing its advantage in speed. A 100mm (4in) brush is a good compromise.

A brush's quality is also important. Avoid the very cheapest types with short, coarse synthetic filament bristles. They don't give good results. Some authorities suggest that you should buy the best you can afford, but that too is a mistake. The very best brushes are designed for the professional, who demands tools that can not only cope with the more traditional 'trade paints', but will also last for years. The needs of the amateur are less demanding, and a middle-of-the-range brush (top-of-the-range in terms of DIY brushes) with long, thick bristles that taper to a wedge when the brush is charged, should be adequate. In all probability, if you were to buy a professional-quality brush, you would be too old to use it by the time you had even 'run it in'.

Good brushes do need a certain amount of 'running in' to produce the best results. It is certainly not a good idea to put a brand new brush straight on to gloss work – the bristles won't have the necessary suppleness and shape. Break them in on primers and undercoats first. New brushes should also be thoroughly washed out in warm, soapy water before use, to soften the bristles and remove any that may be loose. Whether the brush is old or new, before

PAINTBRUSHES

1 *Paint shield*
2 *100mm (4in) wall brush*
3 *150mm (6in) wall brush*
4 *50mm (2in) brush*
5 *25mm (1in) brush*
6 *Cutting-in brush*
7 *Radiator brush*

using it, flirt the bristles through your fingers, and then strop them across the palm of your hand. This removes any remaining loose bristles, and gets rid of dust.

Paint, too, has its own starting ritual. Always wipe over the top of the tin to remove any dust before opening it. Lever off the lid with something that won't damage it and make it difficult to replace. If you are re-opening a partly used tin, don't let chips of dried paint fall in, and carefully cut out and remove any skin that has formed. And always give the paint a good stir to make sure the pigment and binder are uniformly mixed. This applies even to non-drip paints which may tell you not to stir them on the tin. Just let the paint stand undisturbed for an hour or so to regain its non-drip qualities.

Finally, it is well worth decanting the paint into a paint kettle – a sort of shallow metal or plastic bucket – rather than dipping your brush straight into the tin. These are not only lighter and easier to carry around, but also the decanting process allows you to strain the paint to remove any minute bits of debris it may contain. Just pour the paint into the kettle through cheesecloth or nylon. In addition, any dust that gets into the paint from your brush will contaminate only that batch – not the whole tin.

Now for the painting itself. With resin-based paint, the idea is to build up a cohesive film of primer (where appropriate) and undercoat, followed by two or more coats of finish (usually gloss). Traditionally, the undercoat's job is to obliterate the original surface colour, thus ensuring that the colour of the finishing coats will be both uniform and true to the colour chart. It also helps to smooth off the surface, and provide a matt finish to which the finishing coats can stick. What's more, it works out cheaper than applying sufficient top coats to achieve the same effect.

In reality, however, undercoat is not always strictly necessary. Where there is no great colour contrast between the surface and new paint, you can expect the top coat alone to produce a good finish and a true colour after one or two coats (depending on its thickness and quality). And as for the business of needing a matt finish for the top coats to stick, there is some evidence to suggest that, on the contrary, modern resin-based paints stick better to a glossier surface.

Whatever you decide, the basic technique for applying the runnier, more traditional paints (and varnishes) is the same. Dip the brush into the paint until about half the length of its bristles are immersed, then withdraw it and scrape off the surplus paint on the side of the paint kettle. This avoids drips and runs. Next, holding the brush by its metal ferrule in much the same way as you would hold a pen, work the brush lightly up and down, applying the paint to the surface in long strokes, following the direction of the grain if you are working on wood. Your aim at this stage is not to cover the surface completely, but to produce a series of parallel stripes a little apart – a process called 'laying on'.

When the brush starts to run dry, you can move on to the next step – 'brushing out'. This simply means working the

1 *Before using a new paintbrush, 'flirt' the bristles with your fingers and strop it across the palm of your hand to remove any loose bristles and dust which could spoil the finish of your paintwork.*

2 *Dust off the top of the tin before opening it to stop bits falling in the paint. Then lever off the lid carefully with an old screwdriver or similar tool; be careful not to distort it.*

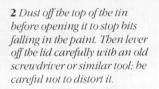

3 *If a skin has formed over the paint, cut all round the edge with a knife and lift it out. Pick out any bits of dry paint you can see, then stir the paint thoroughly (even if it's a non-drip paint).*

4 *Strain the paint from the tin into a paint kettle through a fine sieve to remove any bits remaining in the paint. A kettle is easier to handle than a large tin, and any leftovers at the end of the job can be strained back into the tin again.*

PAINTING WOODWORK

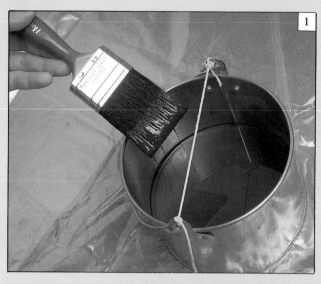

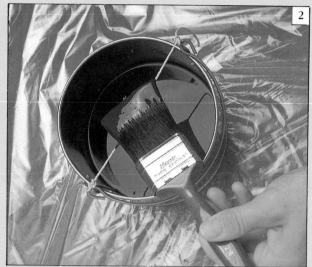

1 & 2 *Dip the brush into the paint to a depth of no more than half the bristle length, then scrape off excess paint by drawing the bristles across a piece of string or wire fixed across the kettle.*

3 & 4 *On surfaces such as doors, apply paint to fiddly bits such as mouldings first. Then paint in the panels, brushing first with the grain and then across it to get good, even coverage. Finish off the area with further light brush strokes parallel with the direction of the grain.*

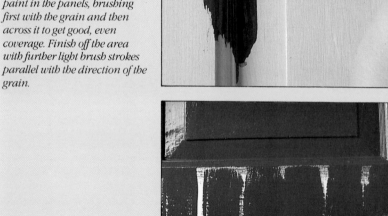

5 & 6 *Tackle other areas in the same way, first applying the paint in parallel strips, then blending them together with brush strokes at right angles to the first ones. Again, finish off each area with light brush strokes parallel with the direction of the wood grain.*

brush at right angles to the stripes to spread the paint into a thin, even layer that covers the surface completely. That done, lightly work the brush over the surface, once again following the direction of the wood grain, to eliminate any obvious brush marks and leave a perfect finish. Having completed one section as described above, recharge the brush and move on to the next, if possible, arranging for the sections to overlap slightly while the paint is still wet, and blend them together while brushing out and finishing off. This prevents the formation of a 'dry line' which might be visible when all the paint has dried.

The technique for non-drip paint is slightly different. The more you work it, the runnier and more difficult to handle it becomes. So, simply dip the brush in to about half the length of the bristles, and, without scraping off the excess, apply it following the direction of any wood grain, aiming for a fairly thick, even coating that completely covers the surface. The paint will then flow out of its own accord to produce a smooth, even finish. You certainly won't be left with brush marks.

With both types of paint, though, you must be careful when working up to an edge. Always work the brush out over an edge. Drag it back, and you could scrape off enough paint to form a ridge of paint or, worse, a run. Working up to a surface that is not to be painted also needs care. It's called 'cutting in', and is generally easiest with a fairly small, preferably worn brush. Charge the brush a little more fully than normal, and position the bristles on the surface a little away from the desired edge of the paint work. Now, draw the brush along parallel to the edge, applying just enough pressure to splay the bristles out until they just reach the surface you don't want painted. After a little practice you will find that by keeping your hand steady and the pressure constant, you can achieve a remarkably straight line with considerable accuracy.

Having successfully applied one complete coat of paint to the surface, allow it to dry completely before applying any subsequent coats that might be required. Once it is hard, it is advisable to rub it down lightly with fine wet-and-dry paper before repainting. This has nothing to do with reducing the thickness of the paint, as some people imagine: it's purpose is partly to provide a key for the next coat, but mainly to flatten off any 'nibs' of paint that have formed around dust particles. In fact, dust is one of the painter's greatest enemies, so do all you can to avoid getting it in the paint. Never work in a dusty atmosphere, and, before applying any paint, give the surface a final sweep using either an old, clean paint brush, or a special, slightly sticky cloth called a tack rag. After rubbing down between coats, wipe off the paint dust with a damp cloth — one moistened with white spirit is best.

Having mastered the above techniques, you can be confident of achieving a good finish on almost any reasonably plain, straightforward surfaces. Unfortunately, few surfaces in real rooms are straightforward. Most present some sort of problem.

Take doors as an example. With a flush door, you should

PAINTING WALLS

1 *The technique for brush-painting walls with emulsion paint is similar to painting woodwork; the main difference is that you use a larger brush — 75 or 100mm (3 or 4 in) wide instead of 25 to 50mm (1 to 2 in). The first stage is to load up the brush as described opposite, and to apply the paint in a series of vertical bands on the wall surface.*

2 *The next step is to brush out the strips applied in stage 1 with horizontal brush strokes, to ensure that the paint covers the wall surface completely and is applied evenly. Don't reload the brush; work with the paint you have already applied.*

3 *Finish off the area with a series of light vertical brush strokes, in the same manner as laying off the paint along the grain when painting wood. Then load up the brush and repeat the process on the next area of wall, working all the time from the wet edge of the paint outwards.*

Painting doors and windows
Starting from the top, paint edges of opening surfaces first, to allow for drying. Paint sills and baseboards last, to avoid picking up dirt from them.

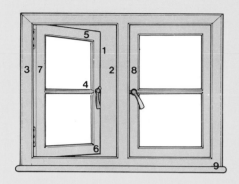

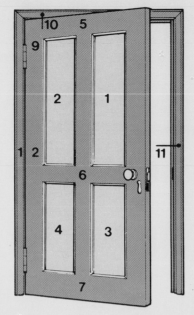

Painting sliding sash windows *Paint the top and bottom edges of the outer sash window with the same type and colour of paint as the outside of the window. Use the same paint and colour as on the inside of the window for the top and bottom edges of the inner sash.*

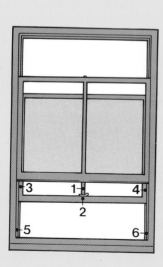

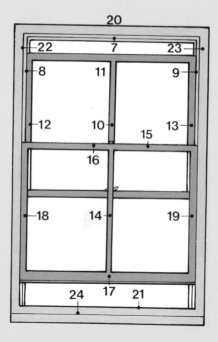

be able to avoid dry lines if you mentally divide the door horizontally into thirds, then divide each third in half vertically to find the sections you should aim to cover with a brushload. With the surface of the door taken care of, you can then tackle the leading or hinge edge, whichever is appropriate. The rule here, incidentally, is that you paint whichever edge is visible from the room when the door is opened in the same colour as the visible door face.

However, there are a couple of practical snags to be overcome. First, if you decided not to lift the flooring before redecorating, you may get paint on it when you come to cut in along the bottom edge of the door. Where carpeting is concerned, you may also get a certain amount of fluff on the new paintwork. If possible, lift the corner of the flooring while you are painting the door, and, in the case of a carpet, leave it folded back until the paint has dried. If for some reason you can't do this, slide newspaper under the door and paint carefully.

There is also the problem of getting in and out of the room while the paint is still wet as, for the best results, you have to remove all door furniture, including the handle. The best solution is to wedge the door open, and keep it open until the paint has dried. It is also well worth jamming a piece of scrap timber into the hole left by the door handle, so that you can use it as a door knob until the door furniture can be replaced. The only trouble with all this is that it allows pets and small children to come and go as they please. And while adults can just about be trusted to understand the meaning of a 'wet paint' sign — even if they insist on touching the paintwork just to make sure — pets and small children are not to be trusted at all in this situation. So, keep an eye on things, or, better still, try to schedule your decorating so that doors can be left to dry unmolested overnight.

More complex pieces of joinery such as panelled doors and windows present even more of a challenge. Since it is almost impossible to paint them without a dry line forming somewhere, you have to use the piece's component parts to disguise the fact, and that means painting the different parts of the door, or whatever, in a special order.

On a panelled door, tackle the panels, together with any associated mouldings, first. Next, paint the rails (the horizontal timbers), starting with the one at the top and working down. Finish off by painting the uprights — the stiles. The only theoretical difficulty here is in deciding where rails end and stiles begin. The answer is to let the wood grain act as your guide. The border line is where the grain changes direction at the joints.

And windows? Ordinary fixed and hinged casement windows are best treated in the same way as a panelled door. Treat each pane of glass as a panel that you don't have to paint. When cutting in around a window pane, though, it is advisable to allow the paint to stray fractionally on to the glass to form a border just under 3mm ($\frac{1}{8}$in) or so wide. This will stop condensation getting under the adjacent paint film and lifting it. Any other paint that strays on to the glass should either be wiped off immediately with a rag dipped in

STAINING/ VARNISHING WOOD

1 & 2 *Start by decanting the wood stain into a small container. Dilute it or mix it with other stains of the same type if required. It's a good idea to wear gloves to keep the stain off your hands. Then apply the first coat with a cloth pad, working along the grain in broad stripes. Don't overlap these, or they will show as dark areas.*

3 & 4 *When the first application of stain has dried fully, sand the surface lightly with fine-grade glasspaper to remove any fibres that have been raised by the stain (this is a particular problem with water-based stains). Then apply a second coat of stain to the surface to deepen colour and ensure even coverage.*

5 & 6 *When the stain has dried, apply the first coat of varnish. It's best to thin this with about 10 per cent white spirit and to apply it with a cloth pad rather than a brush. Then subsequent coats can be applied in the usual way with a brush. Sand the surface down lightly with a fine-grade abrasive between coats to remove dust specks and to ensure good adhesion.*

CLEANING AND STORING BRUSHES

1 *When you have finished painting, brush out as much paint as possible on to sheets of lining paper or newspaper.*

2 *Next, rinse the brush in the appropriate solvent — white spirit, paraffin or a proprietary brush cleaner for solvent-based paints and varnishes, water for emulsion paints.*

3 *Wash the brush carefully in warm, soapy water to remove the last traces of paint (and of white spirit, if you used it earlier). Rinse the brush thoroughly in clean water.*

4 *Wrap the brush in some absorbent paper held in place with a rubber band, and leave to dry. This ensures that the bristles retain their shape, and also keeps the brush clean while it is being stored.*

white spirit, or else scraped off when dry using a razor blade.

You may prefer to make doubly sure that your cutting in around the glass will be accurate. One way of doing this is to use a paint shield — a flat piece of plastic, metal, or stiff card which you hold against the glass with one hand while cutting in with the paint brush in the other. As you might imagine, it is a technique that requires some practice. A simpler alternative is to run masking tape around the glass. This will help neaten the border of paint run on to the glass, and can also be used to secure sheets of newspaper over the glass as a whole. In fact, it is not a bad idea to do this in any case: as well as providing additional insurance against drips of paint, the newspaper will give you some privacy while the windows are without curtains.

Sliding sash windows are trickier still, the snag being that the outer sash is always partially masked by the inner, preventing you from painting it in one go. But there is a solution. Start by partially opening both the inner and outer sashes to leave them roughly in the middle of the window opening with 200-300mm (8-12in) of the outer sash showing. Paint this section of the outer sash, together with the exposed window frame at top and bottom, then pull the inner sash almost completely down, and push the outer sash up far enough to expose that part of it which has yet to be painted. Finish painting the outer sash now, then tackle the inner sash and the rest of the frame in the usual way.

Even skirting boards, architraves and the like can pose problems. If the flooring is still in place you will have the same trouble cutting in along the bottom edge as with a door. Again, the best solution is to peel back the flooring until you have finished painting. If this isn't possible, protect the flooring as far as you can with newspaper or polythene sheeting and masking tape. Masking tape can also be used to stop gloss paint straying on to the surface of the wall. If you intend to paint the walls with emulsion, such mistakes will tend to show. Just be careful not to tear any paper you may have left on the wall when you come to peel the masking tape off.

And what about painting metal? In the case of something like a metal window frame, you can treat it in exactly the same way as woodwork, though, unless you have been thorough over the preparation you may have problems with adhesion. You should also beware of condensation on the surface you are about to paint. Try to work on a warm, dry day to minimize the risk, and, as an extra precaution, wipe over the surface with a dry, lint free cloth.

Condensation is even more likely if you are painting cold radiators and pipework. Equally, though, you shouldn't paint them when they are hot, nor should you allow them to become hot until the paint has completely dried — yet another good reason for tackling this particular job in summer. In addition, choose the paint with care. Any resin based paint is perfectly suitable for pipes and radiators — water-based emulsions are not. Incidentally, if you want to retain the natural look of brass and copper, use a clear lacquer or transparent paint.

Lastly, bear in mind the practical difficulties of painting central heating equipment. If possible, having drained down the system, loosen the union nuts connecting the radiator to the pipework, and tilt them away from the wall so you can paint the back and the wall more easily. Alternatively, use a special radiator brush — a bit like a small, long-handled dustpan brush. When you come to tackle the pipework, work the brush along the pipes rather than around them to stop paint building up on the far sides.

After all that, you will no doubt be relieved to know that painting the walls themselves with a brush is a great deal simpler. All you do is charge the wall brush fairly heavily — that doesn't mean dipping it in deeper; it means scraping off less on the side of the paint kettle — and work it up and down and from side to side to produce a sort of ragged star shape. In fact, the more you work the brush in different directions, the less chance there is of small holes and bumps in the surface leaving unpainted 'shadows'. Keep spreading out the 'star' until the brush starts to run dry, then recharge it and begin another star just to one side of the first, and gradually extend this until the two have merged together. Continue in this way until the entire surface has been covered, switching to a smaller brush where necessary to cut in neatly around the edges.

There are just two final skills you need to acquire concerning painting with a brush, and they are the arts of cleaning brushes properly and storing them in such a way that they are still in good condition when you next decide to decorate. First, cleaning. Always clean your brushes thoroughly when you have finished using them, unless you really are only taking a 'five minute break' in which case you can keep them in a workable condition by wrapping them in polythene secured with an elastic band. Don't allow them to stand in jars of white spirit (or water if using emulsion) until you can resume work or get round to cleaning them. This not only distorts the bristles (and if left long enough the distortion will be permanent), but also leaves the brush so charged with whatever they were standing in that the paint you apply for the first half hour or so will be over-thinned.

To clean them, start by working them back and forth across plenty of clean newspaper to remove the bulk of the paint they contain, then dunk them in the appropriate solvent (water for emulsions; white spirit for resin-based paints) to remove the rest, working it out of the bristles with your fingers and taking special care to remove any that has worked up to where the bristles join the handle. Several changes of solvent may be needed before the brush is really clean. The next step is to wash the brush out in warm soapy water, again using your fingers to clean right to the base of the bristles. This not only flushes out any white spirit, but also helps soften the bristles, thus keeping the brush supple. Finally, dry the bristles off with a clean cloth.

If you won't be needing the brush again for some time, now is the time to think about storage. Carefully shape the bristles into the ideal wedge shape, then wrap them in clean paper — kitchen roll or toilet tissue is ideal — to help

them hold their shape, keeping this in place with an elastic band. They are now ready to be put away in a drawer or cupboard until the next time they are needed. Wherever you store them, make sure it is free from damp, and lay them flat so that the bristles cannot be bent out of shape during the storage period.

Painting with a roller

Whether you are painting walls or ceilings, using a roller will certainly speed things up considerably. However, if you want to be sure of getting a really first-class finish, it is important that you use the right equipment for the job.

The first essential is, of course, the roller itself. Choose a fairly sturdy one with a stout metal frame and a comfortable handle, and make sure that it not only holds the roller sleeve firmly, but also that changing sleeves is straightforward. After all, the sleeve is really the most important part of the tool. It's the sleeve that actually puts the paint on the surface. It is therefore well worth spending some time deciding on the best sleeve to use in a particular situation. There are several types to choose from.

Foam plastic ones are cheapest but do tend to be rather messy in use. Applying too much pressure delivers too much paint to the surface, so avoiding drips and splashes can be difficult. However, on a smooth or lightly textured surface, they do produce quite a reasonable looking finish. For a really fine finish, though, go for a roller with a definite pile — mohair, sheepskin, or synthetic fibre. Mohair sleeves have a very short, fine pile, and will not only give good results with emulsion on smooth or lightly textured surfaces, but also can be used to apply a resin-based paint such as gloss or eggshell. Some synthetic pile sleeves approach this sort of quality, but others, with their longer, coarser fibres, are best reserved for use on textured surfaces. In fact, if you work on the principle that smooth surfaces need smooth sleeves, and rougher surfaces need sleeves with a correspondingly longer pile, you won't go far wrong. From that you can see that sheepskin rollers are for very highly textured surfaces indeed. On a smooth surface, such a long pile tends to produce a rather rough-looking finish.

You will also need a roller tray — the roller's equivalent of a paint kettle. These are made from either metal or plastic, and you will find the latter far easier to clean. Metal trays, however, do have their advantages. They tend to last longer, and many are fitted with hooks allowing you to fit them to the treads of a step ladder, which is obviously handy if you are working on a ceiling or high wall.

Finally, you will need some sort of paint brush. The one thing rollers are not at all good at is cutting in accurately around the edges of the area you want to paint. That's the brush's job.

In addition to this basic tool kit, there are a few special rollers you may find useful. The first is simply an ordinary roller with a very long handle, and is designed to allow you to paint ceilings and high walls without having to set up access equipment. In practice, you will probably find them rather unwieldy, and this, coupled with the fact that you are

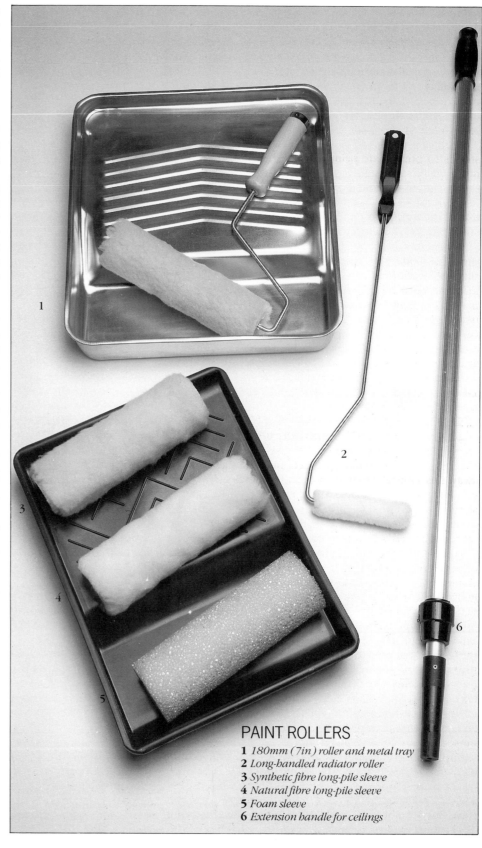

PAINT ROLLERS
1 *180mm (7in) roller and metal tray*
2 *Long-handled radiator roller*
3 *Synthetic fibre long-pile sleeve*
4 *Natural fibre long-pile sleeve*
5 *Foam sleeve*
6 *Extension handle for ceilings*

really too far away from the work to see clearly what you are doing, makes it difficult to obtain a really good finish. More useful is the radiator roller — a small, slim-line roller with a long handle designed to paint behind radiators in the same way as a radiator brush. The third and final type will also come in handy for painting the central heating system. It's called a pipe roller and has two or more small rollers fitted on to a single, flexible shaft so that it can hug the contours of the pipe along which it is run.

As for the technique of actually using a roller, the first step is to pour some paint into the roller tray. Not too much: put just enough into the deep end for the paint level to come a little way up the tray's ramp. And don't forget all the general points about getting paint ready for use mentioned earlier in the section on painting with a brush. They still apply.

You are now ready to charge the roller with paint. Simply run it down into the paint at the deep end of the tray, then run it back and forth over the tray's corrugated ramp a few times to remove the excess before offering the roller up to the wall, ceiling, or whatever. With emulsion paint (don't use a non-drip type with a roller), all you do now is run the roller back and forth in all directions to produce the same sort of ragged star as you would with a wall brush. Here again, when the roller starts to run dry, recharge it, begin another 'star' a little way along, and gradually extend this until it merges with the first 'star', totally covering the surface in between in the process.

There's no need to be too fussy about where one area begins and another ends. It is far more important to obtain an even coverage over the entire surface. You will soon get the hang of it and build up speed, but don't get carried away. It is a mistake to work a roller too quickly. If you do, especially with one that is fully loaded with paint, it will start to spray in much the same way as a car tyre running over a very wet road, and you could end up spattering paint over things best left unpainted.

You should also try to avoid allowing the edges of the area you have painted to dry out before you have had a chance to blend them into the paint film as a whole. With a good quality modern emulsion, such 'dry lines' don't matter so much on the first coat, but where they occur on the final coat of paint they will be noticeable in certain lights. This shouldn't prove too difficult while painting the bulk of the surface, but around the edges where you have to put the roller aside so you can cut in neatly with a brush, it can cause problems. The trick is to put up with the inconvenience of constantly changing tools and to carry out the rolling and cutting in side by side, rather than rolling a large area and going back to brush in over those bits you have missed.

Applying a resin-based paint with a roller is a little more complicated. Matt and semi matt finishes such as eggshell can be treated in the same way as emulsion. Again, don't use a non-drip variety. Gloss is quite another matter. Although a roller will produce a very even coverage, it tends not to leave quite as good a finish as a brush, the main reason

LOADING A ROLLER

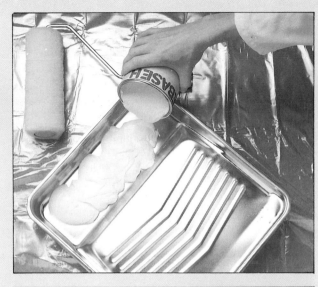

1 *You need a roller tray if you are going to decorate with a paint roller. This has a well at one end to act as a paint reservoir, and a ribbed slope that is used to load the roller evenly. Stir your paint thoroughly, then pour some into the well.*

2 *Push the roller into the well so it picks up some paint on one side. Don't push it in too deeply or you will get paint in the ends of the roller — this can lead to splashes and messy results when you start applying the paint.*

3 *Having picked up the paint on the roller, you simply roll it gently up and down the slope of the tray to disperse the paint evenly throughout the roller pile. Don't press too hard or you will squeeze out too much paint and have to reload more frequently. Excess paint runs back down the slope into the well.*

PAINTING A WALL

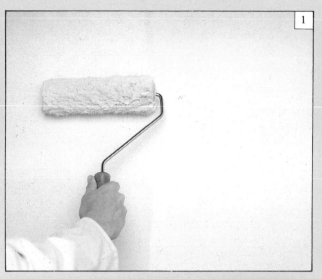

1 & 2 *Start applying the paint by running the roller up and down the wall. Put on several strips side by side; when the roller seems to be running dry, run it over the stripes with a series of horizontal and angled passes to ensure complete coverage and an even distribution of paint.*

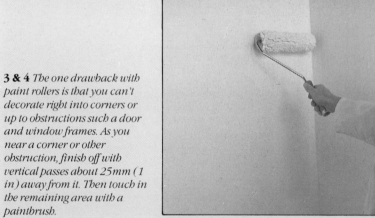

3 & 4 *The one drawback with paint rollers is that you can't decorate right into corners or up to obstructions such a door and window frames. As you near a corner or other obstruction, finish off with vertical passes about 25mm (1 in) away from it. Then touch in the remaining area with a paintbrush.*

APPLYING GLOSS PAINT

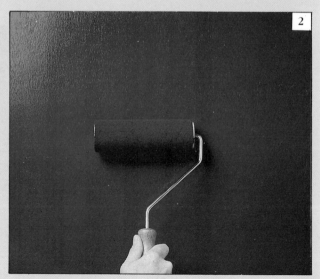

1 & 2 *You can also apply solvent-based paints using a paint roller; sleeves with a natural pile are better than those made from synthetic materials. Load the roller as described on the previous page, then apply the paint first along the grain direction, then across it. Finish off with a light pass parallel with the grain.*

USING SPECIAL ROLLERS

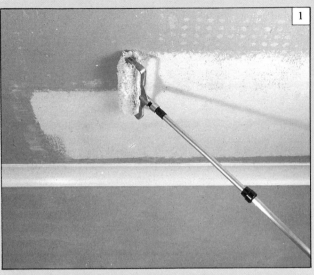

1 & 2 *If you prefer not perch on steps or trestles to paint your ceilings, you can use an extension handle to increase the reach of the roller and work from ground level instead. Use it just like a hand-held roller, first applying paint in stripes and then rolling it out with transverse passes.*

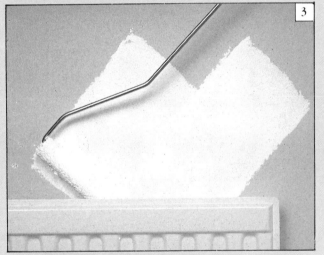

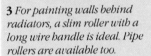

3 *For painting walls behind radiators, a slim roller with a long wire handle is ideal. Pipe rollers are available too.*

CLEANING AND STORING ROLLERS

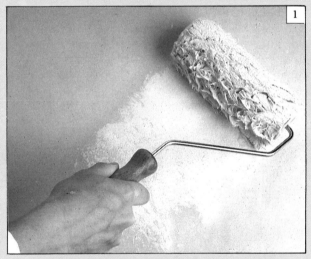

1 *When you have finished decorating, squeeze out as much paint from the sleeve as possible by running it backwards and forwards over a sheet of absorbent paper.*

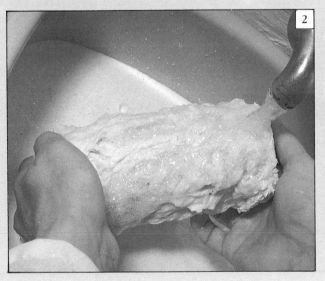

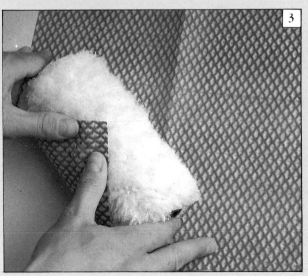

2 & 3 *Rinse out the sleeve thoroughly under a tap if you have been using emulsion paint. Use white spirit, paraffin or proprietary brush cleaner to remove solvent-based paints, and then wash the sleeve in warm, soapy water to remove all traces of the solvent. Allow the sleeve to dry in the open air, away from the direct heat source, then wrap it in clean paper or store it in a polythene bag.*

being that a roller simply doesn't put enough paint on the surface to produce that mirror- like deep shine. One possible answer is to simply overload the roller and apply less pressure when you roll it on. However, drips, runs, sags, spraying, and similar problems are then almost certain to mar the finish in any case. A better option is to use the roller simply as a means of getting the paint on to the surface. Once on, you can then lay the paint off with light, smooth strokes using a brush.

Obviously this is somewhat fiddly and time consuming, since you can only tackle the area in relatively small patches — otherwise the paint will have started to harden before you can brush it out. But it does have one very worthwhile incidental advantage. It allows you to apply the paint using cheap foam rollers, rather than the more expensive mohair ones normally recommended for the job. In fact, these are so cheap you can often afford to throw them away when you've finished — something you will appreciate when you realise how difficult and messy it is to clean resin-based paints out of roller sleeves. Incidentally, the slightly mottled finish produced by foam rollers and resin-based paint isn't all that unattractive — particularly when eggshell is used. You might even decide to keep it instead of brushing it out.

Having taken care of the painting, as always, clean up your tools and equipment. Start by running the roller back and forth over wads of clean newspaper to remove as much of the paint it contains as possible, then turn your attention to the roller tray. Pour back into the tin any paint left over, then wash it out thoroughly using the appropriate solvent — water for emulsions; white spirit for resin-based paints. If you have been applying a resin-based paint, leave some white spirit in the tray when you've finished. You can then run the roller through it, squeezing out the excess just as you would when painting, to give the roller sleeve a preliminary clean. That done, finish cleaning out the tray, remove the sleeve from the roller, and complete the cleaning of both sleeve and roller frame separately. Rinse in soapy water if you have been using white spirit and dry off before storing away for the next decorating session. As with brushes, it is a good idea to wrap sleeves in kitchen towel or something similar — it helps keeps them free of dust.

Painting with a pad

Another alternative to applying paint with a brush that you might like to try is to use a paint pad. These normally consist of a square or rectangular piece of natural or synthetic short-pile material similar to that used for mohair roller sleeves, with a foam plastic backing and mounted in a plastic or metal holder. They are available in a range of sizes — normally from around 65 × 50mm (2½ × 2in) for tackling small surfaces, up to about about 230 x 100mm (9 x 4in) for large areas such as walls — and can be used to apply both emulsions and resin-based paint. Although they are available separately, it is more common to find them sold as 'kits', which is possibly a good thing if you are just starting off, but not so convenient if you want a particular replace-

PAINT PADS

1 *Standard wall pad (minus handle)*
2 *Large wall pad*
3 *Crevice pad*
4 *Cutting-in pad*
5 *Small pad*

ment (though the manufacturers should be able to help here).

The technique for using them is quite straightforward. Begin by decanting the paint into a special tray, having first stirred, strained and prepared it in the usual way (see above). The sort of tray used is similar in principle to that employed with a roller, but different in design. The part that holds the paint reservoir is usually both deeper and narrower, and, instead of having a ramp, the better models come fitted with a grooved plastic roller which can be used to remove excess paint from the pad, and even out the distribution of paint across it. You now just dip the pad lightly into the paint, aiming to load only its pile — in other words, don't just dunk it in so the whole tool is covered in paint. Lightly run it back and forth over the roller a few times until excess paint ceases to come off, then draw the loaded pad gently across the surface you wish to paint, reloading it as necessary when it starts to run dry.

For the best results on a smooth surface such as woodwork or metalwork, cover the area in a series of roughly parallel, barely overlapping strips. On less dependable surfaces such as walls and ceilings, work the pad in as many different directions as possible to prevent lumps and dips leaving unpainted shadows.

You should find that the pad allows you to achieve a far more even coverage than a brush. In fact, in this respect, you can expect results comparable with those achieved using a roller — you will just find the tool easier to control. However, it is not quite as versatile as a paint brush. It tends not to cope well with textured surfaces, and coping with fiddly bits, as well as accurate cutting-in, can also prove difficult. These last two problems, though, can be eased by using special purpose paint pads. There are, for example, special edging pads designed for cutting into internal angles — they have a set of small wheels in their edges which guide the pad by running over the surface you don't want to paint. Similarly, there are very small pads mounted on more manipulable handles designed for tackling awkward corners and more complicated sections.

Cleaning paint pads and their associated equipment can also be rather tricky, particularly if you have been applying a resin-based paint. In this case, it is best to adopt the same strategy as when cleaning a roller. Run the pads over wads of newspaper to remove the bulk of the excess paint, then clean out the pad's tray, fill it with a little white spirit, and use it and its roller (if it has one) to continue the cleaning process. Finally, dismantle the paint pad and treat the various components and accessories separately to ensure that they are really clean. Using disposable pads is, on the whole a better option. If you have been using an emulsion paint, of course, the whole cleaning process is far simpler — merely run everything under a tap until it comes clean. Even so, you may find it difficult to completely clean out the pads themselves, a great deal here depending on how long the pad has been in use (and therefore the amount of ingrained dry paint you have to cope with). Again, it is well worth considering using disposable pads.

LOADING A PAD

1 *Most paint pads come in kits containing several differentsized pads and a special tray with a ribbed roller which you use to load the pads with paint. Start by pouring some stirred and strained paint into the reservoir at one end of the paint tray.*

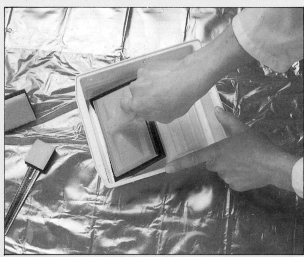

2 *Hold the pad level and dip its pile carefully into the paint reservoir. Don't dip it in too deeply, or you will get paint on the body of the tool and make a mess when you try to paint with it. Take special care with large wall pads — since they nearly fill the reservoir it's easy to push paint up onto the back of the pad as you load it up.*

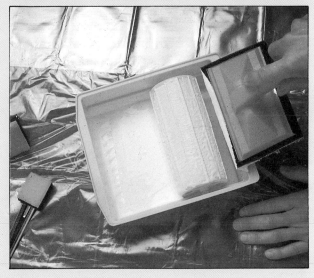

3 *Lift the pad out of the reservoir and run it lightly back and forwards over the ribbed roller to distribute the paint evenly throughout the pile, and to squeeze out excess paint. This then runs back into the reservoir again. Wipe paint off the roller with absorbent paper from time to time to stop it drying and spoiling the pick-up of paint by the pad.*

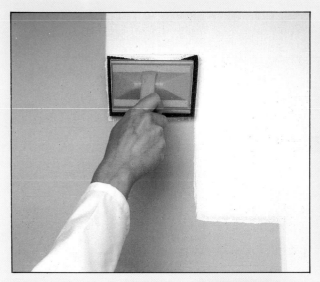

APPLYING PAINT

1 & 2 *If you are applying emulsion paint using a large pad, simply draw it down the wall surface in a series of parallel stripes. Then run the pad over the surface in horizontal and transverse bands to ensure even coverage. Use the smaller pads in the kit for painting awkward areas such a glazing bars.*

3 *Use a long-handled crevice pad for painting hard-to-reach areas such as behind radiators.*

CLEANING AND STORING PADS

1 *When you have finished decorating, press out as much paint as possible from the pad by running it backwards and forwards on some absorbent paper.*

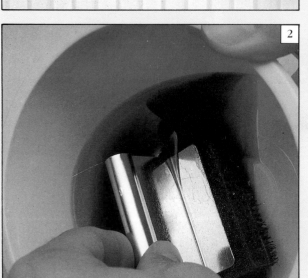

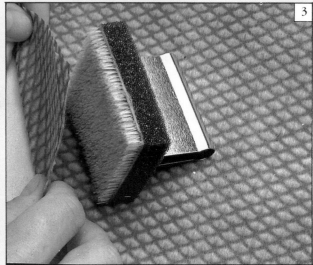

2 & 3 *Next, remove the rest of the paint by rinsing the pad in the appropriate solvent — water for emulsion paints, white spirit, paraffin or proprietary brush cleaner for solvent-based paints. Finally, allow the pile to dry in the open air before wrapping it up and putting it away.*

Spray painting

If brushes, rollers and paint pads don't appeal, why not try a radically different approach to applying paint — spraying it on? It's far quicker, and, with a little practice, you will find you are able to produce a finish far superior (certainly where gloss paint is concerned) to that achieved using any other painting technique.

In terms of tools and equipment, there are two main options. The first is to buy the paint in aerosol form. Although not especially cheap, you will find this an economical method of dealing with most small items such as pieces of furniture and so on, and it does have the additional advantages of being both cleaner (there's no messing about thinning the paint and loading it into the spray gun) and more convenient. The only major snag is that you are limited by what the paint manufacturers choose to sell in this form — generally a fairly basic range of best selling colours in gloss.

The alternative to is hire a full-size spray gun and compressor — the better models are really too expensive to consider buying unless you intend to do a great deal of this sort of work; more than you would find in the average house. But even this is not an especially cheap undertaking, and so you really need to make sure that there is enough work to justify it. Painting the walls and ceiling of a single room probably won't meet this criterion unless the room is very large. Painting a number of rooms or the outside walls of your home almost certainly will, especially if speed is essential — you might, for example, want to give the whole house a quick face lift having just moved in, or smarten it up just before you sell it.

If you do decide to hire spraying equipment, though, there are a few points to bear in mind. First, decide on the type of paint you want to use and let the hire shop advise you on the sort of equipment you need to apply it. So long as you are using ordinary interior resin-based paints and emulsions, you shouldn't have any problems finding suitable equipment. Secondly, decide whether or not you need to work high above the floor. If you do, make sure the equipment comes with a long enough hose between the compressor (which puts the paint under pressure) and the spray gun (which is the bit you hold to actually apply the paint). This will allow you to carry out virtually the entire job from a simple step ladder and/or extension ladder. The alternative is to work from some form of scaffolding arrangement strong enough to raise the compressor to within reach of the work. Finally, make sure you receive adequate instruction on how to operate the equipment — how to set it up, how much (if any) you have to thin the paint, and so on. If you damage the equipment through misuse, you will lose your deposit. Similarly, make sure you know how to clean the equipment before returning it to the shop — they will charge you if they have to clean it themselves.

As for how you set about actually spraying on the paint, the basic technique is broadly the same no matter what equipment you use. Begin by masking off everything in the

SPRAY GUN EQUIPMENT

1 *Spray gun*
2 *Extension nozzle*
3 *Goggles*
4 *Face mask*
5 *Viscosity cup*
6 *Aerosol paint*
7 *Masking tape*
8 *Gloves*

PREPARATION

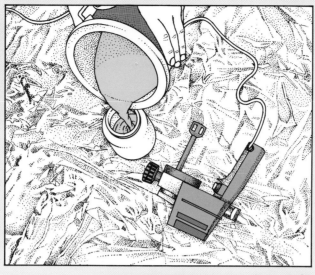

1 & 2 *Lay dust sheets over floors in the area to be painted. Then pour some paint into the reservoir (after thinning it if required) and screw the reservoir to the body of the gun. Finally, attach the appropriate nozzle for the paint being sprayed.*

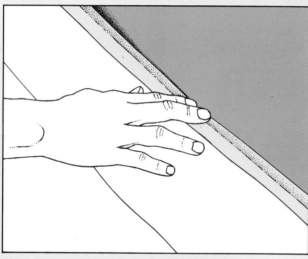

3 & 4 *Protect surfaces such as skirting boards by taping strips of paper or polythene along them with masking tape. Use a similar method to mask off windows. Make sure the tape edge is straight, so that a neat finish is left when it is removed.*

5 & 6 *Smear petroleum jelly over small, awkwardly-shaped fittings such as radiator valves to protect them. The jelly is simply wiped off when painting is complete.*

It is best to spray-paint small objects out of doors.

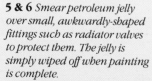

SPRAY PAINTING

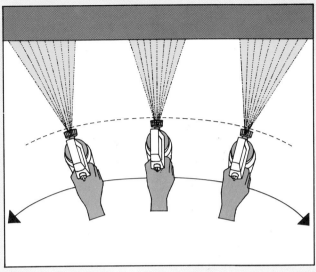
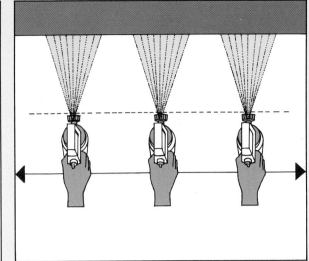

1 & 2 *It's tempting to use the gun by swinging your arm from side to side, but this method applies more paint at the centre point than at the edges of each pass. Instead, move your hand parallel with the surface you're painting.*

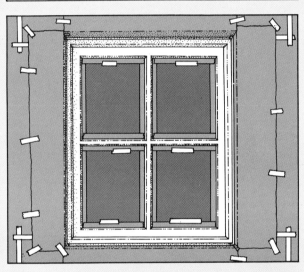

3 & 4 *As you work, overlap successive passes slightly to avoid patchy coverage. Apply two thin coats rather than one thick one. When spraying woodwork, spend time masking off other surfaces that are not to be painted.*

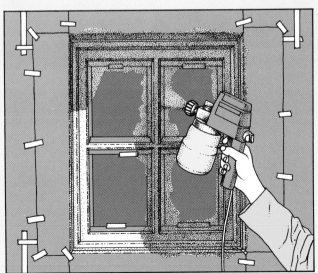

5 & 6 *Spray the exposed surfaces with steady passes of the gun, again applying two thin coats rather than one thick one to avoid runs. Peel off the masking when the paint surface is touch-dry.*

CLEANING A GUN

1 When you have finished decorating, decant any remaining paint from the container back into the original tin. Then squeeze the trigger to expel as much paint as possible.

2 When no more paint emerges from the nozzle, dismantle the gun ready for cleaning. Follow the manufacturer's recommendations here — how much dismantling is needed varies from gun to gun. Make sure that you have unplugged the equipment from the mains before you go any further.

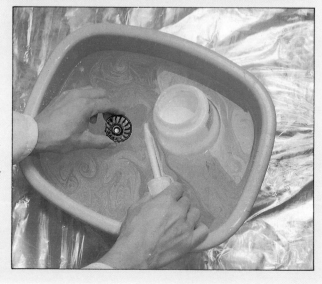

3 Clean all the components of the gun thoroughly in the appropriate solvent — water for emulsion; white spirit, paraffin or a proprietary solvent for gloss and eggshell; special thinners for cellulose paint. Rinse each component in clean solvent, then reassemble the gun and run some clean solvent through it to complete the cleaning process.

vicinity that you don't want painted using a combination of masking tape and newspaper or polythene sheeting — there is no way to cut in accurately with a spray gun. This is incredibly time-consuming, but you must take the trouble to do the job properly, particularly where the various areas are to be painted using different kinds of paint. If, for example, you allow resin paint to stray on to walls that you intend to emulsion later, you may find that the emulsion won't cover the error. Be especially careful when masking off areas you have only just painted. You might, for instance, have painted the ceiling, and wish to mask it in order to spray the walls a different colour. The main thing is to allow the new paintwork to dry out for as long as possible before masking. In addition, be sure to use proper masking tape (not ordinary sticky tape), and remove it as soon as possible after you have finished. This not only produces a cleaner line as it tears through the slightly tacky overlying paint film, but also reduces the risk of it lifting paint off the masked area.

Alternatively, if you are really in a hurry and are prepared to take risks, there is a way to avoid masking. Simply spray as close as you dare to the surface you don't want painted — and the best modern spray guns are sufficiently accurate to allow you to go fairly close — then tackle the final cutting-in with a brush.

Incidentally, don't bother about masking off really fiddly items of hardware. If you cannot remove them before spraying, rub them over with a little petroleum jelly. This stops the paint sticking sufficiently for you to wipe or scrape it off once it is touch-dry.

With the masking out of the way, begin spraying. Starting at the top in one corner, hold the spray nozzle about 300mm (12in) from the surface and push the button. As soon as the paint begins to cover, move the spray gun along at a steady speed to paint a broad, evenly covered stripe. That done, without switching off, spray down a little, then back across the surface to form a second stripe which slightly overlaps the first. Continue in this way until the entire surface has been evenly covered.

Just how fast or slow you work is largely a matter of judgement. The trick is to work slow enough to ensure good coverage, yet not so slow that the paint film gets thick enough to run or sag. Having found the right working speed, keep going as steadily as you can to ensure that the coverage is not only adequate, but also even. It is also important to hold the spray gun at a constant distance from the work along the entire length of each stripe. If you simply hold out your arm and swing it back and forth, the spray nozzle will be closer to the work when spraying the area immediately in front of you than it will be at the ends of the stripes, and this will also result in uneven coverage.

If you have problems in this respect, try turning off the spray gun at the end of each stripe, and work faster rather than slower. You can always apply a second or third coat to achieve the necessary complete coverage and colour density. The drawback with this approach is that, each time you stop and start, you increase the risk of the spray gun 'spluttering' — the resulting uneven coverage obviously defeating the object of the exercise.

With a compressor and spray gun set-up, the answer is to clean out the nozzle at regular intervals following the manufacturer's instructions. Taking care to thin the paint correctly and to mix the resulting mixture to a really smooth consistency will also help. In any case, at the start of each spraying session, it is always worth testing the spray on a wad of newspaper or something similar before directing it at the surface you want to paint. This both helps clear the nozzle, and lets you know that everything is working properly.

The problem of spluttering is more difficult to overcome when using an aerosol. Really all you can do is regularly wipe off around the nozzle with a cloth dipped in white spirit (or cellulose thinners if you are using car retouching spray on metal) and replace the dust cap when the aerosol is not in use. If the jet should start to clog, try inverting the can and spraying on to a wad of newspaper for a few seconds to clear it. Never poke out the nozzle's hole with a pin. You could enlarge or deform it, and thus make matters worse.

Finally, as well as taking good care of the spraying equipment, take good care of yourself. Make sure the room in which you are working is well ventilated — though it should be free from strong draughts that could cause the spray to drift. If spraying resin-based or cellulose paints, keep well away from naked flames. And do wear suitable protective clothing. Goggles and a face mask are certainly to be strongly recommended whatever you are doing. If you are carrying out a lot of spraying in a confined space, they are essential.

Special techniques

By now you should have a fairly good idea of how to set about simply changing the colour of a surface using ordinary interior paints. But there are a few special painting techniques worth knowing about for those situations where you need a finish that's that little bit different.

First, there is the application of a texturing compound or textured paint. The majority of those used for low-to-medium relief finishes are simply applied to the surface with an ordinary wall brush — a fairly wide one is best. Aim to cover an area of about 1sq m (1sq yd) at a time with an even film of the required thickness. This might be 2 or 3mm ($\frac{1}{8}$in) in the case of a texturing compound; the thickness of a rather heavy coat of paint in the case of a textured paint. This, in itself, leaves the surface with a sort of textured effect, but there is a whole host of far more exciting finishes that can be achieved using this sort of product, and to produce them, you need to go back and get to work on the rather plain surface left by the brush.

One of the simplest texturing techniques is to merely run a foam paint roller over the surface. Wrapping coarse string around the roller produces a rather stronger variation on the theme. Sponged finishes are also worth considering. Just dab an ordinary sponge over the surface to pull the

TEXTURING THE SURFACE

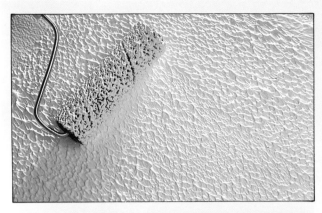

1 *One of the simplest ways of texturing paints of this sort is to run a special texturing roller over the surface. A wide range of different effects can be achieved in this way.*

2 *A wall brush used in a tapping motion will produce overlapping ridges ideal for covering up less-than-perfect wall and ceiling surfaces.*

3 *Another simple effect to achieve is a series of random waves, created by drawing a serrated scraper across the still-wet paint film. Each pass should slightly overlap the previous one.*

4 *By using a wide serrated scraper in a circular motion pivoting around one end, perfect grooved circles can be made, either overlapping or evenly spaced.*

SPONGING

1 *When you're using more than one colour, apply the darkest one first and space the dabs of colour fairly widely to give a sense of depth. Use a genuine marine sponge if possible, rather than a synthetic one, to give the most interesting texture.*

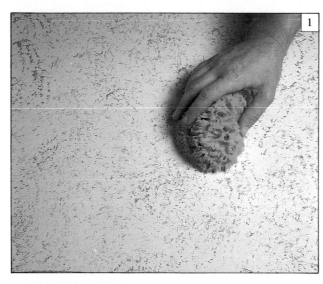

2 *Add the second slightly lighter colour, spacing the colour dabs more closely together this time. Test the effect first on scrap paper each time, to ensure that you have not taken up too much paint on the sponge.*

3 *Apply the third, lightest, colour in the same way to fill in the design. Wash the sponge regularly in water or white spirit (according to the type of paint being used), wringing it out thoroughly every time so you don't dilute the paint.*

4 *Finish off by using a clean sponge to soften the overall effect. Again, rinse the sponge from time to time.*

5 *You can apply the technique to virtually any surface. Here it has been used to disguise the lines of an old radiator.*

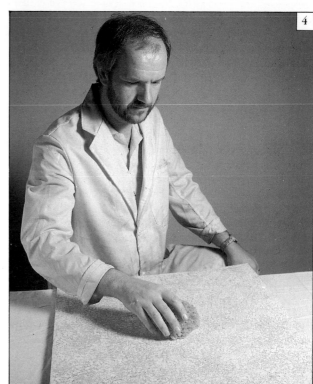

compound out and so produce a random stippled effect. For a more pronounced stipple, try wrapping the sponge in polythene. Give it a twist as you pull it away and you can produce very attractive stippled swirls. Alternatively, use a sponge to drag the compound out into swirls with a wider radius, overlapping arcs that look rather like reptilian scales, zig-zags, or any other pattern that takes your fancy. If you would prefer a more clean-cut finish, use serrated scrapers or metal combs to score out designs. From specialist shops, you can buy a wide variety of such scrapers and combs specially designed for the job in a choice of shapes and sizes, but there is no reason why you cannot obtain equally successful results using improvised equipment — ordinary hair combs, coarse brushes, bits of scrap plastic and metal filed to give a serrated edge, and so on.

Use your imagination, and experiment with the texturing compound on a piece of scrap hardboard or something similar before getting to work on the wall or ceiling. Just avoid creating anything too exotic unless you are absolutely sure that you can live with it for evermore. Remember, texturing compounds are extremely difficult to remove.

Painting murals is something else you might like to try your hand at. You don't have to be another Michelangelo to achieve acceptable results. If you have doubts about your artistic talents, you could limit yourself to creating simple geometric designs — something as basic as a painted stripe at dado or picture rail height can be surprisingly effective — or you could crib from pictures found in magazines.

You don't need much in the way of equipment. A selection of ordinary decorators' paint brushes will cope with most basic designs, but you will need a few smaller 'artists' paint brushes to tackle fine detail. As for paint, any interior emulsion or resin-based paint can be used, though emulsion is generally the best bet for beginners. Don't buy any most basic designs, but you will need a few smaller artist's plus small cans of the primary colours (red, yellow, and blue) will go a long way. Remember, you can mix emulsion quite easily to produce a wide variety of intermediate colours and shades. Paint left over from previous bouts of decorating can also be put to good use, as can the small pots of paint now widely sold as colour samplers — though these can prove expensive. Look out, too, for special dyes purpose made for tinting emulsion. At a pinch, you could even mix in a little children's powder paint, though results cannot be guaranteed.

There are just a few points to bear in mind when mixing paint. Firstly, work out as accurately as you can how much of a given colour you need (allowing for the fact that several coats may be needed to achieve good coverage) and mix it in one batch. If you run out, you will find it almost impossible to achieve exactly the same shade a second time. Next, make sure you mix the paint really thoroughly so as to avoid streaks and other more subtle colour variations throughout the batch. Finally, try the paint out on the wall, allow it to dry, then check that it is exactly the colour you want — the colour of the paint in a mixing bucket isn't a good guide to the finished result. Make sure, too, that you check all the colours in the same light — either daylight or artificial light — or the results of your matching will be unpredictable.

To make a start, prepare the wall in the normal way and paint it completely in a suitable background colour. Ideally, go for a moderately light colour that occupies a lot of space in the finished mural. Failing that, choose a neutral grey or something similar. Once that's dry, you can begin creating the mural in earnest. If you are using your own design, and are confident of your ability, sketch it on to the wall in charcoal to begin with. Any mistakes can then easily be rubbed out with a cloth. Once you are satisfied, go over the lines in soft pencil, felt tipped pen, or diluted paint applied with a small artist's brush. Wash off any excess charcoal dust before continuing.

If you are less sure of being able to draw directly on to the wall, make a preliminary sketch on paper (working to scale) and transfer the design onto the wall in the same way as you would one you had decided to copy from an existing picture. There are two ways in which this can be done. The first is to draw a grid in paint or pencil on the wall, then draw a similar grid, accurately scaled down, on the picture you want to copy. You should then find it relatively easy to transfer the design by hand, a little at a time — the smaller the squares on the grid, the easier it will be. The alternative is to photograph the design in order to get a slide that you can project on to the surface using an ordinary slide projector. You can then merely trace off the relevant features.

Geometric designs are, naturally, rather easier to achieve, and can be safely constructed directly on the wall. For straight lines, either use a long, straight timber batten as a rule, or a chalked line. The latter method is particularly useful for marking out a grid on the wall if you are using that method to transfer a design. Simply rub chalk into a length of soft string (or use a purpose-made chalk line which automatically chalks the string as you pull it from its reel), stretch it along the intended line and snap it against the surface like a bowstring — the result is a neat chalk line.

For circles, either draw round a plate, cup, or something similar, or, if you need a larger circle, make up a 'string and pencil compass'. Push a drawing pin into the wall where the centre of the circle is to be, and tie a piece of string to it. Tie the other end of the string to a pencil so that the length of the string equals the radius of the circle, then start drawing, keeping the string absolutely taut. Pins and string can also be employed to draw ellipses. Stick two pins into the wall this time — the farther they are apart the flatter the ellipse — to anchor an oversize loop of string. Using a pencil, pull out one side of the loop to create a string triangle, then draw the pencil right round both pins keeping the constantly changing string triangle as taut as possible.

One tip: if your design involves repeating the same motif over and over again, draw it on card, cut out the shape, then using this as a template, trace round it on to the wall.

Once the design is on the wall, it is simply a matter of getting to work with paint and brushes to colour in the outline. If you need really precise divisions of colour between

PAINTING A MURAL

1 & 2 *Select a design you want to reproduce, and draw a squared grid over it. Then work out how many times you want to enlarge it, and draw a similar but larger grid on the wall using pencil or charcoal. Use a spirit level to ensure that the grid lines are truly horizontal and vertical.*

3 & 4 *Stick your original up on the wall, and refer to it as you sketch in the outline of the design square by square. Then mix up each colour in turn in a shallow dish, and brush it onto the appropriate areas of the mural.*

5 & 6 *When you have completed the painting, outline the design with fine black lines using an artist's paintbrush or a felt-tipped pen. Allow the paint to dry thoroughly, then wipe off the grid lines and seal the surface with a coat of varnish.*

areas, use masking tape to define each area, paint it in, then peel off the tape when the paint is just tacky.

Of course, a simpler way to paint a pattern on a surface is to use a stencil. You can make up one of your own if you wish, carefully cutting it out of thin card using a very sharp knife. Or you can buy stencils ready made from good craft shops, decorating shops, and department stores — though availability does depend rather a lot on the current fashionability of the technique.

Using the stencil is quite simple. All you need is some masking tape, and a fairly small brush with short, stiff bristles — a purpose made stencil brush is obviously best, but an old, worn paint-brush that fits the description will do. As when painting a mural, no special paint is needed. Use ordinary interior emulsion or resin-based paint, bearing in mind what was said earlier concerning colours. Hold the stencil against the surface or the wall or whatever, and tape it securely in place using the masking tape. Next, load the

brush, aiming to leave little more than a film of paint standing on the very ends of the bristles. You will find this ideal a lot easier to achieve if you pour a very small amount of paint into a shallow dish, rather than a paint kettle — a dish so shallow and containing so little paint that it is physically impossible to dip the brush in too far.

All you do now is apply the paint to the surface through the stencil, working the brush in a series of light stabbing strokes until you have achieved just the right degree of coverage. This is important if you want a really crisp finish. If you don't work the brush absolutely vertically, or if you apply too much paint, there is every chance that paint will find its way under the stencil and blur the outline.

When you have finished, allow the paint to become tacky, then peel off both masking tape and stencil in one clean movement. As when using masking tape on its own, if you remove the stencil too soon, paint may run out beyond the desired outline. Remove it too late, and in tearing the hard-

There is no limit to the results you can achieve with applied decorations. In this kitchen **above left** *a clever 'trompe l'oeil' effect has been used on the cupboard doors to echo the natural stone wall cladding above.*

With murals, simple effects often work best, as with this cleverly painted window **top** *thronged with colourful birds.*

Even a simple splash of colour combined with a striking motif **above** *can bring a room alive, especially where strongly contrasting colours are used.*

STENCILLING

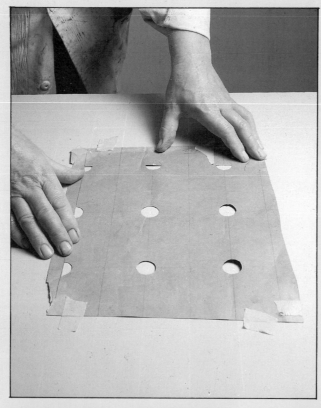

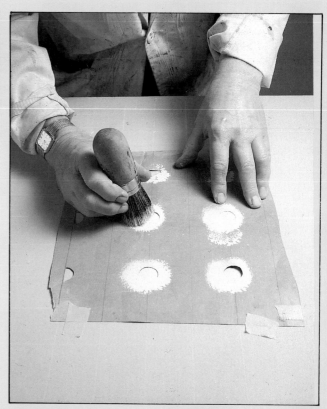

1 & 2 *First, prepare your stencil board, using special stencilling paper. Then stick it firmly in position on the surface you're decorating using masking tape. Apply the paint with a flat-ended stencilling brush, holding it vertically by the ferrule.*

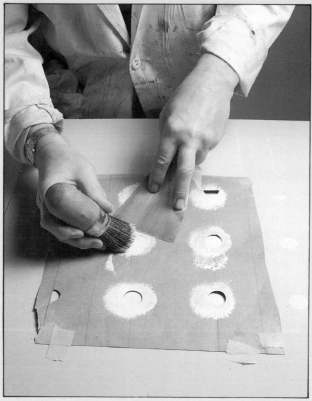

3 & 4 *If the paint shows any signs of getting underneath the edges of the stencil, hold it down while you work with a broad filling knife or similar implement. When the paint is touch-dry, position a stencil with a complementary pattern so you can apply the second colour. Check the alignment carefully before you start.*

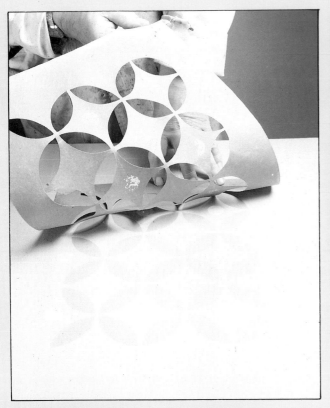

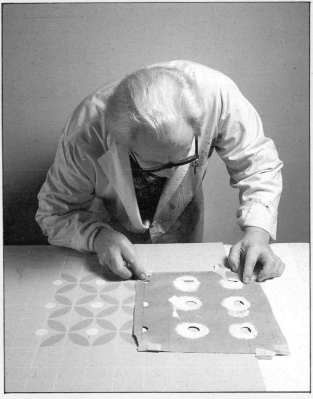

5 & 6 *Peel the stencil away from the paint by lifting it vertically so you don't smudge the paint edges. Wipe off any excess paint before you reposition the stencil to continue the next section of the design. Note here the half-circles cut in the sheet as an aid to accurate alignment.*

7 & 8 *Once stencilling is complete, you can touch up any small defects in the pattern using a small artist's paintbrush. A range of simple stencils can be used to build up quite complex overall designs.*

COMBING

1 Use a soft, long-bristled brush to lay on the base coat, allowing the bristles to form parallel 'trim-lines' in the paint film.

2 Draw a rubber-toothed comb over the paint to straighten the lines.

3 Create a kinked herringbone effect with a stiff fine-toothed comb.

4 Repeat the effect at right angles to give the surface a woven effect.

5 Make short, curved passes with a rubber comb to create a fish-scale pattern.

6 The overall effect closely resembles the three-dimensional effect often used with textured wall and ceiling finishes.

ened paint film, it could pull off paint from within the area of the stencil's design. You therefore need to work fairly quickly if you are using different colours for different parts of the design. To avoid mistakes, either carefully block off with masking tape the holes that do not apply to the colour you are using, or remove the stencil completely when you have finished one colour and wait for the paint to dry before carefully repositioning it and applying the next.

There is one last group of techniques you may like to try out. They are based on the idea of modifying the surface film of paint once it has been brushed onto the wall, either before it has dried or by adding further colour over the top. The step-by-step photographs show how the various methods work, and what sort of effects can be achieved using them.

Having painted the surface in a suitable background colour, take a different coloured paint and mix it with a little of the treacly substance that gives the technique its name — scumble — to form a fairly runny glaze. You now,

brush this on over the painted background, and then wipe it off again with a clean, lint-free cloth, manipulating the cloth as you go to leave just enough of the scumble layer behind to produce the desired effect. For the crisper lines required for woodgraining, combs and sharp points are used to remove the scumble layer. This, of course, is where the skill comes in. It's all too easy to end up with nothing more than a mess. But persevere. For more complex effects, repeat the process with further layers of scumbling in different colours, allowing each to dry thoroughly before applying the next.

If desired, the basic scumbled finish can be used as a base for more extrovert random finish techniques — flicking paint on to the surface with a heavily loaded brush, for example, to produce a spatter effect. Again, with such techniques you need to put in a fair amount of practice before you achieve anything like control over them. And you also need a good eye and sufficient self-restraint to know when enough is enough.

THE COMPLETE PAPERHANGER

THE COMPLETE PAPERHANGER

Paperhanging has, for a long time, had something of a reputation for being one of the more difficult ways to decorate a wall. Certainly it takes a little care to produce good results. But difficult? So long as you start by setting yourself a fairly straightforward stretch of wall to gain confidence, and build up gradually to the more complicated bits of papering, then given the right equipment plus modern pastes and wallcoverings, you will be surprised at just how easy it is — once you know how.

Basic techniques for walls

Your very first job is to decide where to start — where to hang the very first length of paper, or 'drop', as it is called. In years gone by, this was quite a complicated business. The drops overlapped, and it was therefore important to paper in such a way that these overlaps weren't too obvious; the usual practice being to start above and below the room's main window and to work out in both directions around the room. Today, virtually all papers are made so that drops merely butt up against each other. Where you start is therefore up to you, and although there is still something to be said for starting above a main window, or somewhere equally awkward such as in the centre of a chimney breast, this really applies only if you are using a paper with a very large, prominent motif. For the rest, you would do better to start in a corner of the room and tackle a long, uncomplicated wall to get your hand in.

Having chosen a starting place, measure out from the corner and, with the aid of a plumbline, draw a vertical line on the wall to indicate the edge of the first length of paper. This should be about 25mm (1in) less than the paper's width out from the corner of the room. Don't rely on the walls, door frame, or anything else to judge whether the first drop is truly vertical. They are usually out of true, and if you start crooked, things will become progressively more difficult as you paper round the room. You can now use the vertical line as a guide to measure the height of the wall, and therefore the length of paper needed for each drop.

Now cut the first few drops from the roll ready for pasting. It's best to do this on a pasting table — these are not expensive, and really do make paperhanging much easier. Transfer the measured height of the wall on to the paper with a tape measure, add about 100mm (4in) to allow for trimming at top and bottom, and cut across using a pair of long-bladed paperhanger's scissors — another specialist tool well worth buying. To make sure you hang the paper with the pattern the right way up, write 'TOP' on the back of the drop at the appropriate end. To cut subsequent drops to length, use this first one as a guide. Lay it face up on the pasting table, pull more paper from the roll and adjust the latter's position until the patterns match exactly, then

WALLPAPER QUANTITY GUIDE

IMPERIAL

Distance round walls (incl. doors/ windows)	Number of rolls needed						
	Height in feet from skirting						
	7 — 7½	7½ — 8	8 — 8½	8½ — 9	9 — 9½	9½ — 10	10 — 10½
30	4	5	5	5	6	6	6
34	5	5	5	5	6	6	7
38	5	6	6	6	7	7	8
42	6	6	7	7	7	8	8
46	6	7	7	7	8	8	9
50	7	7	8	8	9	9	10
54	7	8	9	9	9	10	10
58	8	8	9	9	10	10	11
62	8	9	10	10	10	11	12
66	9	9	10	10	11	12	13
70	9	10	11	11	12	12	13
74	10	10	12	12	12	13	14
78	10	11	12	12	13	14	15
82	11	11	13	13	14	14	16
86	12	12	14	14	14	15	16
90	12	13	14	14	15	16	17
94	13	13	15	15	15	16	18
98	13	14	15	15	16	17	19

METRIC

Distance round walls (incl. doors/ windows)	Number of rolls needed							
	Height in metres from skirting							
	2 — 2.2	2.2 — 2.5	2.5 — 2.7	2.7 — 3	3 — 3.2	3.2 — 3.5	3.5 — 3.7	3.7 — 4
10	5	5	6	6	7	7	8	8
11	5	6	7	7	8	8	9	9
12	6	6	7	8	8	9	9	10
13	6	7	8	8	9	10	10	10
14	7	7	8	9	10	10	11	11
15	7	8	9	9	10	11	12	12
16	8	8	9	10	11	11	12	13
17	8	9	10	10	11	12	13	14
18	9	9	10	11	12	13	14	15
19	9	10	11	12	13	14	15	16
20	9	10	11	12	13	14	15	16
21	10	11	12	13	14	15	16	17
22	10	11	13	14	15	16	17	18
23	11	12	13	14	15	17	18	19
24	11	12	14	15	16	17	18	20
25	12	13	14	15	17	18	19	20
26	12	13	15	16	17	19	20	21
27	13	14	15	17	18	19	21	22
28	13	14	16	17	19	20	21	23
29	13	15	16	18	19	21	22	24
30	14	15	17	18	20	21	23	24

CUT & PASTE

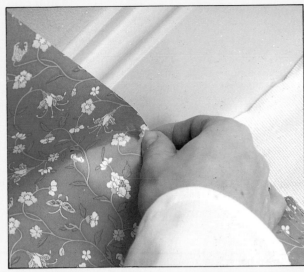

1 & 2 *Unless you are using a ready-mixed tub paste, your first task is to mix up a quantity of powder paste sufficient for the number of rolls you intend to hang. Follow the manufacturer's instructions, mixing the paste carefully to avoid lumps. Then measure out your first length, adding an allowance for trimming.*

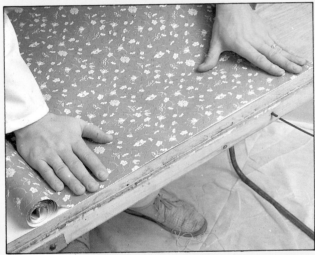
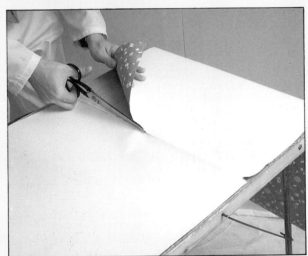

3 & 4 *Fold the paper carefully in line with your length mark, making sure the edges of the paper are parallel to guarantee a square edge to the cut. Then fold the paper out flat on the pasting table and cut carefully along the marked line with your paperhanger's shears.*

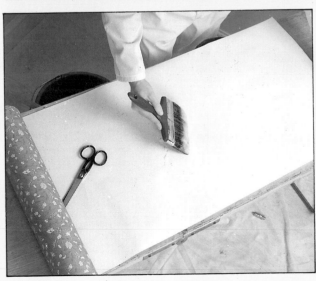

5 & 6 *Brush the paste on to the back of the length generously, making sure you don't miss any parts. As you brush out towards the edges, align the paper with the table edge so that you don't get paste on the table itself (and then on to the face of the wallpaper itself). When you've covered the area on the pasting table, fold over the end pasted side innermost so you can tackle the rest of the length.*

THE COMPLETE PAPERHANGER

BASIC PAPERHANGING

1 & 2 *Measure along the wall from a corner a distance just greater than the width of the wallpaper, and suspend a plumbline at that point. You can make pencil marks on the wall and join them up with a straightedge, or simply work with the plumbline left in position. Then measure the length of the first 'drop', paste it and offer it up.*

3 & 4 *When you have positioned the top of the length, slide it across until its right-hand edge is perfectly aligned with the plumbline. Then use your paperhanger's brush to smooth the length into place. Work from the centre out towards the edges.*

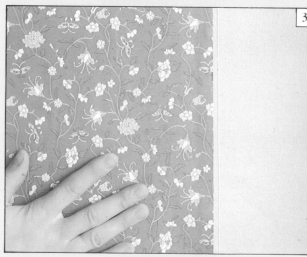

5 & 6 *At the top of the length, use the brush again to tap the paper firmly into the angle between wall and ceiling (or, as here, at picture rail level). Draw the back of the shears along the angle to form a clearly marked crease along the angle, ready for trimming.*

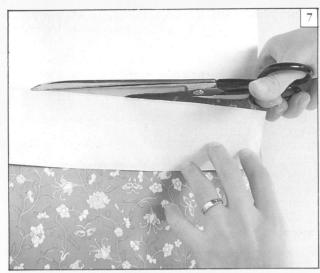

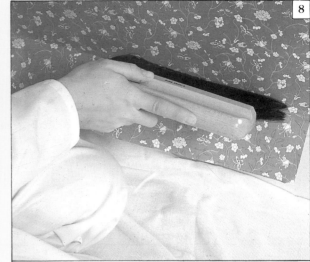

7 & 8 *Peel the top end of the length away from the wall so you can cut along the creased line with the shears, following the profile of the angle precisely. Then brush it back into position on the wall. Repeat the brushing-in process at skirting-board level.*

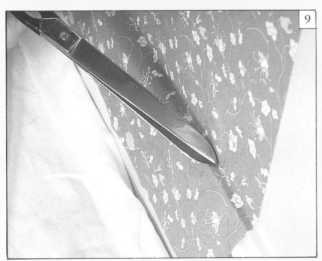

9 & 10 *Once again, use the back of the shears to mark the profile of the angle between wall and skirting board on the paper. Then peel the bottom of the length away from the wall, trim off the excess paper and brush it carefully into place.*

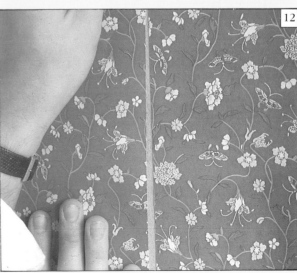

11 & 12 *Cut and paste the second length, take it to the wall and offer it up at the top, aligning it roughly with the edge of the first length. Then slide it carefully into its exact position to form a perfect butt join. Brush the length into place as before, trimming the excess at top and bottom. Repeat the process for subsequent lengths.*

cut it to size; again marking the appropriate end with the word 'TOP'. This makes it easier to achieve an accurate pattern match when the paper is on the wall.

In most cases, you will find that the pattern either runs straight across the two lengths, or else matches if you stagger them slightly (this is known as a drop pattern). But watch for wallcoverings bearing the instructions 'reverse alternate lengths'. This means every other drop is hung upside down, so remember to turn the paper round on the pasting table to obtain the correct pattern match before cutting.

The next job is to paste the first length. Lay it face down on the pasting table and apply an even, liberal coat of paste with a paste brush, taking care not to miss even the smallest patch, and not to get paste on the patterned side of the paper. There are a few tips that will help here. Start by placing the loaded paste brush in the middle of the paper and paste out towards the edges. To paste right up to an edge, adjust the position of the paper so that the edge you are pasting overhangs the table top by about 25mm (1in), and work the paste brush out across it. Never draw the brush back across the edge or paste will be scraped off on to the patterned side of the paper. And do try not to get paste on the surface of the pasting table.

Make sure, too, that you use the right sort of paste. Ordinary paste is fine for light/medium weight papers, but heavyweights, most vinyls and washables, and embossed wallcoverings need a heavy-duty paste. In the case of vinyl and washable wallcoverings — and papers you intend to paint — make sure the paste contains a fungicide. It is also important to mix the paste correctly (unless, of course, you have bought it ready-mixed). You will find full instructions on the pack, but basically, you slowly pour the contents of the packet into a bucket containing a measured amount of cold water, stirring in the paste granules as you go. Give the mix a final, really thorough stir, then leave to stand and thicken for about 15 minutes. It is now ready to use. Tie a length of string between the lugs that take the bucket's handle, to provide a handy brush rest and to allow you to scrape excess paste from the brush.

Having pasted the top half of the paper, take hold of the edge marked 'TOP', and loosely fold it over so you can move the paper along and paste the rest of its length. That done, simply fold the bottom of the paper up towards the edge of the first fold. The only complication is that, where you are pasting a very long drop, you won't be able to paste and fold the bottom section in one go like this. Instead, you must tackle it in sections, pasting as much as you can get on the pasting table at a time, and then folding it concertina fashion under the top fold so you can bring on the next section and paste that. Aim to end up with a neat concertina of paper that can be easily supported over one arm.

When you have finished pasting the first length, put it to one side, and paste a few more in exactly the same way. This is not only a more efficient way to make use of your labour, but also gives the paste a chance to soak in and soften the paper. However, you must judge this softening time quite

carefully. It should be long enough to make the paper supple, yet not so long that it becomes soggy and tears at the least provocation. By trial and error, you should be able to work out a rhythmic cycle of pasting and hanging drops in batches such that, by the time you have finished pasting the last drop in the batch, the first is ready to hang. In addition, subsequent drops in the batch should reach the optimum degree of suppleness just as you finish hanging the preceding length, though in practice, this isn't always possible — the soaking time for thin paper may be less than the time needed to hang a drop; that for thick paper may be much longer.

To hang the first piece of paper, carry it draped over your forearm to where it is needed, open out the top fold, and offer it up to the wall, lining up its edge with the vertical guideline drawn earlier, and allowing a trimming allowance at the top of approximately 50mm (2in) — this enables you to obtain a neat fit even if the ceiling or picture rail is out of true. Hold the drop in place by brushing the top half on to the wall using a paperhanging brush, then open out the bottom fold, and brush out the remainder. The important thing here is to avoid trapping bubbles of air under the paper. Always brush down from the top and out towards the edges.

You can now trim the drop to fit. Run the back of your scissors over the paper, pushing it well into the angle between the wall and ceiling, picture rail, skirting board or whatever, to leave a neat crease. Carefully peel back the trim allowance, together with a little of the paper on the wall, cut along the crease line — it's better to cut off a fraction too little than a fraction too much — and finally brush the trimmed drop back into place. Again, be sure to brush out towards the edges of the paper to avoid trapping air. Neaten the trimmed edges by stabbing at them with the bristles of the brush to push them right into the angle defining the edge of the papered area.

Subsequent drops are hung in exactly the same way, having positioned them to obtain an exact pattern match. You will find this easiest if you brush the top half of the drop into place a little to one side of where it should actually go. If you have pasted the paper properly and sized the wall, you should now be able to slide the paper over to butt up against the edge of the preceding drop, then slide it up or down as required to match the pattern. Use the palms of your hands to manoeuvre the paper — there is then less risk of tearing it.

Hanging convenience wallcoverings

As you will have gathered from the above — although it may sound complicated — hanging ordinary wallpaper isn't really that difficult. And hanging some of the most modern 'convenience' wallcoverings is even easier.

There are the ready-pasted vinyls, for example. With these, instead of laboriously pasting individual lengths, you simply soak them in water for a minute or so to activate the paste coating on the backing paper. Many come with a cardboard trough for the purpose (or you can buy more robust

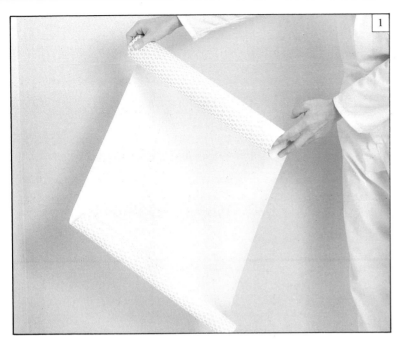

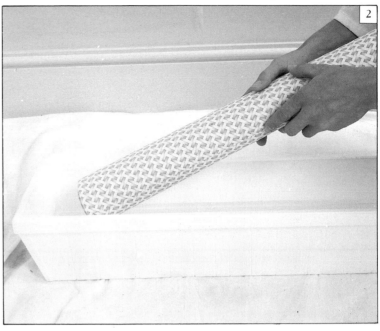

HANGING READY-PASTED PAPERS

1 *Measure the length of paper required for the drop, then roll it up with the bottom of the length innermost.*

2 *Immerse the roll in the soaking trough, which should be positioned at the foot of the wall below the hanging position. Use cold water, and do not exceed the manufacturer's* recommended soaking time.

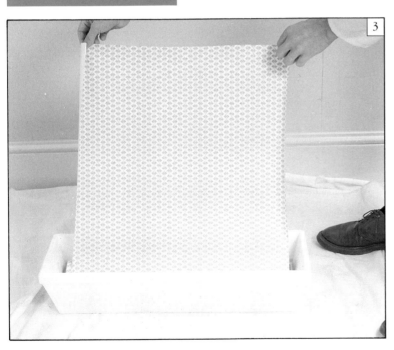

3 *When the soaking time is up, grasp the end of the length and draw it up out of the trough towards the top of the wall. Water will run down the length and back into the trough.*

4 *When most of the water has run off the length, position the top at ceiling level and use a paperhanger's brush (or a sponge with vinyls and* washables) to press it into place. Trim as before.

PAPERING ROUND OBSTACLES

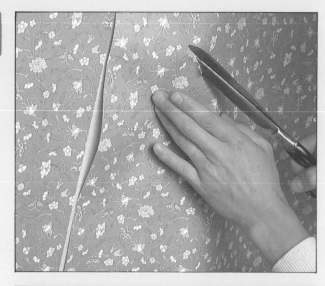

1 *Where the drop hangs over a light switch, power point or similar small obstacle, feel for the centre point of the faceplate and make four short cuts at right angles to each other, radiating outwards from that point, with your paperhanging shears or a smaller pair of scissors.*

2 *Fold back the four tongues formed by the cuts. Then you can either brush them into the angle between the faceplate and the wall and trim them off along the marked line, or tuck them behind the faceplate — see below.*

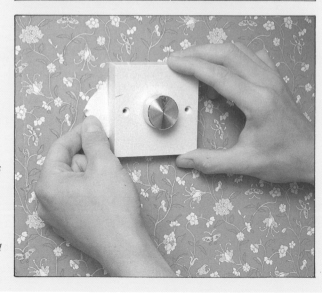

3 *The neatest effect is achieved by snipping off about two-thirds of each triangular tongue and tucking the remainder behind the faceplate of the switch or power point. If this is being done, it is essential that the current to the circuit is switched off at the mains before the faceplate is unscrewed.*

metal and plastic troughs), but, in practice, it is best to use these solely to carry the drops to where they are needed. You can then speed up the work by having a number of drops in the process of soaking, say, in the bath. To hang the paper, just take hold of the top edge, offer it up to the wall — it will simply unroll from the trough — and smooth it into place with a moist sponge. The only snag is that, when dealing with especially tricky parts of the room, you may find that the paste dries out and refuses to stick. The answer is to have a bucket of conventional paste standing by so you can brush a little fresh paste on to the appropriate sections as required.

Getting the wallcovering to stick where drops have to overlap – at a corner, for example – can also be a problem. Since paste doesn't produce a particularly strong bond, stick down the overlaps as a separate operation using a clear, rubber-based household adhesive such as Copydex.

Another 'convenience' wallcovering that is much easier to hang than ordinary types is Novamura. This contains no paper; it's made from foamed polyethylene (polythene) and is stuck to the wall with a specially-formulated ready-mixed adhesive. The two major points of difference here are that you brush the adhesive onto the wall, not the wallcovering, and that, because the material is so light, you can work with the complete roll rather than separate lengths. You simply let the roll lie on the floor below the position of the next drop, draw it up into position (not forgetting the trim allowance), smooth it into place with a damp sponge and trim off the excess at skirting board level before returning to the top edge and trimming there too.

Tackling awkard areas

Once you have mastered the basic techniques for papering plain, flat walls, you can set about tackling the trickier parts of the room.

Light switches and similar wall-mounted fittings are among the first obstacles you will have to get round. The trick is to brush the paper down as far as the switch, and let the rest of the drop hang loosely over it. You then feel through the paper for the switch, poke your scissors through at what you judge to be the middle, and then make a snip out towards each of the switch's corners — or, in the case of a round fitting, several snips to form a circular star of cuts. The idea is to allow the switch to poke through the cuts as you now brush the rest of the drop into place. The triangles of waste paper left around the outline of the switch can now be trimmed off in the usual way. Simply score with the back of your scissors and then cut along the crease. For a really neat finish, loosen the retaining screws in the switch's faceplate just enough to allow the trimmed edges of the paper to be poked underneath with the paperhanging brush. However, if you do tamper with the faceplate, play safe and turn off the electricity supply at the mains first.

Corners are another common problem. You simply cannot count on the room's walls being sufficiently true to paper straight round them. The answer is to trim the width

TURNING CORNERS

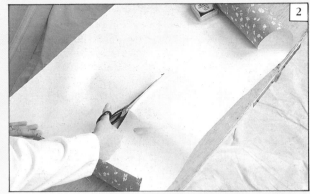

1 & 2 *Measure the distance from the edge of the last complete drop to the corner. Add about 25mm (1 in) to this measurement and cut a strip of paper to match it.*

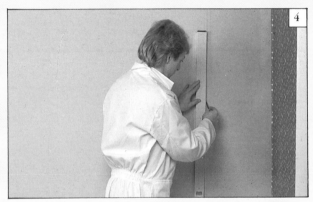

3 & 4 *Paste and hang the narrow strip in the usual way, butting its right-hand edge against the length already hung and brushing the other edge into the angle so it just turns onto the other wall. Then mark a plumbed line on the wall just less than the width of the rest of the strip from the corner.*

5 & 6 *Paste the off-cut part of the length and hang it to the plumbed line, brushing the overlap well into the angle for a perfect finish. At an external corner, again cut the length concerned so about 25mm (1 in) will turn onto the adjacent wall face.*

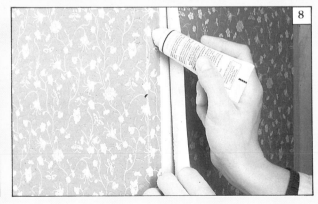

7 & 8 *Hang the rest of the strip so that it overlaps the turned edge by a few millimetres, and brush it into position. If you are hanging a washable or vinyl wallcovering, use a special vinyl overlap adhesive to ensure that the overlapping part is well stuck down.*

of the drop so that it turns the corner by only about 25mm (1in). The next drop — the one around the corner — is then hung absolutely vertically (strike a guide line with the aid of a plumb line in the same way as when you first started papering) so that it covers as much of this overlap as possible. The only snag is that this method makes it quite difficult to achieve a good pattern match at the corner. Using the off-cut from the first drop to start on the second wall can sometimes help — though, in this case, it needs to be fairly wide, and you must trim the first drop to width very carefully indeed to leave the off-cut with a clean, straight edge — but really the fault lies with the walls, rather than the method. You simply have to aim for the best pattern match you can in the circumstances.

And doors? These are usually one of the simplest obstacles to paper round. As usual, brush the top of the drop on to the wall, and let the rest hang down over the door surround. Almost invariably, part of the drop will lie above the surround, and part over the flat wall at the side of the door, so, with a paperhanging brush, push the loose paper well into the angle formed by the top of the door surround's architrave, crease along it with the back of your scissors, and cut along the crease as far as the architrave's corner. Finish brushing the paper above the door into place, then hinge back the flap created by the freeing cut you have just made, and brush the rest of the drop on to the wall. Run the back of your scissors down the angle formed between the architrave and the wall at the side of the door, then, finally, use the resulting crease to accurately trim off the flap of excess paper. The drop should now fit snugly round the door surround, and the remainder of the wall above the door can then be covered with a number of short drops in the usual way.

The same technique can be adapted to paper round flush windows. Simply make additional freeing cuts so you can fit the bottom of the drop around the window sill and turn it on to the wall beneath the sill where it can be brushed into place. Then, in addition to hanging short drops to cover the wall above the window frame, all you need do is hang similarly short drops to cover the wall below. The only trouble with this very simple approach is that where the window acts as a visual focal point for the room, and where you are using a paper with a fairly prominent motif, the result can look rather lop-sided. It is better to hang a drop centrally above the window to centre the motif, and to work outwards from there to paper the rest of the wall. Any discrepancy in pattern match between this wall and the plain walls you have already papered can generally be 'lost' or corrected at the corners.

Starting with a central drop in this way is, in any case, essential if you wish to paper neatly around a window set back in a reveal — one of the most difficult papering jobs you are ever likely to meet. Begin by measuring the width of the reveal on the wall above the window to find its exact middle, and mark this with a pencil. From this centre point, you must now measure out towards the end of the reveal in units equal to the paper's width, marking the edge of each

PAPERING ROUND DOORS AND WINDOWS

1 *When papering across a window or door reveal, hang the length as shown so it overlaps the opening. Ideally the part overlapping the opening should be wide enough to reach to the back of the reveal when the release cuts are made.*

2 *Mark the trimming cut at ceiling or picture rail level, and make the first release cut level with the top edge of the reveal. Make a similar release cut further down the length, level with the window sill.*

3 *Brush the central 'tongue' back onto the side wall of the reveal, crease its rear edge with the shears where it butts up against the window frame and trim off any excess material before brushing the tongue back into place. If it doesn't reach the frame, cut and hang a narrow strip of paper to fill the gap.*

4 & 5 *Hang the next length over the reveal in the same way. With a reveal wider than this a short length may be needed above the centre of the window before the next full-length drop is hung. The underside of the reveal head is then papered with short lengths that overlap on to the wall above the opening.*

6 & 7 *At a doorway with a projecting architrave, brush the edge of the length over the corner of the door frame, and mark where this comes on the paper. Then make a cut with your shears at an angle of 45° from the edge of the paper up to the mark.*

8 & 9 *Brush the freed sections of paper into the angles between the wall surface and the edge of the architrave, and mark and trim them in the usual way. Then hang a short length of paper on the wall above the door opening before hanging another full-length drop at its far side.*

imaginary drop as you go — a spare roll of paper makes a convenient gauge for this. The question you must now ask yourself is whether, with the drops arranged in this fashion, it is possible to turn those at each side of the window round on to the reveal in order to cover it. If the answer is no, with the aid of a plumb line, strike a vertical guide line to indicate the edge of the first drop to be hung above the window, half the width of the paper to the right or left of the reveal's centre point. If the answer is yes, strike the guide line through the centre point.

Working to this line, you can now paper the wall above the window reveal with short drops. Provided the reveal isn't too badly out of square, these can in fact be turned into the reveal to cover the soffit (the reveal's 'ceiling') as well. However, if the reveal is badly askew (or if you are using a pattern that highlights the slightest inaccuracy), merely turn these drops about 25mm (1in) on to the soffit, and paper the soffit separately with drops hung at right angles to the window frame.

The next step is to tackle the drops at each side of the reveal. Brush these into place at the top of the wall and let the rest of the drop hang loosely over the reveal in the same way as when papering round a door. You must now make two freeing cuts in the paper hanging over the window in order to produce a flap that can be turned on to the reveal. The first should be about 12mm ($\frac{1}{2}$in) below the level of the soffit; the second exactly level with the top of the window sill. Brush this flap into place, then make further freeing cuts as necessary to allow the rest of the drop to be fitted around the window sill and brushed out on to the wall beneath. The reveal should now be completely papered (unless very deep, in which case additional thin drops may be needed to extend the side flaps to cover its sides), save for the very ends of the soffit.

To cover these, make a vertical freeing cut in line with the side of the reveal, up through the strip of unstuck paper produced by making the side flap's top freeing cut 12mm ($\frac{1}{2}$in) below soffit level. This strip can then be turned on to the soffit and stuck down — as is common when tackling complicated papering jobs, you will probably have to apply a little fresh paste here to make it stick. Now, cover the remaining bare soffit with a small patch of paper, cut to turn down on to the sides of the reveal by about 12mm ($\frac{1}{2}$in). Peel back the paper already covering the side of the reveal at these points, to allow these small turns to be tucked away neatly out of sight.

To complete the job, cover the wall beneath the window sill with short drops of paper hung in the normal way. Here, though, you should start with drops butted against the full length drops at each side of the window, and work in towards the centre.

Another situation where it is advisable to begin papering with a central drop is where you are using a paper with a bold motif on a chimney breast. It can look very odd if the design isn't exactly centred, and since a chimney breast is often the main focal point of the room, any inaccuracy here can have an effect on the look of the room as a whole. As

with the window reveal, you should start by measuring up to find the exact centre of the breast, and step out from this point in 'paper-width' units to find out where the joins between drops fall in relation to the chimney breast's external corners. The aim this time, though, is for as much as possible of the drops turning these corners to lie on the chimney breast's face, yet still allowing a reasonable amount to turn on to the breast's sides. Accordingly, you must decide whether to hang a drop in the centre of the chimney breast's face – that is, hung to a vertical guide line half a paper-width to the right or left of the centre point – or to start with two drops hung on each side of a vertical line drawn through the centre point itself.

Once you have made that decision, paper the face of the chimney breast in the normal way, allowing the outer drops to turn on to the side walls by about 25mm (1in). Next, paper the side walls, covering the overlaps in the process, and turning about 25mm (1in) on to the walls of the alcoves. As usual when turning a corner, these drops should be hung to a vertical guide line, but, if the chimney breast is very shallow, there may not be room. In this case, use a plumb-line to check directly that the front edges of the drops are exactly vertical. Finally, paper the alcoves — yet again hanging the drops there to a vertical guide line so that they overlap the paper turning off the chimney breast's side walls. It sounds straightforward, and so it is if the fireplace in the chimney breast has been blocked off. But what if you are faced with papering around a complicated fire surround?

This can be a very fiddly job, but it's not difficult. Basically, all you do is brush the paper down flat on the wall as far as you can (probably level with the top mantelshelf), then make a freeing cut in the same way as when papering round a door in order to allow you to brush out a little more of the drop. If the fire surround widens out beyond this point, simply repeat the procedure. Brush down as far as you can, make a freeing cut, then brush down the rest of the drop until you meet another obstacle. If the surround narrows — say, where it cuts in beneath a long shelf — merely brush the flap created by the previous freeing cut into the gap, and, starting at the top, carefully trim to fit the side of the fireplace.

Where 'cut-backs' of this sort are fairly large, take them into account when working out where to hang the first drop on the chimney breast, making sure that the arrangement of drops you settle on produces a sufficiently large flap when the freeing cuts are made to fill the 'cut-back' without the need to resort to using odd-looking strips in order to cover the wall there. It is more likely, however, that your problem will be having to cope with too much excess paper. This can make it very difficult to make freeing cuts accurately. The way round the problem is to cut off the bulk of the waste before any freeing cuts are made. So long as you are careful not to remove too much at this stage, you will find trimming the paper exactly to fit much easier and much less messy. This applies when tackling any obstacle — not just fireplaces.

Papering stairwells

Although most stairwells contain lots of large, flat walls, papering them — indeed decorating them at all — can still be a real problem. How do you reach to the very top of the well? You cannot simply stand a ladder on the stairs. Clearly, some more effective means of access must be found.

The traditional method is to improvise using a combination of scaffold boards, a step ladder, a single section ladder, and a 'hop up' — essentially a small, portable staircase with two steps, which you can either buy, or make yourself from chipboard or natural timber. The idea is to arrange the hop up, ladder, and steps so that they can support the scaffold boards at the required working height. However, the arrangement does have to be carefully thought out, moving it to tackle another section of stairwell is a major operation (you usually have to dismantle everything and start again from scratch in the new location), and there is the question of safety.

You must certainly make sure that all the components of the set-up are securely joined with ropes and G-cramps to make sure that nothing slips out of place. Similarly, you must make sure that the feet of ladders (and steps where they are being used closed as a mini-ladder) are securely anchored, either by using the stairs themselves to resist any tendency to slip, or timber battens screwed temporarily to the floor. Even then, walking about on a couple of scaffold boards at the top of a stairwell is not everyone's idea of fun.

You might therefore prefer a simpler alternative. One possibility is a combination ladder — a step ladder that can be opened out to form a straight ladder if desired. The more complex models also convert into a sort of scaffold arrangement, and in many cases can be set up quite safely on the stairs. Perhaps a better bet though, is to hire an indoor scaffold tower — many allow you to extend the legs on one side so they will stand on a flight of stairs. This arrangement is, admittedly, slightly inconvenient in that it allows you to tackle only a relatively small section of wall at any time, and moving the tower along to tackle the next section is only slightly less arduous than dismantling and moving the traditional, make-shift arrangement mentioned earlier. But, if you follow the manufacturer's recommendations covering assembly and moving, it should be completely safe. The fact that you can construct a tower with a safety rail around the working platform is an added bonus if you are not very good with heights.

But reaching the heights of a stairwell isn't the only problem you are likely to encounter. The fact that you are dealing, for the most part, with very long drops of paper can also prove a burden. They are difficult to paste, difficult to handle, and difficult to hang unless you are careful not to let the paper stretch unevenly as you brush it into place — by the time you have reached the bottom of the drop, it may have stretched to the point where the pattern no longer matches that on the preceding length.

As far as the pasting is concerned, there isn't a great deal you can do to make life easier. Just be especially careful to

Access equipment for papering stairwells

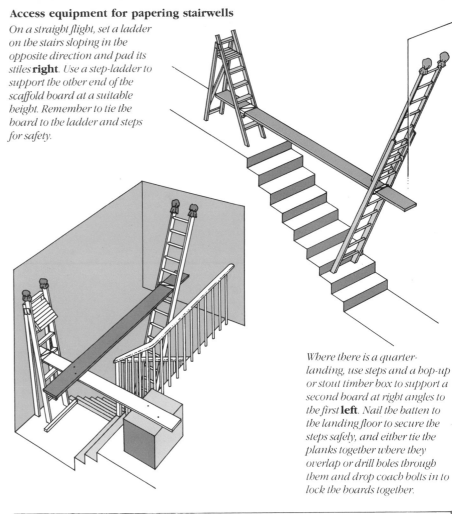

On a straight flight, set a ladder on the stairs sloping in the opposite direction and pad its stiles **right**. *Use a step-ladder to support the other end of the scaffold board at a suitable height. Remember to tie the board to the ladder and steps for safety.*

Where there is a quarter-landing, use steps and a hop-up or stout timber box to support a second board at right angles to the first **left**. *Nail the batten to the landing floor to secure the steps safely, and either tie the planks together where they overlap or drill holes through them and drop coach bolts in to lock the boards together.*

Papering sequence for stairwells

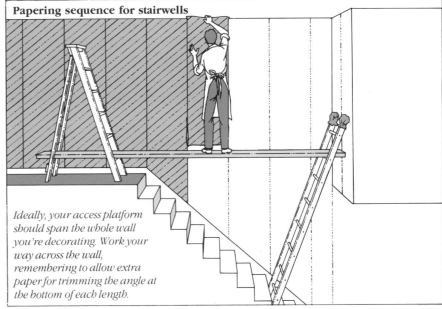

Ideally, your access platform should span the whole wall you're decorating. Work your way across the wall, remembering to allow extra paper for trimming the angle at the bottom of each length.

fold the drop into a neat, manageable concertina, and try to avoid allowing the paper to soak for too long — soggy paper is more likely to stretch unevenly. The handling you can make a lot easier by getting a helper to support the bulk of the drop while you concentrate on hanging it. Having an assistant to take care of the pasting is, in any case, a good idea. It will save you a lot of climbing up and down, and allows you to store the drops waiting to be hung safely out of the way. Working single-handed, the alternatives are either to take an entire batch of drops with you up on to the scaffold (in which case you risk treading on them), or to put them to one side and then fetch each drop as you need it (which entails even more climbing up and down).

And what about the actual hanging technique? As already mentioned, the main thing to avoid is uneven stretching, so do try to brush each drop into place in a uniform manner, without varying the pressure of the paperhanging brush. However, it must be said that some papers, notably the thinner ones, are especially prone to stretching, so avoid using these in stairwells unless you have to. The only other thing to watch is the trimming. This is carried out in exactly the same way as when papering any other wall, but do remember that you obviously need a far larger trim allowance at the bottom of each drop to accommodate the slope of the stairs.

Papering a ceiling

Mention papering a ceiling, and most people immediately conjure up visions of chaotic slapstick comedy routines in which gravity triumphs over paste and paper. But in reality, it's a relatively simple task. After all, how many other surfaces in your home can you think of that are so uncomplicated? Of course, the fact that you do have gravity working against you has to be taken into account, and handling the sort of long lengths of paper generally needed for the job creates a certain amount of difficulty in itself. However, don't be put off. With a little know how and organization, all of the problems you are likely to encounter are easily overcome. There are really two keys to success.

The first is good preparation. In order to disprove the old adage 'what goes up must come down' it is obviously vital to do all you can to ensure that the paper sticks properly. And it won't stick properly on a surface that has not been adequately and correctly prepared. Sizing — that is sealing the surface with a coat of dilute wallpaper paste — is also essential. This not only helps improve adhesion, but also makes it a good deal easier to manoeuvre lengths of paper into place without stretching and tearing them.

The second is arranging good access. In this case, however, good access is not simply a question of coming up with a way to reach the ceiling comfortably and in safety – though, obviously, neither factor can be ignored. Step ladders and access towers are not much help here. While they would enable you to brush the start of each length into place without much difficulty, what happens then? The answer is that you have to climb down, move the steps or

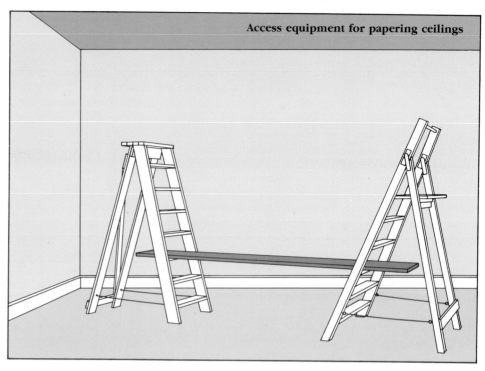

Access equipment for papering ceilings

When papering a ceiling, you need to be able to move freely across the room as you position each length of paper. The best method is to use two step-ladders with a scaffold board set between them.

tower along, and climb back up before you can continue work. The chances are that at some stage during that process, your neat concertina of pasted paper would unravel into a tangled mess, and it is virtually certain that the weight of unhung paper would simply pull down the section already in place. What you need, therefore, is some sort of access equipment that allows you to walk from one side of the room to the other, brushing a length of paper into place on the ceiling as you go.

There is only one piece of equipment that fits the bill — long scaffold boards supported at each end by step ladders, decorator's trestles, access towers, or a combination of any two of these. The necessary boards can be hired quite easily from a good tool hire shop, together with the necessary supporting steps, trestles, or whatever. For safety's sake, though, do hire a pair of boards, and set them up side by side to form a reasonably wide catwalk. And don't be tempted to improvise by using ordinary planks instead of purpose-made scaffold boards — they won't be strong enough.

Having sorted out the access equipment, you can turn your attention to actually hanging the paper, and the first question you have to answer is: where should you start? The traditional advice is to start with a drop hung parallel to the wall containing the room's main window, and to work out from there across the room. However, as with the comparable advice on where to start papering walls, this way of doing things was originally devised to help make the overlapping joins between old-fashioned ceiling papers less obvious. Since virtually all modern papers simply butt together at the joints, it consequently no longer applies. You can start against any wall you choose. Pick one adjacent

PASTING AND FOLDING

1 & 2 *Because of the length of paper needed to cover the width of a room, you have to paste and fold ceiling paper differently. Paste the first part of the length, then fold a short section over on itself. Continue to paste and fold in this way until you have created a series of concertina-like folds.*

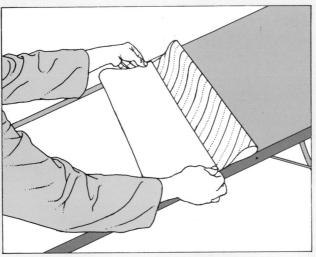
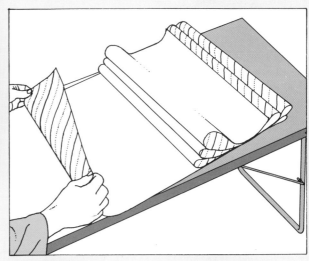

HANGING CEILING PAPER

1 & 2 *Use a string line pinned across the ceiling to mark a guide line on its surface. This should be just less than the paper's width from the edge of the room, to allow the long edge to be trimmed precisely to fit. Unfold the concertinas and brush the first length into place against the line.*

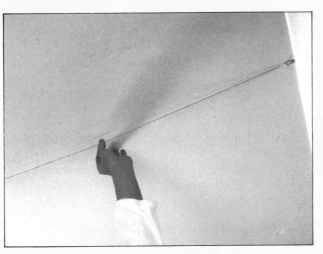

3 & 4 *Crease the ends of the length (and the long side edge of the first and last lengths hung) into the angle between ceiling and coving, then peel them back and trim off the excess. Hang subsequent lengths in the same way, with neat butt joins between lengths.*

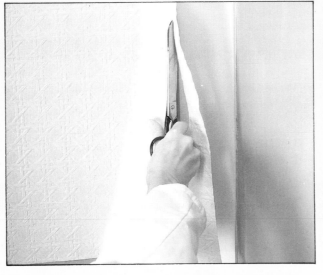
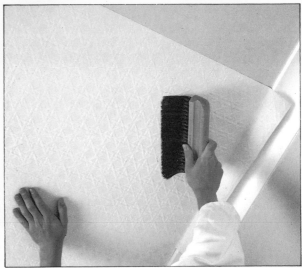

THE COMPLETE PAPERHANGER

to a nice long, uninterrupted stretch of totally flat ceiling. You will find, though, that the old timers were right in one sense — ceiling paper does somehow look better if hung parallel to the wall containing the room's largest window.

You must now draw a line on the ceiling parallel to the wall to indicate where the edge of the first drop is to go. This should be about 50mm (2in) less than the width of the paper from the wall to allow a reasonable trimming allowance to turn down on to the wall. To draw the line, you could simply mark the appropriate measurement at various points across the ceiling and joint up these points using a long, straight batten as a ruler. However, that's not very accurate — the wall may not be straight. A better method is to use a chalked line. You can buy these from good decorating shops. The line comes on a reel designed to chalk the string as it is pulled out. Alternative, just take a length of soft string and rub a dark coloured chalk into the fibres. Mark the line's position on the ceiling at opposite ends of the wall, stretch the line tightly between these two points, then snap it against the ceiling like a bowstring to leave a dead straight chalked line.

Using this line as a guide, cut the first few drops to length, allowing an extra 100mm (4in) or so at each end for trimming. Paste them in the usual way, folding each drop into a neat concertina, then when they have soaked for the required time, carry the first drop to where it is needed, open out the top fold, and offer it up to the ceiling — you will find this a lot easier if you support the concertina on a spare roll of paper or something similar. Position its edge against the guide line, remembering to allow the trim allowance at the ends to turn down on to the wall, then brush the first section in place just as you would if you were brushing it on to a wall, at the same time poking the trim allowance at the side well into the angle between wall and ceiling using the tip of your paperhanging brush.

Once a little less than a metre of paper has been brushed into place, it should stay there, allowing you to open out a little more of the concertina and brush the next section into position. Continue in this way, aiming to unfold and brush the paper into place in one smooth movement as you walk the length of the scaffold board, until the entire drop is in position. You can now trim the paper to fit along the side and end wall. This is done in the usual way by running the back of your scissors along the angle between wall and ceiling to leave a score line to which you can cut, but take care when peeling back the paper for the final cut not to peel back so much that the entire drop starts to come away. Make sure, too, when brushing the paper back into place after trimming, that it really does stick. If you find the paste has dried out, brush on a little fresh paste to achieve a really strong bond.

With the first drop in place, you now simply move your access equipment along as necessary to hang the second and subsequent drops, butting each one tightly against its predecessor to achieve a good pattern match, just as you would if you were papering a wall. On most ceilings, there are just two problems you are likely to encounter. To begin

PAPERING ROUND CEILING OBSTACLES

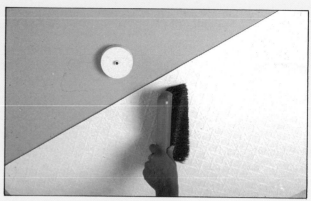

1 *If you have pendant light fittings, turn off the power and remove the pendant before you start decorating. Hang the length of paper adjacent to the ceiling rose in the usual way; then hang the length that will lie over it.*

2 *Brush the paper over the rose position so you can mark its centre point. Then use your shears or a smaller pair of scissors to make a series of short cuts out from the centre point to just beyond the perimeter of the rose itself.*

3 *Crease the tongues neatly against the edge of the rose, and trim them off with scissors or a sharp knife. Alternatively, unscrew the rose cover and tuck the trimmed ends of the tongues behind it for a neat finish.*

SLOPING CEILINGS

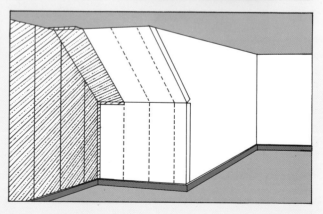

Where a sloping ceiling is being decorated with the same paper as a wall, it's easier to hang separate pieces on the sloping and vertical surfaces. Allow a generous turn onto adjacent surfaces to avoid gaps.

with you will probably have to paper round a pendant light at some point. This is done in more or less the same way you would paper round a light switch. Brush the paper up to the ceiling rose, hold the next section of paper loosely over the rose — you will have to hold the light flex out of the way while you do this — then push the scissors through at the point you judge to be the rose's centre, and make a star-shaped series of freeing cuts out towards the ceiling rose's circumference. You then drop the light flex and bulb holder through the resulting hole, brush that section of the paper firmly on to the ceiling and trim off the little triangles of waste paper around the rose's rim. As with light switches, for a really neat finish, you can loosen the screws holding the rose to the ceiling just enough to push the trimmed edges of the paper underneath. These fixing screws are located on the terminal plate beneath the rose's screw-on cover, though, so do turn off the electricity at the mains before removing the cover, and don't turn it back on again until the cover has been screwed back in place.

The second thing you may have trouble with is hanging the very last drop. If this is too narrow, the weight of waste paper turning down the wall tends to pull it away before you can trim it accurately to size. The solution is to cut the paper approximately to width before attempting to hang it — allow about 50mm (2in) extra to turn down on to the wall. Even then, a very narrow strip of paper can be tricky. It is therefore a good idea to work out how wide this final drop will be before you start papering. You can then adjust its size by moving the starting guide line closer to the wall, increasing the side trim allowance on the first drop by the amount you want to increase the width of the last. Again, if this trim allowance proves unmanageably large, trim off the bulk of it before brushing the first drop into place.

Hanging lining paper

People often wonder how professionals manage to achieve such a smooth, even finish using paint and wallcoverings. Part of their answer is obviously that constant practice gives them rather more skill than the average amateur. However, that aside, much of their success is actually due to the fact that they will line the wall prior to decorating if it shows the slightest imperfection, where an amateur might not bother.

That's an example you should follow. Lining paper isn't that expensive, nor is it particularly difficult to hang. If you are planning to paint over the lining paper, put it up in exactly the same way as ordinary paper. Where you wish to paper over it, however, it is much better to cross-line — that is, to hang the paper horizontally instead of vertically. There are two main reasons for this. Hung vertically, there is a risk that the joins between lengths will match up with those between the drops of the finishing paper. That would leave a weakness in the finish and the paper could peel off. More importantly, with the lining and top paper running in opposite directions, the layer as a whole tends to do a better job of smoothing out imperfections in the surface. Hanging both papers in the same direction can sometimes

HANGING LINING PAPER

1 *Lining paper is hung horizontally on wall surfaces, starting at the top of the wall. Paste it and fold it into concertinas as for ceiling paper, then brush the paper onto the wall parallel with the top edge.*

2 *At corners, crease the paper into the angle and trim it so it just turns on to the surface of the adjacent wall. Use the same principle where the paper has to turn an external corner.*

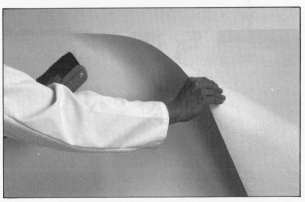

3 *Hang subsequent lengths in the same way, butting the top edge of each length up against the bottom edge of the previous one. Take care not to let the edges overlap, since this would show through the final wallcovering; if anything, it's preferable to leave a slight gap between the lengths.*

4 *Finish off the wall by cutting and hanging a narrow strip at skirting board level. This will have to be creased into the angle between wall and skirting board before being trimmed all the way along.*

highlight lumps and bumps instead of concealing them. There is just one other method of lining a surface. It's called double lining, and is generally reserved for walls and ceilings so rough that a single layer of lining paper will not produce a smooth base for the finishing paper. All it involves is hanging one layer of lining paper vertically, and then cross-lining over the top.

Hanging paper horizontally for cross-lining is obviously not as simple as hanging relatively short vertical drops, but it is not nearly as difficult as you might imagine. The trick is in the way the paper is folded when pasted. Fold it concertina fashion in the same way as any other long drop, but make smaller folds than you might otherwise — small enough to allow you to hold the entire concertina in one hand. Starting at the top right-hand side of the wall (or top left if you are left-handed), pull off a couple of folds from the concertina, press the end of the paper on to the wall until it holds, then smooth it into place properly with a paperhanger's brush.

Once the end is securely in place, you can merely walk the length of the wall, unravelling the concertina and brushing the paper into place as you go, in much the same way as when papering a ceiling. There is no need, incidentally, to strike a guide line for the first drop unless you want to be really particular. Remember, the lining paper won't show when the wall is finished. Equally, you need not worry too much about accurate trimming, nor about achieving really neat butt joins between lengths. However, don't be too slap-dash. Major imperfections in the lining paper layer will show through the covering layer of paper.

The only other thing to consider when lining is the choice of lining paper. You will find several different types in a good decorating store. Some are thick; some are thin. Some have a beautifully smooth finish; others use a somewhat rougher paper. As a general rule, the smoother quality papers are made to receive a painted finish. Beneath a finishing layer of wallcovering, the roughness of the cheaper paper's doesn't show. Choosing the correct thickness of paper, on the other hand, is rather more a matter of judgement. The rougher the surface of the wall or ceiling, the thicker the paper needs to be if it is to smooth out the imperfections.

Hanging relief decorations

For the most part, hanging a relief wallcovering is no different to hanging any other kind of wallcovering. The basic techniques of pasting, hanging, and trimming still apply. However, for the very best results, there are a few additional points to bear in mind.

To begin with, watch the soaking times of pasted drops waiting to be hung. Embossed wallcoverings tend to be a good deal thicker than the average plain wallcovering, and it therefore takes a lot longer for the paste to soak in and make them supple. At the same time, bear in mind that they will also soak up a good deal more paste in the process, so be sure to apply a slightly thicker coat than you would normally during the initial pasting. This helps stop the paste

drying out while the paper is soaking. Even so, drying out may still be a problem around the edges of each drop, so keep a bucket of paste handy when hanging the drops. You can brush a little extra paste on to any sections of the wallcovering that need it — or brush paste on to the appropriate bit of wall if that's more convenient. Working on a surface that has been thoroughly sized will also help alleviate the problem. And while we are on the subject of pasting, you really do paste the whole of the drop. Work it right into the indentations formed by the embossing. Take care, too, when folding the drop. The thicker wallcoverings will still be fairly stiff at this stage, and if you try to force them into too tight a fold, they could bend, leaving a crease mark across the embossed surface.

The relief pattern of the thinner embossed wallcoverings is even more vulnerable once the paper has become supple. Take care when brushing the drop on to the wall or ceiling that you aren't too heavy handed or you could 'iron out' sections of the relief. Similarly, try not to slip when using the back of your scissor to crease the line to which the wallcovering will be trimmed. Such accidental creases remain far more obvious in a relief decoration than in an ordinary wallcovering. At the same time, don't be too gentle. The wallcovering must be stuck firmly in place, and you must be able to see guide creases to which you want to cut.

With embossed wallcoverings, it is also even more important than usual to obtain a really exact pattern match, and really tight butt joints between drops. Inaccuracies in either department are not only rather more obvious than with an ordinary wallcovering, but also rather more permanent, since the heavier embossed wallcoverings designed to be painted over (those in the Anaglypta family, for example) are not the sort of thing you want to strip off each time you redecorate. Nor should you need to. They are designed to be semi-permanent wallcoverings. Just try to make sure they are semi-permanent monuments to your paperhanging skill, not semi-permanent catalogues of your mistakes.

There is just one other important difference between hanging embossed wallcoverings and hanging flat ones. With the latter, when turning a corner, papering into a window reveal, or something similar, you can safely afford to overlap adjacent drops in order to compensate for variations in the squareness of the walls. Apart from the occasional mis-match in the pattern, such overlapping joints hardly notice, and if they do look too bulky for your taste, you can always flatten them out with a wooden or plastic seam roller. Not so with an embossed wallcovering: given the thickness of the pattern, any overlap between drops will be very noticeable indeed, and not particularly attractive. A seam roller won't help either. That would only flatten out the design.

How then do you avoid overlaps? Let's suppose that you have just papered round a corner and are ready to hang the first drop on the adjacent wall. What you must do is straighten up the edge of the drop turning the corner so that the next drop can be butted up against its edge. Remember that this second drop must be hung absolutely vertical, so the

HANGING UNBACKED FABRICS

1 & 2 *Measure and cut each drop in turn, allowing for trimming top and bottom, and then roll the fabric right side in and bottom end first on to a cardboard tube. Apply ready-mixed tub paste to the wall surface.*

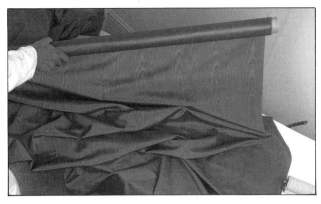

3 & 4 *Align the top edge of the fabric with the plumbline and let the tube unroll down the wall surface, then use a hard felt roller to press the fabric gently into the adhesive. Don't press too hard or you will stretch it.*

5 & 6 *Hang subsequent lengths with a slight overlap, rolling the material firmly into place. Then use a straightedge and a very sharp handyman's knife to cut off the excess fabric at ceiling and skirting board level.*

7 & 8 *Where adjacent lengths overlap, position a straightedge over the centre line and cut through both layers of fabric from top to bottom of the seam. Pull away the offcut of the upper layer of material, then lift its edge and peel away the strip underneath. Finally roll the seam for a perfect finish.*

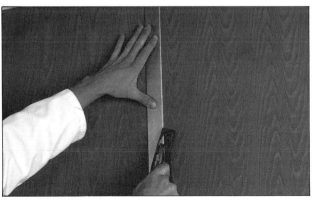

edge of the first drop must be trued up with a sharp knife (guide the blade using a long, straight batten to ensure a straight cut), or a pair of scissors. Check where the cut should be made using a plumb-line, and, if you are using a knife, make sure it is absolutely razor sharp. A slightly blunt blade will merely tear the wet paper and leave a ragged edge.

The big snag with this method is, of course, that success depends almost entirely on your ability to cut a clean, straight line, so you may prefer to try a variation on the technique where this is less important. What you do is allow the two drops to overlap temporarily, and then use a knife (again guided along a batten) to cut a vertical line through the double thickness of paper. If you then remove the waste from both drops (you have to peel back the overlying drop to do this), you should find that they now butt together perfectly. Only try this on a wallcovering that will be painted over, though. The temporary overlap usually leaves a paste stain on the surface of the first drop.

Hanging fabrics

Another type of specialist wallcovering you might wish to hang is fabric. Hessian, grasscloth, and silk are widely available paper-backed, and hanging these isn't so very different from hanging ordinary wallpaper.

Apply a liberal coat of paste to each drop in the usual way, taking extra care not to get paste on the fabric-covered face, then allow to soak for around four minutes to allow the paper backing to soften. Do follow the manufacturer's recommendations on the sort of paste you use. Traditional starch-based and modern ready-mixed pastes are generally preferred. When you come to hang the drops, smooth them on to the wall with a foam or felt-covered roller rather than a brush, and trim at top and bottom using a very sharp knife and a straightedge in preference to scissors — using the normal method of trimming wallpaper, any crease you manage to get in this sort of wallcovering is usually too vague to be of much use for accurate trimming. And what about overlapping drops? As with embossed wallcoverings, overlaps will be very obvious so avoid them in exactly the same way. Once again, takes great care not to get paste on the surface of the fabric. It will leave a prominent, messy-looking stain. If you do have an accident, wipe off the paste immediately with a damp cloth, then wipe over the area a second time using a cloth moistened with a little methylated spirit.

Fabric wallcoverings that don't have a paper backing are another possibility — the most common is hessian. To hang these, although the basic principles of paperhanging still apply, the details of the technique are a little different.

The first and most obvious difference is that you paste the wall, not the wallcovering. As with paper-backed fabric wallcoverings, starch paste or ready-mixed paste is normally used for the job, but do follow the manufacturer's recommendations over the choice of adhesive.

There are other important differences that relate to hanging this sort of wallcovering. Always use a soft roller to smooth the fabric on to the wall; never a paperhanging brush. And do take care not to stretch the fabric unevenly with the roller in such a way that the cloth's weave becomes crooked. In addition, you will not be able simply to butt adjacent drops together — the edges of the fabric are often frayed, making it impossible to obtain a neat join. Instead, allow each drop to overlap its predecessor by about 12mm (½in). You can then obtain a good join by cutting through the double thickness of fabric using a sharp knife and straightedge, peeling away the waste fabric from both drops, and then smoothing the newly cut edges back on to the wall — this will almost certainly need another application of paste to make the edges stick. Complete the join by running over it with a seam roller.

The same techniques are used to avoid overlapping joins at corners, but here there are a couple of additional points to bear in mind. Firstly, when turning external corners, be sure to carry round a fairly wide strip of fabric on to the second wall – 50 to 75mm (2 to 3in) at least. Hessian in particular is quite likely to fray at the edges, and where the edge is close to a join, fraying is not only more likely, but also far more obvious. Secondly, when tackling internal corners, bear in mind that the fabric may shrink and pull out of the angle as it dries. To avoid this, make a neat butt joint along the line where the two walls meet, rather than allowing a single drop to turn the corner.

Incidentally, if you want to paint over plain hessian — and the effect is both unusual and not unattractive — do make sure you allow adequate time for the paste to dry. Anything over 48 hours is usually safe. Apply the paint, either emulsion or a resin-based paint, using a long piled roller to work the paint right into the fabric's weave.

Another pasted-on fabric wallcovering you may wish to hang is paper-backed felt. This is treated in more or less the same way as unbacked hessian, except that having rolled joins smooth, you can use a fine wire brush (a suede brush will do) to disguise them almost totally by teasing fibres from each drop to cover the line between it and its neighbour. There is, unfortunately, one major snag. Unlike hessian, paper-backed felt is normally very wide, and very heavy. In fact, so awkward is it to handle that even with a helper you will probably have trouble. But there is a way round the problem. Cut each drop approximately to length, roll it up, with the paper backing facing outwards, around a long, stout timber batten, and support this in front of the wall you wish to cover on a pair of step ladders or decorator's trestles. You can then paste that section of wall and smooth the felt into place, starting at the bottom. You should find that, as you work upwards, the felt unrolls itself off the batten, allowing you to concentrate on hanging it rather than on supporting its weight.

Finally, it is possible to decorate walls with other types of fabric. In fact, you can use almost any fabric you wish — though furnishing fabrics obviously wear better. And that is just as well if you are looking for a really bright, patterned finish, for the majority of purpose-made fabric wallcoverings either come in plain, rather muted colours, or else are incredibly expensive — so expensive it's probably not worth taking the risk of hanging them yourself. How is it done? There are two main options.

The first is to paste it into place in much the same way as unbacked hessian, using a thick ready-mixed wallpaper adhesive. The only major difference is that where the fabric has a pattern you must obviously try to achieve as good a match as possible between adjacent drops. This generally proves far more difficult than matching patterns on a wallpaper — it's so easy to stretch the fabric unevenly as you roll it out on to the wall. And there's no easy solution to the problem. You simply have to work as carefully as you can. What's more, fabrics not specifically made for the job are far more likely to shrink drastically as the paste dries out. Applying the bare minimum of paste to the wall will help, and this is worth doing in any case to avoid the risk of paste soaking through the fabric and staining its surface. But some shrinkage will almost certainly occur even then, so you must allow for this when hanging. The best way to do that, is to hang the fabric without trimming it — not even at the overlapping joins between drops. If you then allow plenty of time for the paste to dry, by which time the fabric will have shrunk as much as it is going to, you can trim with absolute confidence, tackling the entire room in one go.

The second fixing option is to staple the fabric in place using a heavy-duty staple gun. This is generally a good deal safer than pasting, and makes it a lot easier to obtain an accurate pattern match. What's more, there is nothing to stop you using the staples to hold the fabric in pleats, ruches, and so on, if you wish for a really luxurious effect. Don't fix the fabric directly on to the wall, though. Staple it to thin 25mm x 6mm (1 x ⅟₄in) timber battens.

Starting in one corner of the room, cut the first drop of fabric about 50mm (2in) longer than the height of the wall. Staple one edge to the edge of a batten cut to match the wall's height exactly (centre the 50mm/2in trim allowance); then, having tucked the trim allowance over the ends, fix the batten in place by nailing through its face into the wall (or staple if your staple gun is up to the job). If you now pull the fabric over the batten's face, none of the fixings will show. To secure the other edge of the fabric, fix a second batten to the wall at the appropriate distance from the first, pull the fabric taut, and staple to the batten's edge.

If you now repeat the whole process for the second and subsequent drops, you will find that the first batten of each drop effectively conceals the final fixings of the drop before. That is, until you reach the far end of the wall. Here, you have no choice but to staple the fabric to the batten's face. Do this as close to the edge as possible. In this way, if you are continuing around the corner, the first drop on the adjacent wall will cover the staples. If not, you can cover them with a strip of decorative beading or something similar, pinned in place. To make this cover-up less obvious, it's a good idea to frame each wall with the same beading.

Friezes and borders
Although decorative friezes and borders are no longer as popular as was once the case, they are by no means old fash-

HANGING FRIEZES AND BORDERS

1 *Friezes and borders are cut to length and hung just like extremely narrow lengths of wallpaper. To border a wall, hang the vertical sections first, brushing them into place in the corner. If the corner is not true, hang it to a plumbed line.*

2 *Offer up the horzontal sections next, and cut them to length. If you want an accurate pattern match in the corners, work out precisely where the mitred cuts will fall. Make the mitred cuts with a knife and sliding bevel or combination square for accuracy.*

3 *Offer up the mitred cut end into the angle to check its fit and to make sure the pattern will match accurately. Then paste the length carefully and carry it to the wall.*

4 *Slide the length into place so that the neatly-mitred corners meet precisely and the pattern matches. Then brush out the rest of the length. Alternatively, overlap the corners as you hang them and trim the mitres in situ with a straightedge and a sharp knife.*

A small pattern can be used on both walls and ceilings to dramatic effect **left,** especially if the colours are chosen to complement those of the furnishings.

A tiny, repetitive motif on the wallpaper can echo a larger design on furnishing fabrics **above.** A slim frieze frames each wall to perfection.

Wallcoverings can be used to create contrast too. Here an alcove **above right** has been papered to add interest to the room.

Strong vertical stripes combined with a light-coloured ceiling **right** help to give an illusion of height in a low-ceilinged room.

ioned. On the contrary, they can still do a very useful job in any decorating scheme, helping to break up large areas and highlight architectural features by simply forming dados and 'picture rails', or more complex effects such as forming a frame around an entire wall.

In principle, putting them up is no different to putting up an ordinary wallcovering. Just cut them approximately to length, paste them, allow them to soak for a while, then brush them into place, and finally trim off any excess. There are, however, a few additional tips worth knowing.

If you are hanging them horizontally, make sure they are truly horizontal. Hang them to a guide line drawn lightly in pencil with the aid of a spirit-level and a long, straight batten — rested on top of the spirit-level, the batten effectively increases the length of the spirit level. Similarly, if you want a vertical border hang it to a guide line drawn with the aid of a plumb-line.

If you are laying the frieze or border on top of some other wallcovering — the one covering the bulk of the wall or ceiling — don't apply any more paste than is needed to ensure that it sticks. If you do, it could ooze out as you brush the frieze or border into place and leave a nasty stain.

Finally, if you want to create a frame using a paper border, do mitre the corners — it looks so much neater. This isn't as difficult as it may sound. At each corner, allow the borders to overlap (don't paste the ends), then cut through the double thickness of paper with a sharp knife following a straightedge held to draw an imaginary line between the frame's internal and external corners. Remove the waste paper from both layers, then finish off by brushing a little paste on to the unpasted sections of each border and smooth them into place.

*This gloomy and uninviting hall and staircase **above, right** has been transformed by the use of a bright, lightly patterned wallpaper and gleaming white paintwork. Small details such as the carpet runner and the table cloth add highlights of colour.*

THE COMPLETE TILER

Tiles of one sort or another have been used to decorate homes since the days of the Romans. And when you think about it, it's easy to see just why they have remained so popular for so long. Quite apart from the hardwearing, easy-clean qualities of ceramic tiling, tiles in general provide one of the quickest, simplest cover-ups for walls and ceilings there is.

Basic techniques

Let's start by looking at ceramic tiling. The simplest way to get a feel for the job is to tackle a straightforward tiled area such as a splashback behind a bath or basin.

Having prepared the surface thoroughly, the first step is to tackle what's know as the 'setting out' — that is, working out the approximate position of every tile on the wall; the aim being to come up with an arrangement that is both symmetrical, and that avoids the need for unsightly, awkward-to-cut tiles around the edges and other obstacles. This sounds fairly tedious, and so beginners often rush through it in their eagerness to get a few tiles on to the wall. But it really is worth taking the time and trouble to do the job properly. Get the setting out right, and you will save yourself a great deal of trouble in the long run. It makes putting up the tiles so much easier, and you get a better looking end result.

Start by drawing a horizontal pencil line on the wall to indicate the position of the bottom edge of the bottom row of tiles. Use a spirit-level and a long timber batten here to ensure that this line really is straight and absolutely horizontal, then carefully measure it and make a mark at a point exactly half way along its length. This represents the midpoint of the tiled area — the point at which you will begin tiling, and from which you will work out towards the edges of the tiled area in order that all the tiles and joints are arranged symmetrically. You must now check that starting at this point will leave cut tiles of a reasonable width around the edges of the tiled area, so step off along the line in units equal to one whole tile plus the width of a grout line, and indicate the position of each grout line on the wall. If you find that cut tiles less than about 25mm (1in) wide are needed at the edges, move the starting point half a tile width to the left or right and try again.

Now, obviously, if you do all this by carefully measuring to find each point, even using a tile as a gauge, it will take some time, and inaccuracies are likely to creep into your calculations. It's therefore better to use something called a gauge rod. You can make this yourself. Arrange a number of tiles in a row on the floor, taking care to leave the correct spacing for grout between each one. Then lay a long, straight timber batten next to the row, and mark the positions of the tile edges on its edge to form a handy 'ruler'

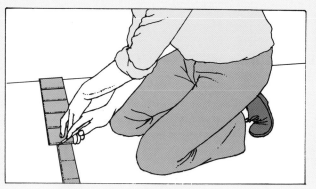

1 *Begin by laying out a row of tiles (plus spacers if necessary) on the floor, and mark the tile spacings on a long, straight timber batten to make a tile gauge.*

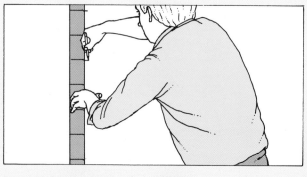

2 *Use this to work out where cut tiles will fall, in both vertical and horizontal rows. Don't be afraid to adjust your starting point to avoid very narrow cut pieces at the end of rows.*

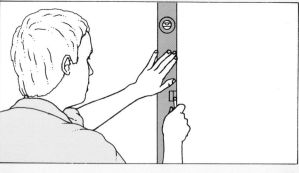

3 *When you have found a satisfactory arrangement, draw a vertical line through the centre point of the area to be tiled. Use a spirit-level to ensure that it is truly vertical.*

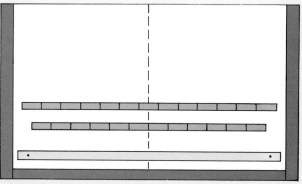

4 *Fix a horizontal batten across the bottom of the area to be tiled, with its top edge in line with the bottom edge of the lowest row of whole tiles. Note the effect of fixing the first tile across or at one side of the centre line.*

graduated in tile-plus-grout-line units.

Once you are satisfied with the arrangement of the vertical joints between tiles, use either a plumb-line, or a spirit-level that allows you to check verticals as well as horizontals — the latter is more convenient — to strike a vertical line through the point you have selected as the best place to start. Then, working up from the horizontal line representing the bottom of the tiled area, work out the positions of the horizontal joins, again using the gauge rod. As when checking the vertical tile positions, if you find that any cut tiles needed at the top are less than about 25mm (1in) wide, adjust the position of the starting point — this time moving it up half the width of a tile — and restrike the horizontal line. One tip: whenever you have to make an adjustment during the setting out, scribble out those marks that no longer apply so that they cannot confuse you when you are ready to move on to the next stage — fixing the tiles on to the wall.

Begin tiling at the intersection of the vertical and horizontal guide lines. Apply a thin coat of tiling adhesive to the wall using a notched plastic spreader (often provided with the adhesive), aiming to cover an area equivalent to about half a dozen whole tiles — you can increase this as you become more proficient. If you have done this properly, you should be left with the bare wall more or less showing between the ridges of adhesive left by the spreader's notches. You now simply take the first tile, and press it on to the wall, lining its edges up with the vertical and horizontal guide line. That done, take a second tile, position this on the horizontal line, and press it into place next to the first tile. Continue adding tiles in this way, spreading on more adhesive as required, until you have a row of whole tiles running the length of the horizontal guide line (don't worry about the cut tiles at this stage). Repeat to produce a row along

TILE QUANTITY CHART

Area to be tiled (sq m)	Number of tiles needed			
	10×10	15×15	10×20	30×30
1	100	44	50	12
2	200	87	100	23
3	300	130	150	34
4	400	174	200	45
5	500	217	250	56
6	600	260	300	67
7	700	303	350	78
8	800	347	400	89
9	900	390	450	100

MARKING UP

1 *Always start tiling by marking a true horizontal line on the wall, in line with the bottom edge of the lowest row of whole tiles. This is especially important if you are tiling a whole room, to ensure each row is at the same level when you get back to your starting point. Don't rely on skirtings being level.*

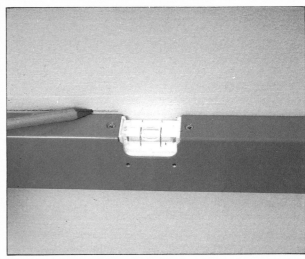

2 *Measure the width of the tiled area, and halve the answer. Then measure this distance along your horizontal line from one edge of the area and mark the exact midpoint. Use your spirit level (or a plumbline) to draw a truly vertical line through this point.*

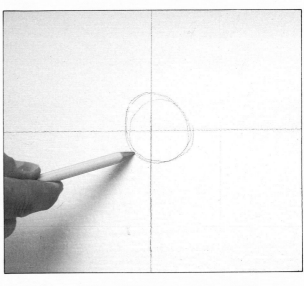

3 *Identify the point where the lines cross as the midpoint of the tiled area by circling the intersection. You can then use your tiling gauge to check whether cut pieces of sensible width will be left at each edge of the area. If they are, the first tiles will be fixed in the angle between the lines; if not, the vertical line is moved half a tile width along the horizontal line.*

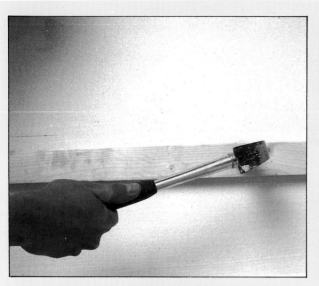

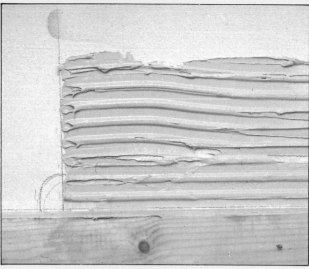

FIXING TILES

1 & 2 *When you have completed the setting-out to your satisfaction, fix timber battens to the wall immediately below the marked line to support the first row of tiles. Pin them in place with partly-driven masonry nails so you can remove them easily later. Then spread the first band of adhesive on the wall with a notched spreader.*

3 & 4 *Bed the first tile in place by resting its bottom edge on the batten and then raising it to the vertical. Press it firmly into the adhesive. Unless the tiles you are using have small spacer lugs on each edge, you must insert a tile spacer — either a proprietary plastic cross or a piece of matchstick or card.*

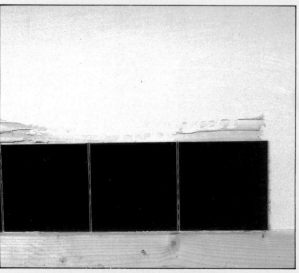

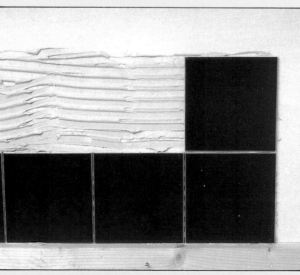

5 & 6 *Continue placing tiles in the first row until you reach the edge of the tiled area (or the corner of the room). Complete the row to the left of the start point. Then spread another band of tile adhesive on the wall and start bedding the second row of tiles. Again, use spacers if necessary.*

CUTTING TILES

1 & 2 *To cut edge pieces of exactly the right width, offer up a whole tile into the angle and mark the required width, remembering to acount for the joint thickness. Then use a carbide-tipped tile cutter to score the glaze along the cutting line. Try to make just one clean pass with the cutter — repeated cuts can cause the glaze to craze.*

3 & 4 *The simplest way to break the tile once the glaze has been scored is to slip a matchstick under each end of the scored line and then to press down firmly on each side of the tile with the balls of your thumbs. Don't exert too much force, though, or you could crack the tile in the other direction. Don't use this method to cut strips less than about a quarter of a tile wide.*

5 & 6 *A tile-cutting machine is an easier (and more accurate) way of cutting tiles, especially where very narrow cut pieces are required. The tile is simply lined up on the base of the machine, and the cutting wheel is run across its surface. Then the protruding part is simply snapped off by hand. Test the cut piece for fit, then spread some adhesive on its back and press it into place.*

GROUTING TILES

1 *When the tile adhesive has set, mix up some grout (or buy ready-mixed grout) and use a flexible squeegee to press it into the joint lines between the tiles, tackling a small area at a time. Scrape excess grout off the faces of the tiles as you work to minimize the amount of cleaning-up that will be needed later.*

2 *Remove excess grout from the joints by drawing a rounded object such as a piece of dowel along each joint line in turn. Don't use your fingers for this; grout is surprisingly abrasive, and will soon cause very sore fingertips.*

3 *Leave the grout to dry for the time recommended by the manufacturer. Then polish the surface of the tiles with a clean, dry cloth to remove surplus grout from the faces of the tiles and leave the tiled area looking fresh and sparkling. Here, special plastic tile-edging strips have been used to create a neat finish round the edges of the window reveal — see opposite.*

the vertical guide lines, then fill in as much of the remaining tiled area as you can using whole tiles.

There are just two points to watch. Unless the bottom row of tiles is supported by, say, the bath, basin, or whatever, it may slip. You should therefore provide it with temporary support, where necessary, by nailing a timber batten to the wall with its top edge just level with the horizontal starting line. This can be removed once the adhesive has set. Secondly, as you press tiles on to the wall, make sure they are correctly spaced to leave an even grout line 2-3mm ($\frac{1}{8}$in) wide. With many modern tiles, you can achieve this simply by butting each tile hard up against its neighbour. The tile's edges either have built-in spacing lugs, or else slope to leave exactly the right gap for grouting automatically. You may come across a few tiles with plain, square edges, however, and with these it is up to you to ensure the correct spacing. The simplest way to do this is to space the tiles out by inserting matchsticks or special plastic spacers.

Now you can fill in round the edges with cut tiles. These are put up in exactly the same way as whole tiles, except that you may find it easier to spread adhesive on to the tile back, rather than on to a narrow strip of wall. The big question, of course, is: how do you cut a ceramic tile? This is another of those jobs that beginners dread. But try it. The first tile you cut will show you just how easy it really is. Naturally you may have a few accidents (usually once your new found skill has tempted you to over-confidence), but even professional tilers break the occasional tile.

The first step is to measure up to find the width of the cut tile. Take two readings for this — one at the top of the space to be filled, and another at the bottom. This allows for the fact that whatever it is you are tiling up to may be out of square. Transfer both measurements on to the face of the tile (making sure you get them the right way round) then, with the tile laid on a flat surface, lay a straightedge between these two points to indicate the line of the cut. All you do now is run a tile cutter along the line with sufficient pressure to cut through the glaze, carrying the cut down both edges of the tile to score through any glaze there. Don't try to cut right through the tile. And don't worry if you have to run over the line a few times. The important thing is to finish with a clean score line that goes right through the glaze along its entire length. Now for the moment of truth. Place the tile face up on a table so that the table's edge lies immediately underneath the line scored in the tile's glaze. Hold the tile firmly on the table top with one hand, press down on the overhang with the other, and the tile should snap cleanly in two along the line. And that's it.

It's all a question of confidence. If you feel happier about it, you don't have to snap the tile over a table edge. You can snap it over a pencil or a couple of matchsticks. Alternatively, you will find a variety of tile cutting tools that will take care of the snapping as well as the scoring stages of the job — some are also designed to help with the transfer of measurements on to the tile's face.

Once all the cut tiles are in position, allow the adhesive to set completely — leaving it overnight is usually sufficient —

then finish off by filling in the gaps between tiles with grout. Mix this up according to the manufacturer's instructions to a thick, creamy consistency (or buy it ready-mixed) and apply it to the tile joints with a plastic spreader (often provided with the grout). Don't worry about getting grout on the face of the tiles. Just make sure you push it right into the gaps. Once you have covered about 1sq m/1 sq yd (by that time the grout should have started to harden) go back and smooth off the surface of the grout joins by running down them with a wet dowel, pencil or even your finger. If you do use your finger, though, wear rubber gloves to protect your skin from the cement most grouts contain.

Having treated the entire surface in this way, leave the grout to harden for 12 to 24 hours (see the instructions on the pack), and then wash down with plenty of clean water to remove the surplus grout still clinging to the surface of the tiles. Repeat the washing process as necessary until the water comes off clean, then allow to dry. As the surface dries, watch for a fine 'bloom' of grout residue to appear on the surface of the tiles. This is quite normal and can be polished off when completely dry using a soft cloth. Don't try to wash it off as each time you leave the tiling to dry it will reappear.

Tiling tricky areas

Many real life tiling situations are, of course, a little more complicated than the simple splashback described above. Tiling a whole room, for example, can prove very awkward indeed. But it's rare to find a tiling problem that cannot be overcome. The key to success in this sort of situation is to be found in the setting out. You simply have to take as much time and trouble as necessary to make sure you get it absolutely right before putting a single tile on to the wall.

The principles of setting out mentioned above still apply.

Starting points *On walls with two windows, start tiling from a centre line drawn between them unless the space between them is exactly equal to a number of whole tiles.*

If a door is centrally placed, start tiling from a line drawn through the centre of the door. If it is near a corner, start one tile's width away from the door frame and work outwards from there.

You must aim for symmetry and avoid the need for awkward, unsightly, narrow cut tiles. And to these two basic tenets you can add a third — aim for an arrangement that makes tiling around obstacles such as taps, light switches, windows, and so on, as simple as possible. So, assuming you are tiling a whole room, where should you start?

The best bet is usually the room's main window. Creating a symmetrical arrangement about this not only makes for easy tiling, but also, because that window is a natural focal point within the room, helps give the tiled effect as a whole a more balanced look. With the aid of a plumb-line or spirit-level, draw a vertical line on the wall above and below the window to indicate half the window's width, then, using a gauge rod, step out from this line along the window's top and bottom edges to see how the vertical tile joints will fall in relation to the window's sides.

Ideally, unless you are lucky enough to have a window that is an exact number of whole tiles wide, the corners of

TILING CORNERS AND EDGES

1 *Where tiling continues on the next wall, begin each row with the offcut from the end of the preceding row. Leave a small gap between the edge of the cut piece and the wall to allow the joint to be grouted later; if the pieces are butted tightly together, any slight movement in the wall could cause the tiles to crack.*

2 *To finish off external corners neatly when using universal tiles, you can bed special plastic edging strips in the adhesive and butt the edges of the last row of tiles up to them. Similar strips are available for edging areas that are tiled only for part of their height or width — splashbacks, for example.*

the window (or its reveal) should come roughly half way along a whole tile, though, in practice, any split that leaves more than about 25mm (1in) of a whole tile extending beyond the width of the window or reveal is acceptable. You see, this dimension is also the width of the cut tiles needed to fill in along the sides of the window, and quite apart from the fact that strips narrower than 25mm (1in) are difficult to cut, you must allow for the fact the an L-shaped tile may well be needed at the corners. The less tile you have to remove to produce the L-shape, the easier it will be to end up with a cut tile that is both strong and attractive. If you find that you are left with tiles that over-run by less than 25mm (1in), move the vertical starting line half a tile width to the right or left, and try again.

Having sorted out where the vertical columns of tiles are to go, turn your attention to the horizontal rows. You will find this easier if you strike a second, temporary vertical guide line a little to one side of the window or reveal. Mark a point on the line about 50mm (2in) above the floor or skirting board that defines the lower edge of the tiled area, to represent the bottom edge of the bottom row of tiles. Why not start the bottom row off along the skirting board or floor? The reason is that there is no guarantee that such fixtures are absolutely straight and level. You could, there-fore, end up with crooked tiling, or with some very awkward cutting to make a horizontal row of tiles fit in around any dips and bumps. From this starting point, now use the gauge rod to work out the positions of the tile rows in relation to the top and bottom of the window or reveal, then continue up to the ceiling and check the width of any cut tiles needed to fill in there.

Where the top and bottom of the window are concerned, bear in mind the points mentioned in connection with its width. Don't worry too much about achieving perfect symmetry, though. Any arrangement that is approximately symmetrical is usually good enough, so try to visualize how the finished tiling will look and make up your own mind as to whether or not it looks reasonable. At the ceiling, the ideal is to end up with a row of cut tiles of about the same depth as the cut tiles filling in along the bottom of the wall, though again small deviations from perfect symmetry are generally acceptable so long as the end result looks right. Whatever you do, avoid finishing at the ceiling with a row of whole tiles. Ceilings are no more likely to be straight and level than floors and skirting boards.

Having said all that, you will be very lucky indeed if you arrive at the perfect arrangement at the first attempt. Indeed, even after several tries, each time starting with the bottom row of tiles in a slightly different position, there is no guarantee that you will be able to satisfy all of the condi-tions outlined. In such cases, you simply have to use your own judgement, settling on the arrangement that comes closest to the ideal.

To complete the setting out around the window, finally work out the positions of the tiles that will line any reveal, starting with one set so that its edge is flush with the faces of the tiles covering the main wall. As usual, you should avoid

TILING WINDOW REVEALS

1 *When tiling up to and within a window reveal, fix the tiles on the facing wall first. If you are using edging strips, bed these in the adhesive before fixing the last row of tiles. Then tile the sill, beginning with a row of whole tiles butting up to the angle trim.*

2 *When all the whole tiles have been laid across the sill, cut and fit narrow pieces to fill the gap between the whole tiles and the window frame. As with internal corners, leave a slight gap between the cut pieces and the frame to allow for any movement that might occur in the future.*

3 *Tile the sides of the reveal in a similar manner, fixing whole tiles first and then adding cut pieces as required. If edge trim is not being used, simply position the whole tiles so that they overlap the edges of those on the face of the wall. Finish off the reveal by tiling the underside of the reveal head; you may need to support the tiles by propping an offcut of timber across them until the adhesive sets.*

the need for narrow cut tiles as you fill in the window side of the reveal. In this case, though, you cannot adjust the starting position to correct errors. Instead, be prepared to cut the first line of tiles down in depth, in order to increase the depth of those running back to the window frame.

There is, unfortunately, one major snag with this arrangement. It allows you to see the edges of the tiles lining the reveal. If those edges are unglazed, let alone unglazed and studded with spacing lugs, the result is obviously not going to be very attractive. So, is there an alternative? After all, the same problem will occur when tiling around any external corner.

The traditional solution to this problem was to use a special kind of tile, called an RE tile. Unlike the field tiles used to cover the bulk of the surface (which had square cut, unglazed edges), RE tiles had one edge not only glazed, but also slightly rounded to give the corner (or the edge of an isolated tiled area) a smoothly contoured finish. There were REX tiles too — tiles with two rounded, glazed edges designed to produce a neat corner. The snag is that RE and REX tiles are now rare. In fact, virtually the only tiles now made using this three tile system are a few of the thicker, more traditional types of ceramic floor tile — quarry tiles, and the like. On walls, their job has largely been taken over by the continental two-tile system, comprising field tiles and edging tiles (the latter basically just field tiles with one or more edges glazed), and by the more recently introduced universal tiles – tiles with four sloping edges glazed, the edge slope providing automatic spacing.

There is, however, another possibility, and that is to use special quadrant tiles — essentially the ceramic equivalent of timber quadrant beading. These come in straight lengths, plus mitred pairs for internal and external corners, but the choice of colours is limited, and you may therefore experience some difficulty in finding quadrant tiles that match the tiles chosen for the rest of the wall. In this case, consider choosing quadrants in a strongly contrasting colour, rather than settling for a near miss. There is one other thing to remember if you do decide to use quadrant tiles. Be sure to allow for them when working out the sizes and positions of cut tiles leading up to the corner.

Having worked out the optimum tiling arrangement for the area around the window, restrike the starting horizontal guide line at the foot of the wall and extend it right round the room. If it runs past any noticeable changes in the level of the floor or ceiling, use your gauge rod to see how these changes relate to the positions of the horizontal rows at that point. If you discover a potential problem — for example, if extra narrow cut tiles become necessary — decide whether or not it is worth starting all over again with a slightly adjusted starting point beneath the window.

Similarly, if the line runs past (or up against) an obstacle mounted on the wall — a bath, for example — work out how the tile rows will fit round it. Again, if such obstacles pose severe problems, you may decide it is worth adjusting the starting point at the window to make things easier. Incidentally, where such obstacles prevent you continuing

TILING ROUND OBSTACLES

1 When you have to fit tiles round obstacles such as light switches, or where L-shaped pieces of tile are required at the corners of window openings, the easiest way of ensuring an accurate, crack-free cut is to use a special tile saw — rather like a coping saw for woodwork. Grip the tile securely in a vice and cut steadily along the marked line.

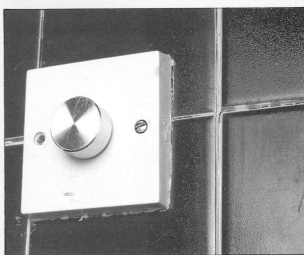

2 Test each cut piece carefully for fit round the obstacle, and trim it slightly if necessary using a tile file or similar abrasive. Then butter some adhesive on to its rear face and press it into position. Check that it sits flush with its neighbours, then grout the joints neatly to complete the job. If the faceplate screws are long enough, you can release them and set the tile edges behind the faceplate.

the guide line along the foot of the wall, strike a vertical guide line, measure up this in whole tile-plus-grout units to a point above the obstacle, then restart the horizontal guide line from there. Reverse the procedure to return the guide line to the foot of the wall once you are past the obstacle.

The final stage of the setting out procedure for complete rooms is to work out how the vertical columns of tiles fit in with the room's corners and any other obstacles. Starting at the vertical guide line beneath the window, merely use the gauge rod to step off tile widths along the horizontal guide line. As usual, the aim is to come up with an arrangement that avoids the need for awkward fitting and narrow cut tiles. Here, however, if you encounter a problem on any wall other than the one containing the window, there is usually no need to go right back to the beginning and try a slightly different starting point. Instead, for the purpose of setting out tile columns, you can treat each wall as a separate entity, adjusting the column's positions as necessary to achieve an easy-to-tile, reasonably symmetrical arrangement.

Whatever you do, take care at the corners of the room. If the finished wall is to look right, it is important to maintain some visual continuity between the tiling on the two adjacent walls. In theory, the best way to do this is to use the off-cuts from the tiles on one wall to begin tiling on the next — this having the added advantage of saving work as well as saving tiles. However, it is not always such a good idea in practice. If the walls are out of square, the off-cuts may need some delicate trimming before they fit. What's more, the use of off-cuts in this way may not give the best column arrangement on the second wall. Once again, you will have to use your own judgement. Make use of off-cuts to fill in by all means, but not to the detriment of the tiling as a whole.

Now that you know, more or less, the position of every tile in the room, you can move on to the actual tiling. This is carried out in just the same way as when tiling a small splashback. However, you will need to know how to cut more complex tile shapes. Let's start with the L-shapes needed around windows, doors, and similar obstacles. Mark out the line along which the cut is to be made in pencil, then score along it with a tile cutter, as usual remembering to score through any glaze on the tile edges to ensure a clean break. You now take a pair of carpenter's pincers and nibble away the waste material a little at the time. You will find it easier to nibble away the waste area of tile if you cross-hatch it first using your tile cutter. When you have removed as much as you can safely with the pliers — there is a risk of snapping the tile in two — neaten the cut edges with a file.

The same technique can be adapted to cut more complex shapes in the edges of tiles. Alternatively, consider using a special saw. The most widely available type is a bit like a fretsaw, fitted with a specially hardened blade similar to an *Abrafile*. But what about cutting round something like a pipe that passes through the middle of a tile? The trick is to cut the tile neatly in two along a line running through the centre of the desired hole, then to cut the outline of half the hole in each half of the tile using the technique described above. Once the tile has been stuck in place on the wall, the join between the halves of the tile will hardly show.

Applying mosaics

Mosaics have to be among the oldest of all forms of interior decoration, but to produce one these days, you don't have to mess about chipping bits of marble exactly to fit, or set each piece in by hand, laboriously building up the finished design fragment by fragment. Instead, you can buy modern ceramic mosaics. These are made up, not of stone, but of a series of small glazed ceramic tiles. The really clever thing about them is that you don't have to assemble the surface bit by bit. The tiny tiles come already arranged in the correct order, temporarily stuck in place on a backing sheet of fabric or covered with a facing sheet of paper.

Creating a perfect mosaic-covered surface is therefore almost as easy as hanging wallpaper. Measure up the area you wish to cover, taking two or three readings in different places for both the length and breadth just in case it is out of square. Now, working to the smallest reading for each dimension, cut the mosaic sheet to size with a pair of scissors, following the gaps between the rows of tiles — leave the sheet fractionally undersize if necessary, rather than make it too large.

If the resulting trimmed sheet is too large to be handled comfortably, cut it up into sections and lay each one separately. In this case, though, do take care to leave the correct gap between the tiny tiles at the edges of the sections when you come to reassemble the mosaic on the surface. With the sections still stuck to their backing sheets, you can usually judge this by eye, taking the spacings between tiles in the centre of each sheet as a guide. And if the mosaic has to fit round an obstruction such as a tap? Just lay the sheet in its final position on the surface, and snip out as many whole fragments as necessary to obtain the best possible fit.

The next step is to apply a layer of the recommended adhesive to the surface with a serrated spreader (often provided), covering an area the same size as the trimmed mosaic sheet. Now, just lay the sheet in place (paper-facing uppermost, fabric down) aiming to centre it on the area it is to cover, and smooth it over with a soft cloth or soft paint roller to bed each of the small tiles in place. Once the adhesive has set, carefully peel back away the backing paper (you may need to soak it first) and begin filling in any wide gaps around the edges with cut tiles.

This has the potential for being a rather fiddly chore, but fortunately, since minor inaccuracies tend not to show, you don't have to be too particular. Just nibble away at the tiles — taken from an off-cut of the main sheet — using a pair of carpenter's pincers until they fit. You may find this easier if you grip the tile you are working on in a pair of pliers. Constantly check the fit of each piece as you work, and when you are satisfied, coat the back with a little adhesive and pop it into place.

Once you have completed the mosaic, all that remains is to grout the joins between tiles — grout can also be used to fill gaps around the edges that proved too small to fill with tiles. Don't bother to treat each join individually as you would with full-size ceramic tiles. Apply the grout thickly over the entire surface, scraping off the bulk of the excess and working the grout right down into the gaps with the spreader as you go. Similarly, don't attempt to neaten individual joins. When the grout has hardened sufficiently, just wipe over the surface with a damp sponge or cloth. That done, all that remains is to wait until the grout has hardened completely, and then wash and polish the surface down in the usual way.

Cork tiling

Cork tiles are also worth considering as a finish for walls. As well as being attractive, and thick enough to cover up minor imperfections in the surface, they can help to deaden echoes within the room (useful if the room has a hard floor-

LAYING MOSAICS

1 & 2 *Fabric-backed mosaics are bonded to a net backing for ease of handling, but are laid in the same way as other ceramic tiles. Start by marking setting-out lines on the surface to be tiled. Then spread an area of adhesive slightly larger than the sheet, and bed it in place. Press it down firmly into the adhesive for a good bond.*

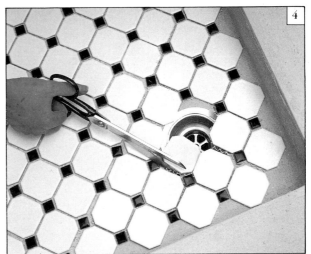

3 & 4 *Cut through the mesh backing with scissors to remove unwanted areas of the mosaic at the edges of the tiled area. Small cut pieces of mosaic will fill any gaps that are left. With obstacles such as a shower waste outlet, lay the sheet over it and then snip away whole pieces of mosaic as required.*

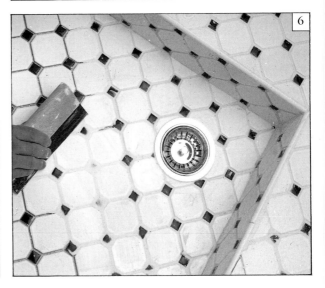

5 & 6 *Cut small pieces of mosaic to fit gaps at edges and round obstacles by nibbling away the unwanted portions wih pincers or special tile nibblers. Then stick each cut piece in position with a blob of adhesive. When all the mosaics are in place, grout the whole area as for ordinary tiling, and polish the surface with a cloth.*

FIXING CORK TILES

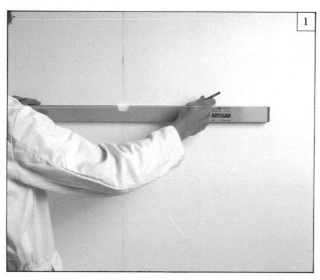

1 & 2 *When fixing cork tiles to a wall surface, start by marking out a true horizontal line across the wall. Then find the midpoint and draw a vertical line here to indicate your starting point. Move it half a tile width to one side if the layout requires very narrow strips at the edge of the tiled area. Then apply adhesive to the wall.*

3 & 4 *Spread a thin layer of adhesive on the back of each tile using the notched spreader supplied. Then press the first tile into place on the wall, lining it up carefully with the vertical and horizontal guidelines. Make sure that it is well stuck by pressing it all over with the palms of your hands.*

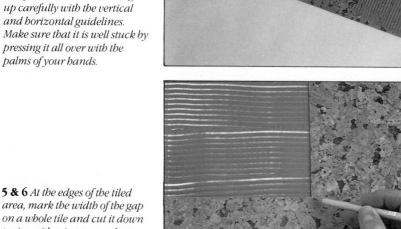

5 & 6 *At the edges of the tiled area, mark the width of the gap on a whole tile and cut it down to size with scissors or a sharp craft knife. Test its fit, then spread adhesive on its rear face and press it into position. Where you are tiling round an external corner, fit a corner trim of wood, metal or plastic to protect the crumbly edges of the tiles from damage.*

covering), and warm up the surface. However, don't choose them solely because you want to improve the wall's sound and/or thermal insulation. They are not nearly thick enough to stop unwanted noise entering the room, nor for that matter are they usually thick enough to prevent heat escaping.

You should also think twice about using this type of wall-covering as a cure for condensation. Although it should provide sufficient insulation to warm the wall to the point where condensation will no longer form on the surface, this cannot be guaranteed. You could just end up with soggy cork tiles, instead of damp wallpaper. In addition, there is a chance that this sort of treatment for condensation could make matters worse elsewhere, unless you also take steps to tackle the root cause of the problem — high humidity levels — by improving your home's heating and ventilation.

How do you put them up? As when using ceramic tiles, start with some setting out. Let's suppose you are tiling a single wall as a special feature of the decor. Strike a vertical guide line exactly half way along the wall using either a plumb-line or a spirit-level that will test verticals. Now with the aid of a spirit-level, strike a horizontal guide line through this exactly half way along its length — in other words, exactly half way up the wall. If you now start tiling with four tiles set around the intersection of these two lines, you will finish with the perfectly symmetrical arrangement you need.

But don't start tiling just yet. First check on the sizes of any cut tiles needed to fill in at the top, bottom, and sides of the wall. Simply step off along both the horizontal and verti-cal guide lines in whole tile widths marking the positions of the joins between tiles as you go. You can use a spare tile as a gauge for this. Cork tiles simply butt together, so there is no need to bother with a gauge rod to ensure an even grouting allowance. If you find that the cut tiles needed are too narrow to be cut easily — treat 25-50mm (1-2in) as a practical minimum — move the appropriate guide line by the width of half a whole tile. To correct for narrow tiles at the top and bottom, move the horizontal guide line up or down. To correct for narrow tiles at the sides, move the vertical guide line to the left or right.

Now you can start tiling, starting with the four tiles that cluster around the intersection of the horizontal and verti-cal guide lines. Simply spread a thin coat of contact adhesive on to the wall with a smooth plastic spreader, aim-ing to cover an area equivalent to about four whole tiles at a time, then apply a similarly thin coat to the back of each tile, and allow the adhesive on both tile and wall to become almost touch dry. Offer the tile up to the wall, with its edge just touching the surface so you can check its position, then 'hinge' it down flat against the surface and smooth into place with a soft clean cloth. If you are using very thin, flexi-ble tiles, begin smoothing in the centre and work out towards the edges to avoid trapping bubbles of air.

Although obviously slightly inaccurate, this method of positioning the tile with only its edge touching the surface is necessary. Most contact adhesives grip hard the moment the two layers of adhesive come together. Even if you go for a contact adhesive that claims to allow some adjustment after the surfaces are brought together, you will find that the amount of adjustment possible tends to be rather small.

There is one other point to consider when choosing the adhesive. Most conventional contacts use petroleum-based solvent, and therefore give off fairly heady and highly inflammable fumes as they dry out. So, if you decide to use this type, make sure the room is really well ventilated, and don't allow naked lights to come anywhere near. Certain mixtures of solvent fumes and air are more than inflamm-able — they can explode. If you cannot meet these safety requirements for any reason, be sure to choose one of the more modern water-based contact adhesives. You may, in any case, find using these more comfortable, because with these the 'fumes' are nothing more than water vapour.

Once the first four tiles are in place, continue tiling out along the four arms of the cross formed by the guide line, butting each tile tight against its neighbour, until you reach the point where cut tiles are needed to fill in around the edges of the wall. You should now go back and cover the rest of the wall as far as you can using whole tiles. This may sound a slightly strange way to set about things, but you should find it appreciably quicker than simply working out-wards for the four centre tiles in a more or less *ad hoc* fashion.

With all the whole tiles in place, turn your attention to filling in the gaps around the edges with cut tiles. As with ceramic tiling, measure the width of each cut tile at both sides to allow for the fact that the wall may be out of square and transfer these measurements, the right way round, on to the face of the tile with a pencil. Finally, join up with a pencil line to indicate the line of the cut. As for actually cutting the tile, so long as the tile is not too thick, a pair of strong scissors will do the job. However, some cork tiles are rather crumbly, and so you will probably find that a sharp craft knife leaves a far neater edge. Simply place the tile on a flat surface — a sheet of scrap hardboard is ideal, because it doesn't matter if it gets scratched as the knife breaks through — lay a metal straightedge along the line of the cut, and run the knife along its edge two or three times until you are through. The cut tile can then be stuck in place on the wall in the normal way.

To complete the tiling, vacuum the surface of the wall to remove any dirt and dust clinging to the tiles and inspect it closely for gaps, and chipped edges. This is not to suggest that your workmanship is at fault. Some tiles crumble so easily it's very difficult to put them up without doing a cer-tain amount of damage, and this, coupled with the fact that few cork tiles are absolutely square, makes a few defects of this sort almost inevitable. Often effective repairs can be made merely by breaking chips of cork from waste off-cuts and glueing them into place with a little PVA woodworking adhesive — any that oozes out should be wiped off immedi-ately with a damp cloth. Very narrow gaps, unfortunately, don't respond easily to this treatment. Really all you can do is camouflage them with a little paint.

All that remains is to seal the surface. Unless you have bought ready-sealed tiles, the cork needs some protection against airborne moisture and dirt. A polyurethane varnish is perhaps the best choice for the job as it also helps strengthen the cork against physical damage. It's up to you whether you use one with a gloss, matt, or satin finish, but you will need at least two or three coats to obtain a satisfactory result. Dilute the first coat with a little white spirit according to the manufacturer's instructions and lightly rub this into the cork with a soft, lint-free cloth, taking care not to damage the tiles in the process. This should effectively seal the surface ready for the finishing coats, which you apply unthinned using an ordinary paint brush. For the best results, allow each coat to dry thoroughly before applying the next. On smooth cork tiles, it is also worth lightly rubbing down the surface between coats using fine grade wire wool, glasspaper, or silicon carbide abrasive used dry. In this case, wipe over with a damp cloth to remove dust, and leave to dry off before continuing.

Tiling ceilings

Just as tiles offer a speedy and effective cover-up for less than perfect walls, so too can they be used to give a ceiling that's in poor condition an attractive decorative finish. There are two types of tile commonly used for the purpose — expanded polystyrene tiles, and tongued-and-grooved fibre tiles. Both are put up in an entirely different way, so let's take them one at a time, starting with the procedure for those in polystyrene.

Start with the setting out. This is carried out in broadly the same way as for cork wall tiling. Measure up the room and, using a chalked line, strike guide lines on the ceiling between the mid-points of opposite walls. They will cross

in the exact centre of the room, and this is where you should begin tiling, with four tiles set in the angles between the chalk guide lines, in order to give the tiled ceiling an attractive looking symmetry. There is, however, one possible exception to this rule, and that is where a pendant light forms the dominant feature of the ceiling. In this case, decide whether the ceiling might not look better with a group of tiles clustered around the ceiling rose. If you think it does, work out as accurately as you can where the edges of these tiles will fall and restrike the guide lines accordingly — in line with the outer edges of two of these tiles, so that you don't have to start the tiling with the fiddly job of cutting tiles to shape.

As usual, though, before putting up a single tile, check that the cut tiles needed around the edge of the room are a reasonable size — anything over 25mm (1in) is about right — by stepping off whole tile widths along the guide lines. Where there are chimney breasts to be fitted round, and alcoves and window bays to be tiled into, check what will happen to the tiles there. Reposition the starting guide lines as necessary until you have achieved a satisfactory arrangement — one that gives a reasonable constant border of adequately wide cut tiles around the walls, and one that avoids awkward cutting in around chimney breasts and other external angles.

There is one last check to make, and that is to ensure that the final guide lines look right. If the room is badly out of square, tiles laid to guide lines that are correct according to the text book can sometimes look rather odd, and in such circumstances it is usually worth cheating a little, restriking the lines in a compromise position that fits in better with the shape of the room. Just make sure that the guide lines end up crossing each other at right-angles.

You can now start putting up the tiles, following the same order of work as described for cork tiling a wall. Begin with the tiles at the intersection of the two guide lines, then lay a row of tiles along each guide line, fill in between the arms of this tiled cross as far as possible using whole tiles, then finish off by filling in around the edges of the room with cut tiles tailored to fit. You'll find actually cutting very easy indeed. Just use a sharp knife and a straightedge in the same way as when cutting cork tiles. But do take care not to mark the tiles as you press them into place — they are quite soft. Don't use your hands for this job. Instead, make up a flat pressing board from scrap plywood with a block of softwood for a handle. If you must use your hands, at least protect the tile you are fixing by covering it with a spare tile to spread the load. It is also worth making sure your hands are clean before handling the tiles — they get dirty easily and finger marks are not easily washed off.

There are just a few final points to watch concerning the long-term safety of the ceiling. Always buy good quality tiles — ones containing a fire retardant. Always use an adhesive specially designed for use with polystyrene tiles, and follow the maker's recommendations on using it — the usual recommendation these days is to set the tiles in a continuous bed of adhesive rather than with a blob of adhesive in

Setting out ceiling tiles *Find the centre point of the room by joining the mid-points of opposite walls, and start tiling in the angles between the chalk lines. Work outwards from this centre point in triangles.*

FIXING POLYSTYRENE CEILING TILES

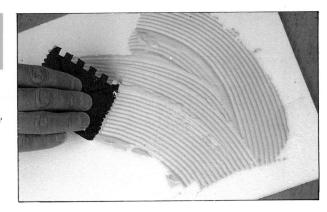

1 *When you have completed the setting-out and know where tiling will start on the ceiling, spread special polystyrene adhesive all over the back of each tile; don't rely on just a blob at each corner of the tile.*

2 *Start fixing the tiles against your guidelines, working from the centre of the room out towards the walls. Where there is a central ceiling rose, trim the corners of the tiles to fit round it.*

3 *Press each tile into place carefully, aligning it with its neighbours. Beware of denting the tiles with your fingers; it's better to use an offcut of hardboard or something similar to press them into position.*

4 *At the perimeter of the ceiling, measure and cut narrow strips to fit the gap. Test the fit dry first, then spread adhesive on the back and press the strip into place carefully.*

each corner as was once common practice. Finally, never paint polystyrene tiles. If you do and there is a fire in the room, the paint film will counteract the safety effects of the two previous precautions. It really is very dangerous.

And what about tongued-and-grooved fibre tiles? There are two main differences between using these and putting up any other kind of tile. The first is that they are not stuck in place. They are fixed to slim timber battens. Secondly, you should begin fixing them in one corner of the room, rather than in the centre of the ceiling.

You still need to set the tiles out properly though. Strike chalk guide lines in the usual way to determine the size and position of the ceiling's cut tile border, then use panel pins to fix a 50 x 12mm (2 x ½in) softwood batten parallel to a wall adjoining the corner at which you intend to begin tiling. Use sawn softwood battens, incidentally – their rough finish will be covered by the tiles, and they are cheaper. But how do you decide which wall to place the batten against? Obviously it is preferable not to choose one containing obstacles such as chimney breasts and alcoves, but there is another consideration. The timber battens must be run at right-angles to the ceiling joists so that their fixing pins can be driven securely into the joists' timber, rather than into the ceiling's plasterboard or lath and plaster skin – they won't grip otherwise.

You must therefore take the time to locate the exact position of each joist, and having found them, it's a good idea to mark the lines of their centres on the ceiling's surface with a chalk line. Locating the joists in an upstairs room where you have access to the loft is easiest. Once in the loft you can poke through the ceiling with a bradawl or something similar to indicate the position of each side of any given joist. There is no need to mark every joist in this way. Once you know the spacing between a pair of joists and the direction in which they run, you can measure to find the line of the remainder on the ceiling below – they are generally parallel and evenly spaced. And if you cannot gain direct access to the joists? All you can do is drill a series of test holes up through the ceiling until you strike wood.

Once the first tiling batten is in position, fix a second along the line of the joints between the cut tile border and the first row of whole tiles. You now continue adding battens across the ceiling with their centres one whole tile apart. Measure the first gap using an actual tile. For the rest, you will find spacing quicker if you make up a gauge from scrap softwood. Simply recess the ends of this with a saw so that the distance between the recesses is equal to the distance between battens. By running the gauge along between battens you can also check that they are parallel to each other.

Having completed the battening, cut a tile to fit the corner of the cut tile border, and secure this to the first and second battens using either small panel pins or a heavy-duty stapler – the latter is quicker and allows you to work one-handed. Those that form the fixing to the second batten should be driven through the top lip of the tile's grooved edge. Now, work out from this corner tile along

This unusual bathroom **left** makes excellent use of the water resistance of ceramic tiles. They have been used to tile the custom-built bath and shower area, and the same tiles have been taken up the walls to shoulder height as a splashback. Note that the size of the bath has been gauged to avoid the need for cut tiles.

Tiles provide the perfect decoration for this combined bath and basin surround **above** and their use on the walls above give the whole room a unified look. Again, careful planning has avoided unnecessary tile cutting.

Floor-to-ceiling tiling is the perfect answer for a modern style washing area such as this **right**. The pale overall colour is brightened by the unusual use of surface-mounted conduits for the light and power supplies.

FIXING CEILING TILES TO BATTENS

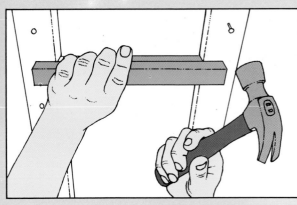

1 *Start by nailing slim timber battens to the ceiling surface at right angles to the joists. Use a timber spacer to ensure that the battens are truly parallel and the right distance apart.*

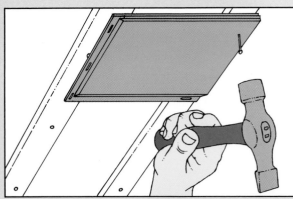

2 *Begin tiling at one edge of the room, pinning through the face of the tile into the perimeter batten. Punch the pin head just below the surface and disguise it with filler.*

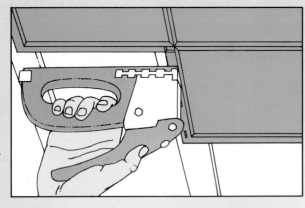

3 *Continue tiling by locating the groove of each tile over the exposed tongue of the previous one, and stapling through its tongue into the batten beneath. A staple gun is essential, as it leaves the other hand free to position the tile.*

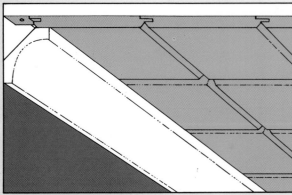

4 *Either fill the last row with small pieces of cut tile, or disguise the edges of the tiles by fixing a decorative cornice right round the room. Lightweight types can be fixed in place with adhesive.*

both adjacent walls, fixing the remaining cut tiles in place in the same way, again with their tongued edges pointing in towards the centre of the room.

With these two rows in place, it's a relatively simple matter to tile outwards from the corner, using whole tiles. Simply slot their tongues into the grooves of the preceding tile, and secure their tongued edges to a batten with pins or staples. The only likely hitch will come when you reach a pendant light fitting. The rose will have to be removed and remounted on the surface of the tiles. This can wait until the tiling is complete, but for now, turn off the power at the mains, remove the ceiling rose, and draw the cables that come out of the ceiling through a hole cut in the tile at that point just before you fix it in place. Once all the whole tiles have been put up, finish off the ceiling by fixing cut tiles along the two remaining sides of the room, securing them to battens run along the ceiling next to the walls. You will probably have to cut these slightly undersize in order to locate their tongued edges in the grooves of the adjacent whole tiles, but this gap can be easily concealed beneath a decorative coving. It is, in any case, a good idea to use coving to neaten all the edges of the ceiling. It will cover up any accidental gaps between cut tiles and wall, as well as concealing the exposed heads of the pins used to fix the cut tiles to the wall battens.

THE COMPLETE PANELLER

When it comes to finding a way to both decorate and cover up a wall or ceiling that's in really poor condition, panelling is hard to beat. It's not a particularly cheap treatment and to do it properly does involve a fair amount of hard work, but then, unlike so many other forms of decoration, you can view it as a more or less permanent addition to your home – a genuine improvement. And it is undeniably attractive.

There are basically two types of material you can use for the job. For genuine timber cladding, tongued and grooved softwood matchboarding is the usual choice. Widely available from good timber yards and DIY stores it allows you a number of subtle variations on the basic theme. For example, you can alter the look of the cladding by staining it, or by putting it up in an unusual way – perhaps diagonally to form chevrons. Even the type of varnish you choose to seal it, whether gloss, matt or satin finish, can have a surprisingly great effect.

This is, unfortunately, one of the most expensive forms of cladding, but even if your budget won't stretch to it, you can still achieve the same sort of look using the second cladding option – wallboards. These are basically sheets of tough plywood or hardboard printed or veneered to look like a genuine article. The surface is usually embossed to create the illusion of tongued and grooved joints between planks, but you are not restricted solely to a matchboarding finish: wallboards are also available with tile effects, as well as in plain colours for where you want a really chic lacquered look.

Whichever you choose, you will find that although putting it up takes time, it's not very difficult. Let's look at how you would set about creating a single clad feature wall.

Cladding walls

Although wallboards will cover-up a good many faults, they won't tolerate dampness, so do make sure that the wall you intend to clad is free from penetrating and rising damp. As an additional precaution, line an *exterior* wall with heavy-gauge polyethylene (polythene) sheeting. This can be taped into place (the cladding will provide a more permanent fixing) provided adjacent sheets overlap by at least 150mm (6in). To complete the final preparation, remove all skirting boards and picture rails, plus door and window architraves, from the relevant wall.

If you are putting up genuine matchboarding, you must cover the wall with a framework of softwood battens to provide suitable fixing points for the cladding – 50 x 25mm (2 x 1in) sawn softwood is adequate. For vertical cladding, fix one batten at the top of the wall and one at the bottom, then add further intermediate battens at roughly 600mm (24in) centres. For horizontal cladding, fix the battens vertically – one at each end of the wall; then at approximately 600mm (24in) centres in between.

Use a spirit-level/plumb-line to make sure the battens are truly horizontal/vertical, and check that the faces of the battens represent a reasonably flat surface to which the cladding can be fixed. Any inaccuracies in the wall can simply be corrected by inserting packing pieces of scrap plywood behind the battens before fixing them in place. For speed, secure the battens to masonry walls using masonry nails; on stud partition walls use ordinary wood nails, but do make sure you drive these into the wall's timber framework, not just into the plasterboard skin. The framework's vertical studs are generally spaced about 600mm (24in) apart and can be located by drilling test holes through the plasterboard with a drill and a small diameter twist bit. Tapping the wall gives a good indication of where to start drilling – it sounds less hollow over a stud (a vertical baulk of timber to which plasterboard is nailed).

With all the battens in place, begin putting up the cladding. Start at one edge of the wall and position the first board with its grooved edge facing into the corner, securing this edge to the battens by driving small panel pins at an angle through one lip of the groove. Fix the tongued edge to the battens by driving in further pins just where the tongue emerges from the body of the board. Again drive these at an angle so that they emerge obliquely through the underside of the board's body. This is called 'secret nailing' and allows you to secure the second board merely by sliding its groove over the first board's tongue. The tongued edge of this second board is now pinned to the battens using the same secret nailing technique. If you find secret nailing difficult, special clips are available which allow you to secure the tongued edges of the boarding without it.

Continue in this way until you come to the very last board; it almost certainly won't fit, so plane its tongued edge down until it does, then remove just enough extra to allow its groove to be located over the neighbouring board's tongue. Finally, secure the remaining free edge – the one you planed – with pins driven into the battens through the face of the board. Their exposed heads, together with any gaps around the cladding due to inaccurate cutting or variations in the line of adjacent walls, can be covered with decorative wooden moulding. Similar defects at the top of the wall can be covered by ceiling coving, while those at the bottom will be hidden when you replace the skirting board.

Once you know how to clad a single wall, it is but a small step to apply the technique to a room as a whole. In fact, the only real difference is that you need to know how to get round obstacles such as doors and windows, and how to turn internal and external corners. The methods described

FIXING BATTENS

1 *The first stage in cladding a wall with tongued-and-grooved timber is to fix a network of supporting battens to the wall surface. Begin by fixing horizontal battens at floor and ceiling level; then add a batten at each edge of the wall. Remove skirting boards and architraves if they're fitted.*

2 *Add further intermediate battens at roughly 600mm (24in) centres to provide extra support for the cladding. Here the boards will be fixed vertically, so horizontal battens are used. An offcut of timber helps to ensure even spacing.*

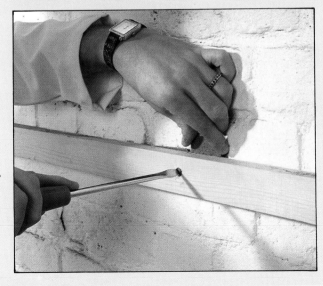

3 *To get a true finished surface to the cladding on an uneven wall, the battens may have to be packed out. Test them with a straightedge; where hollows are found, release the screws and insert packing pieces of hardboard or thick card before tightening up the fixing screws again.*

below are for vertical matchboarding, but if your cladding is horizontal, you should have no difficult whatsoever in adapting them to suit.

Let's start with external corners. Having butt-jointed the battens at that point to provide adequate support, clad up to the corner as far as the last board, then begin cladding the adjacent wall in the usual way. You can now finish off the cladding on the first wall, planing the tongued edge of its final board flush with the cladding around the corner. Fix this free edge by pinning through the board's face into the tongued edge of the first board on the second wall. Much the same technique is used for internal corners. Here though, it is simply a matter of planing down the tongued edge of the last board on the first wall until it fits into the gap left once the first board on the adjacent wall has been fixed in place.

Doors and windows can be a little trickier. The simplest way to clad round them is to surround them completely with battens, then clad round these in the same way as an external corner to leave a neat finish. Alternatively, with a door, you can widen the door lining to leave it flush with the clad surface, and neaten the join by covering it with architrave. In this case, the door must obviously be re-hung. There is another option, too, for windows set into a reveal. If the window frame is thick enough, you can turn the cladding into the reveal and rely on the frame to conceal the final edge — a decorative beading should help. Lastly, don't forget about light switches. It's best to resite these, together with their mounting boxes, so that they finish flush with the surface of the cladding, but to do this, the cladding will need extra support, so frame the old switch position with battens.

And what about wallboards? Like matchboarding, these can be simply pinned in place on battens. But there is an easier alternative, and that is to stick them in place directly to the wall using a special gap-filling panel adhesive. The adhesive comes in cartridges from which it is extruded with a special gun in the same way as mastic and caulking. All you do is apply it to the wall in stripes (though do check the manufacturer's instructions), and press the cut-to-size board firmly into place.

This method does, however, pre-suppose that the walls are in reasonably good condition. If they are not, consider getting the best of both worlds by combining the two techniques — glueing the wallboards to battening. The battens help accommodate any defects in the wall, and the adhesive gives you an invisible fixing.

Cladding ceilings

The exact method used to clad a ceiling tends to depend not so much on what type of cladding you intend to use, as on why you want to clad the ceiling in the first place. If it is simply a question of giving the surface a tongued and grooved look, then you can proceed in the same way as when cladding a wall — pin the cladding in place; don't rely on adhesive. There are only three important differences. First, you will have to remount any ceiling roses on the sur-

FIXING CLADDING

1 & 2 *Cut the first board to be fitted to length, and offer its tongued edge up to the side wall so you can see how uneven this is. If there are gaps here and there, it's best to scribe the wall profile on to the board with a pencil and a small block of wood, and to saw along the line with a jigsaw or padsaw to ensure a perfect fit.*

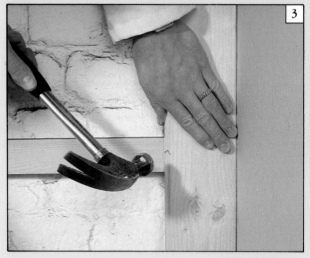

3 & 4 *Offer the scribed board up into the corner, checking that it is tightly butted against the other wall, and drive pins through the tongue into the battens to hold it in place. Then slide the groove of the second board over the tongue of the first, and tap it home using a cladding offcut to protect the tongue. Pin as before.*

5 & 6 *When the last whole plank has been pinned in place, mark the width of the narrow strip needed to complete the cladding. If the wall surface is uneven, scribe and saw its long edge first. Then offer the strip up and fix it in place by driving pins through the face of the board into the battens. Punch in the nail heads.*

face of the cladding. This is done in much the same way as when repositioning a lightswitch on a wall. Second, there is no need to worry too much about concealing gaps and exposed nail heads around the perimeter of the clad area — framing the ceiling with a decorative wooden moulding used in the same way as ordinary coving gives excellent results. And finally, you must make sure that the supporting timber battens are nailed to the ceiling joists for the same reason that, when cladding a stud partition wall, you must make the fixings into the wall's supporting studs — the plasterboard or lath-and-plaster skin doesn't provide a strong enough anchorage.

If, on the other hand, your reason for choosing cladding as a finish is that you want to physically lower the ceiling level in order to alter the proportions of the room, then a slightly different approach is required. The fact is that the thickness of ordinary battens and cladding are unlikely to make a great deal of difference. Instead, you must construct what's known as a suspended ceiling — more accurately, a false ceiling set well below the level of the original. In this case, although the method of applying the cladding remains the same, the system of battening required is rather more complex — mainly because it needs to be a good deal stronger in order to carry the weight of the cladding all on its own.

You should therefore start by deciding on the new ceiling height and by drawing a line right round the walls of the room at the appropriate level, less the thickness of the cladding, with the aid of a spirit-level and a long, straight timber batten. This line can now be used as a guide to positioning the ceiling's main supports — lengths of 75 x 50mm (3 x 2in) sawn softwood screwed to the walls. Known as wallplates, these must be very firmly fixed indeed. This means that, as usual, if you are dealing with a stud partition you must make the fixings into the the wall's supporting timber studs. If you are fixing to a masonry wall, the use of good quality wallplugs should give sufficient strength.

You see, the wallplates' job is to carry the weight of the new joists used to support the ceiling's cladding. Also made from 75 x 50mm (3 x 2in) softwood, these should be spaced at roughly 400mm (16in) centres and fixed to the wallplates on opposite walls using simple halving joints. You must therefore work out the best arrangement for the suspended ceiling's structural timber work at an early stage in order to notch the wallplates ready to receive the joists, before any of the timbers are fixed in place.

There is another reason for carefully planning the job before you start work. Joists of this size have a tendency to sag under their own weight and the weight of the cladding. If they are made to span a distance of more than about 2m (80in), this sag can be significant, so, on most ceilings, additional support must be provided. This additional support comes in the form of vertical timbers called hangers — hence the name, suspended ceiling. Fixed between the new timberwork and the original ceiling, they simply transfer some of the load to the latter's heavier supporting joists.

No complicated joints are needed here. The hangers can

COPING WITH OBSTACLES AND CORNERS

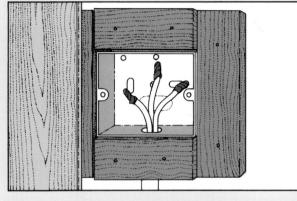

1 Where the cladding will be fixed round obstacles such as light switches and power points, fix short lengths of batten to the wall to support the cladding. If you have flush-mounted fittings, they must be repositioned so the edge of the mounting box is flush with the cladding.

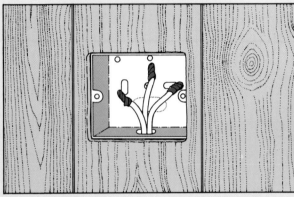

2 Mark the size of cut-out needed in each length of cladding surrounding the obstacle, then make the cut-outs with a jigsaw or coping saw. Pin each piece in place to the battens, then reconnect the faceplate and attach it to the box before restoring the power supply.

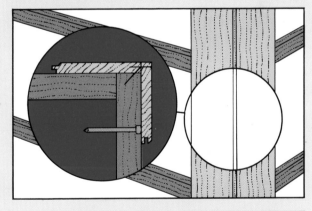

3 At external corners, fix a complete strip to the second face of the wall with its edge flush with the surface of the battens on the first face (A). Then saw or plane down the tongued edge of another strip (B) and pin it in place so it overlaps the edge of strip (A).

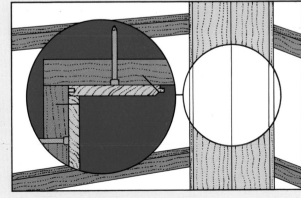

4 At internal corners, use a similar technique. Fit the whole strip (A) to the second wall first, then cut a strip down to width to complete the first wall (B). Pin it in place through its face.

FINISHING TOUCHES

1 *Either fit completely new skirting boards across the newly-clad wall, or else re-fix original cladding that was removed earlier.*

2 *If the edges of the cladding look a little ragged, you can improve their appearance by pinning slim quadrant or scotia beading all the way round. Punch in the heads of the fixing nails ready for filling.*

3 *Use wood stopping in a colour that matches the cladding to fill any visible nail holes. Press it in with a filling knife, leave to harden, then sand smooth for an almost invisible repair.*

4 *Finish off the cladding by giving it three coats of clear polyurethane varnish. Apply the first with a cloth pad, after thinning the varnish with about 10 per cent white spirit. Then brush on the next two coats, making sure that the joints are well treated. Sand lightly between coats.*

merely be screwed on to the sides of the new ceiling joists. There is, however, a choice of methods when it comes to fixing the hangers to the original ceiling joists, and you must decide which is most convenient in the circumstances. If you can gain access to the void above the original ceiling, the simplest method is to just poke the hangers through the old ceiling's skin and screw them directly to the sides of the original joists. The success of this method, though, obviously depends on the old and new joist being in just the right place. You could try deliberately arranging things so that the new timbers are in just the right position, but, in practice, this approach tends to be harder work than adopting the alternative fixing technique.

This is simply to fix the hangers to yet another timber — one on the underside of the old ceiling, held in place by stout screws driven through the ceiling's skin into the joists above. The obvious snag with this method is that you have to locate the exact positions of the old ceiling's joists, but as we have already seen elsewhere in this book, that's not difficult. Just drill a series of test holes through the ceiling with an electric drill and a small diameter bit until you bore into the timber of a joist. A more real problem is that, where the new joists run at right angles to the originals, you are unlikely to find an original joist in exactly the right position — that is along the line of the joist hangers. There are ways to obtain a secure fixing for the joist hangers' support timber in spite of this (involving yet more timberwork above or below the ceiling's skin), but it is generally simpler to make the fixing to the old joist closest to the optimum position. This shouldn't weaken the structure too much, but if you are worried, build in an additional set of hangers to bring the unsupported joist span within acceptable limits.

There is just one final point to bear in mind. It concerns the fixing of the cladding itself. Instead of using a pin hammer and panel pins, it is well worth considering using a heavy-duty staple gun to fix the matchboarding or wallboards in place. There are plenty of models capable of firing the necessary extra long staples through wood, and if you don't think it worth buying one just for this job, you shouldn't have too much difficulty in hiring a suitable tool.

Of course, all that timberwork does put up the cost of your new ceiling, but at least the result is every bit as permanent as the original. What's more, with the structural timberwork in place, you are actually not restricted merely to cladding the ceiling. You can build a genuinely new ceiling by covering the joists with sheets of plasterboard.

Starting in one corner of the room, put up as many whole sheets as you can — standard sheets of plasterboard measure 2440 x 1220mm (8 x 4ft) so you will need help — fixing it to the new joists with plasterboard nails. Complete the 'row' with a cut sheet, then use the off-cut from this to begin a second row, the idea being to stagger the joins between sheets as far as possible. Completely cover the ceiling in this way then neaten the joints between boards using joint filler, joint tape and joint finish – this is a good deal easier if you use taper-edged plasterboard. Basically, all you do is fill the depression created by the taper where two

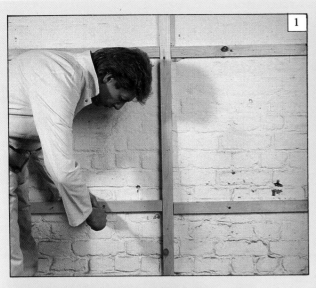

FIXING WALLBOARDS

1 & 2 *Wallboards need support at the edges and at intervals in between. Fix battens to the wall surface at spacings to suit the board dimensions, and back out any low spots. Then measure the floor-to-ceiling height, cut the first board to length and offer it up to the battens.*

3 & 4 *Line the board up with the centre of the vertical batten and drive in the fixing pins. Use more pins to secure the board to the intermediate supporting battens. Where only part of a board is needed to finish off the wall, the quickest way of cutting it to size is with a power jigsaw.*

5 & 6 *Complete the cladding by offering up the cut-to-size section and pinning it to the battens. Finish off the area if necessary by pinning beading round the perimeter.*

If the wall surface is flat and true, the panels can be fixed in place with special panel adhesive instead of being pinned to battens. Simply apply the adhesive to the wall and press the panel into position.

boards meet, bed the tape into the filler while it is still wet, then, when the filler has set, cover with a layer of joint finish, feathering this out across the adjacent boards with a damp sponge. When that has set, apply a second coat of finishing compound to further neaten the joint, then apply a slurry of joint finish over the entire ceiling to leave the surface completely smooth. Full details on how to do the job,

together with advice on the specialist tools you need can be found on the filler and finish compound's pack, or ask the plasterboard's manufacturer for their advice.

The new ceiling can now be decorated using the same sort of finish as you would use on any other ceiling — just be sure to prime it with all-surface primer if you intend to apply a resin-based paint.

Squares and rectangles of varnished plywood have been used to create an unusual panelled effect in this bedroom. The same material has been used to face the built-in units.

THE COMPLETE FLOORER

Tiling floors 152

Laying sheet vinyls 159

People expect a great deal of the floorcoverings in their home. After all, a flooring is expected to be attractive, yet hardwearing; comfortable, yet easy to keep clean. That's asking a lot of a single material, so it's not really surprising that most floorings on the market are better in respect of some of these qualities than in others. Choosing a flooring for a particular room is therefore largely a matter of choosing 'horses for courses'. In the kitchen, for example, it's more important to have a durable, easy-to-clean floor than it is to have one that is comfortable. That's why 'hard' floorings such as tiles and sheet vinyls are usually preferred to carpet. In a bedroom, on the other hand, comfort is everything, since bedroom floors are not usually subjected to heavy soiling or heavy traffic. And that's why most people go for carpet rather than a spartan, 'practical' floorcovering.

You can apply the same sort of logic to choosing the flooring for every room in the house, and so long as you strike the right balance in rooms, such as the lounge, where you need a flooring that is both durable and comfortable, your new flooring should prove a very worthwhile investment — assuming, that is, you lay it correctly.

Tiling floors

Tiling is perhaps the easiest way to get a new floor, and, thanks to the wide variety of flooring tiles now available, it's a technique you can apply to almost any room in the house. There are cork tiles, wooden tiles, carpet tiles, vinyl tiles, glazed ceramic tiles, unglazed ceramic tiles, and many more besides. Obviously, each of these is laid in a slightly different way. But all floor tiling has one thing in common — the setting out.

This is carried out in the same way as on a ceiling. Measure up and use a chalked line to strike guide lines between opposite walls so that they cross exactly in the centre of the room. It's best to ignore ancillary features such as window bays or chimney breast alcoves when doing this. Since the object of the exercise is to give the tiling a symmetrical appearance, what you are really after is the centre of the bulk of the tiled area. For the same reason, if you are tiling the floor of a room that has some sort of fitting occupying most of one wall — say, a bath, or a line of built-in wardrobes — you should treat the fitting as if it was a wall, and adjust the position of the relevant guide line accordingly.

Now, step out from the centre of this cross in whole tile units (or whole tile plus grout line units as measured with a gauge rod if you are using ceramic tiles), and see what happens around the edges of the room. Ideally, the cut tiles needed to fill in here should all be of a reasonable width — certainly no less than 25mm (1in), and preferably a lot more. If they are not, move the relevant guide line along by half the width of a tile and try again. As a final check that the floor tiles will be both easy to lay, and attractively set out, work out how any awkward corners and obstacles fit within the tile arrangement. Further adjustments in the positioning of the starting guide lines may be necessary to avoid over-awkward cutting in.

And what about actually laying the tiles? Vinyl tiles are simplest. You merely coat the floor with contact adhesive using a notched spreader, aiming to cover roughly a square metre at a time, and then press each tile into place, smoothing it over finally with a soft cloth. As always, begin with four tiles set into the angles at the centre of the cross where the chalk guide lines intersect. Next lay as many whole tiles as you can along each arm of the cross, then cover the remainder of the floor as far as possible with more whole tiles before filling in the gaps left around the edges of the room with cut tiles individually tailored to fit.

Now there is a little dodge you may find useful. It saves you having to measure up for each cut tile — and no matter how careful you are, when transferring measurements there is always the chance of a mistake. What you do is lay the tile you wish to cut exactly on top of the whole tile that comes before the gap you want to fill. If you now place a spare whole tile on top of that, this time positioning it with one edge butted tight against the skirting board, (or whatever else it is you are tiling up to) you will find that exposed portion of the tile you wish to cut is exactly the right size to fill the gap. So, start by drawing a line on the tile to be cut using the edge of the uppermost tile as a straightedge. Place the tile to be cut on a sheet of scrap hardboard or something similar to protect the new flooring, then lay a metal straightedge along the guide line and cut along the line using a sharp knife.

The same trick, with slight modifications, also enables you to mark out tiles due to be fitted into an internal angle, or around an external angle. In the former case, position the tile to be cut over the whole tile nearest to the angle, then mark it first with the uppermost gauge tile butted against one wall, then again with the gauge tile butted against the second wall. This transfers not only the size of the cut tile, but also the angles of the wall just in case these are out of square. Similarly, for an external corner, mark the cut tile to fit against one wall just as if there were no corner there at all. That done, move the cut tile around the corner (without rotating it), and mark it to fit against the wall there, again just if the corner did not exist. These two sets of guide lines now perfectly describe the outline of an L-shaped cut tile that will fit the corner like a glove.

Awkwardly shaped obstacles such WCs are more difficult to cut round. The simplest way to mark out the cut tile is with a template. Take a tile-sized sheet of paper, and posi-

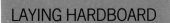

LAYING HARDBOARD

1 *Hardboard forms the perfect underlay for many floorcoverings, masking uneven boards and the gaps between them.*

2 *Lay manageable sections — say 1220mm (4ft) squares — in a row along one edge of the room. Make cut-outs where necessary to allow the sheets to fit round obstacles.*

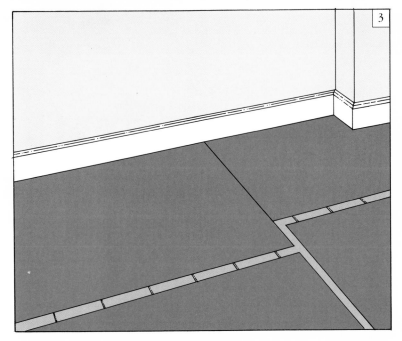

3 *Try to stagger the joins between rows as you lay the boards. Butt them tightly together and pin them to the subfloor at 150mm (6in) intervals all over.*

SETTING OUT

Find the centre point of the room by joining the mid-points of opposite walls with string lines. Start by fixing the first tile in the angle formed by the lines.

LAYING WHOLE TILES

1 Mark out the floor to give a centre point. Then spread some adhesive in the angle betwen the guidelines.

2 Lay the first tile in the angle, offering it up to the lines and lowering it into place. Bed it down with firm hand pressure, and check its alignment again.

3 Position the next tile alongside the first one, aligning it and bedding it into the adhesive as before. Use spacers to ensure an even gap between the tiles.

4 As you work, use a spirit level to keep checking that the tiles are level in both directions and that they are lying absolutely flush with their neighbours.

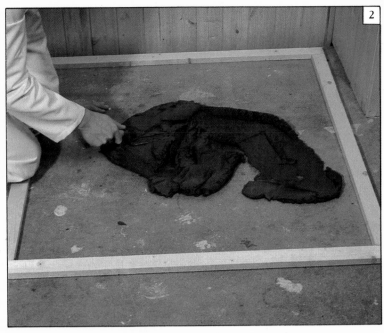

LAYING QUARRY TILES

1 *Quarry tiles are laid in a mortar bed. Set out battens to form bays big enough to take, say, nine tiles.*

2 *Check that the battens are level using your spirit level, adding packing if necessary where the floor dips, and nail them in place. Then spread mortar in the bay.*

3 *Bed each tile securely in the mortar bed using firm hand pressure, and check regularly with a spirit level or straightedge to ensure that tiles are level with the battens and each other.*

4 *When you have completed one bay, lift and reposition the battens to form the next one. Note that the edge of the first bay forms one side of the second bay.*

LAYING BORDER TILES

 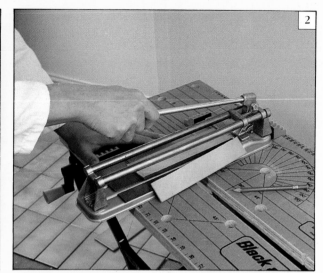

1 & 2 *Mark the width of the border pieces at each point on a whole tile butted up against the skirting. Then cut the tile with a tile-cutting machine rather than a hand tile-cutter.*

3 & 4 *Test the cut piece for fit, then butter some tile adhesive on to its rear face and bed it in position. Fit spacers if necessary to maintain the grouting gap, and check that the border piece is level with its neighbours.*

5 & 6 *At external corners, an L-shaped cut tile will be needed. Mark the position of the cut on one edge of the tile first, then on the other edge, and remove the waste with a tile saw or by nibbling it away carefully with pincers.*

tion it just as you would the tile you wish to cut. Obviously it won't go in, so make a few freeing cuts to fit it neatly round the obstacle, folding back the waste and creasing it around the obstacle's outline in much the same way as you would if hanging wallpaper. If you now carefully cut around this crease, you will be left with a piece of paper exactly the same size and shape as the cut tile required.

As for cork and wooden tiles, these are laid in exactly the same way, but do remember to finish off the floor by protecting the surface with a tough polyurethane varnish. This is even more important here than on cork wall tiling. In fact, the more coats you apply the better. You will certainly need to brush on at least three, in addition to the initial thinned sealing coat rubbed in with a cloth. Take special care to avoid getting dust in the finish, though. Before applying any of the coats, wipe the floor over with a damp cloth, allow to dry, then vacuum up any dust that has resettled.

And carpet tiles? The main difference with these is that the majority do not need to be stuck down. Their backing, aided by their weight and the restraint imposed by the neighbouring tiles, is normally sufficient to keep them in place. It is, however, worth sticking down cut tiles plus a row of whole tiles around the perimeter of the room. Use double-sided sticky tape for this, putting it down in 'tram-lines' so that it grips the edges of the carpet tiles. There is just one other thing to watch. With carpet tiles, it is best to measure up to find the size of each cut tile. If you use the gauge tile trick, you will find that the carpet pile allows sufficient movement in the tile 'sandwich' for inaccuracies to creep in. In addition, be sure to do the marking out on the back of the tile in pencil (not felt-tipped pen because of the risk of getting it on the pile), and take care when cutting the tile, not to shave off the pile next to the cut edge. You may find this easier to avoid if you cut the tiles with scissors.

Finally, there are ceramic tiles. Putting down glazed versions is really no different to tiling a wall, except that you are likely to have more trouble in cutting tiles to fit. Most floor tiles are too thick to be snapped in two. Instead, having scored through the glaze in the usual way, tap along the line with a hammer and a cold chisel, gradually working round and round the tile until it breaks. Unglazed ceramic tiles — quarry tiles — are quite another matter. These are set, not in adhesive, but in a thick mortar bed. Temporarily fix timber battens around the walls of the room along a line corresponding to the outer edge of the whole tiles there, then divide off a strip of the room (about four tiles wide) with another batten. Hold the battens in place with blobs of mortar spaced about 600mm (2ft) apart. Use battens equal in thickness to the mortar bed plus the thickness of a tile. Check that these battens are absolutely level, using a spirit level, and pack out beneath them with scrap timber or card as necessary until they are. Now put down about a square metre (sq yd) of the mortar bed within this battened-off bay, set in the tiles, and use the upper edges of the battens as a guide to levelling them.

Continue in this way until the entire bay has been tiled, then remove the batten nearest the centre of the floor and

GROUTING

1 *When all the tiles have been placed and levelled, use a squeegee or sponge to force the grout into the gaps between them. Scrape off excess grout as you work.*

2 *Then use a piece of dowel or some similar implement to neaten all the grout lines. Don't scrape out too much grout, or you will leave dust-gathering depressions.*

3 *Finally, wash off the grout stains from the surface of the tiles with a damp cloth. Work diagonally rather than along the grout lines to avoid disturbing the grout.*

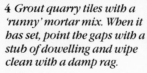

4 *Grout quarry tiles with a 'runny' mortar mix. When it has set, point the gaps with a stub of dowelling and wipe clean with a damp rag.*

SEALING QUARRY TILES

1 & 2 *Ordinary quarry tiles need sealing to make them stain — and waterproof. Use a clear floor sealer for this, and apply the first coat with a cloth pad. Then roughen the surface with abrasive paper to ensure a good bond between coats.*

3 *Finally, brush on a second (and possibly a third) coat.*

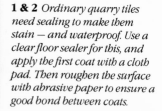
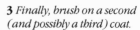

COPING WITH THRESHOLDS

1 *You can protect the tile edging at doorways by nailing down a proprietary threshold strip. Do this before laying the tiles, so you can butt them neatly up against the edge of the strip as you work.*

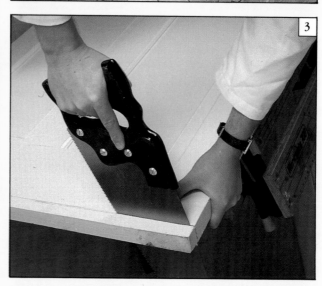

2 & 3 *An alternative to the metal threshold strip is to shape a piece of hardwood and secure this to the floor against the edge of the tiled area. Finish it with three coats of clear varnish.*
Remember that a tiled floor is relatively thick, so you will have to saw off some wood from the bottom of doors to the tiled room. Remove the doors before you start tiling.

The natural colour and surface texture of quarry tiles provide the perfect floorcovering for this conservatory. A frost-proof type has been selected, so the same tile could be laid as a surround to the outdoor pool beyond.

move it along to create a new bay ready for tiling. When you have covered as much of the floor as possible with whole tiles, remove the edging battens, and fill in the gaps with cut tiles. Grout the gaps between quarry tiles with a 'runny' mortar mix. When the grouting has set firm, but not hard, point the gaps with a stub of dowelling and wipe off excess mortar with a damp rag.

Laying sheet vinyls

While laying a sheet vinyl flooring is, in theory, both quicker and easier than laying tiles, a lot depends on the room — its size, its shape, and on the number of obstacles it contains. It is therefore well worth running through the job in your head before you buy the flooring, to identify the likely problems, and work out how best to overcome them.

In this respect, the main thing to consider is the need for joins between adjacent lengths. In general, they are best avoided. They complicate the job of laying, they don't look particularly attractive, and they introduce an unwanted weakness into what is otherwise a very durable, water-proof, easy-to-clean surface. This is where extra-wide vinyl floorings come in. At 4m (12ft) wide, they make it possible to cover the floors of most small rooms without any joins at all. Even on a larger, long, narrow room you may be able to avoid joins by simply laying the vinyl starting against one of the narrower walls.

In some rooms, though, no matter what you do, at least one join is inevitable, and in this case it is important to plan things so that the join is positioned where it will be least noticeable, and will do least damage. In particular, avoid having joins in heavy traffic areas — around doorways, in the centre of the room, and in the area immediately in front of

LAYING SHEET VINYL

1 *Start laying against the longest straight wall in the room. Butt the end of the roll up against the skirting and check to see whether the long wall undulates.*

2 *If it does, you have to scribe the edge of the sheet so you can trim it to match the profile of the wall. Use a pencil and a block of wood slightly wider than the widest gap, drawing the block along the skirting to mark the cutting line.*

3 *Slide the length away from the skirting board and cut carefully along the scribed line with a sharp handyman's knife. Peel away and discard the offcut strip.*

4 *Slide the vinyl sheet back into position to check the fit, and make any minor trimming adjustments that may still be needed. You can then trim the other end of the length neatly to butt up against the skirting at the other end of the room.*

the family sofa and armchairs. Joins in this sort of position tend to wear very rapidly, and as they wear, there is every chance that they will lift and create a trip hazard. What's more, if someone should trip over the edge of the vinyl, the flooring will chip and/or tear and be completely ruined. If possible, therefore, arrange for joins to fall off to one side of the room, preferably so that they run beneath some large, little-moved piece of furniture that will both help to protect and conceal the vinyl's vulnerable edges.

You are now almost ready to begin laying. There is just one final bit of preparation to be attended to – when you get the vinyl home, loosen the roll as much as you can and leave it in a warm room for 12 to 24 hours. You will then find that, when you come to start laying it, the now warm, 'relaxed' vinyl is a lot easier to handle. In fact, so great is the effect of temperature on the vinyl's flexibility that, in winter, it is well worth thoroughly warming up the room before you start work. This is particularly important at the trimming stage. If the flooring is extremely cold, it has a tendency to crack rather than bend.

Once the vinyl is warm enough, lay the roll down in a corner of the room, and line it up against the wall opposite the one you have chosen as your starting point. Now take a firm grip on the free edge, and start pulling the flooring off the roll by walking back across the room. Having unrolled rather more than you need to cover the floor between the walls, cut the vinyl roughly to length, allowing an extra 50mm (2in) or so trim allowance at each end, and move the remainder of the roll out of the way. You must now straighten up the vinyl, using the walls as a guide, at the same time positioning it so that a 50mm (2in) trim allowance turns up the third wall at that end of the room. If the vinyl is actually large enough to cover the entire floor, then simply centre it as accurately as you can.

The next step is to make enough freeing cuts for the vinyl to be more or less flattened out. At internal corners simply cut off the corner of the vinyl there at an angle of about 45 degrees so that as you settle the vinyl in place, a separate trim allowance turns up the adjacent walls. Deciding on the position of the freeing cut at this stage is of course largely a matter of guesswork, but the important thing is not to cut off too much. It is therefore best to make a few preliminary freeing cuts, testing the fit of each one, and gradually paring the vinyl back to the optimum line.

External corners – say, those of a chimney breast – require a slightly different approach. Here your first priority is to make a freeing cut that will allow you to continue smoothing out the vinyl into the alcove, window bay, or whatever beyond. A straight cut from the edge of the vinyl to the point where it meets the corner will do the trick, and again you must decide where to end the cut by a process of trial and error. However, make sure you angle the cut so that it runs through vinyl you know beyond a shadow of a doubt will be waste – on a chimney breast, that will be the vinyl running up the the breast's face. In this way, as you smooth the vinyl past the corner, a trim allowance will be left to turn up the side wall, thus giving you the opportunity

COPING WITH INTERNAL CORNERS

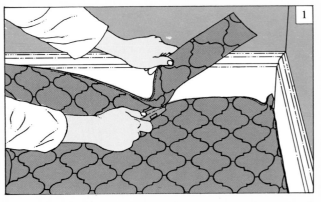

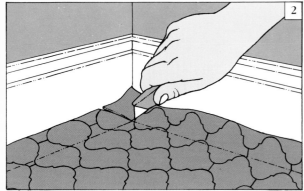

1 & 2 *Start by removing most of the waste material from the edge of the sheet with a sharp knife. Then lift the corner and make a diagonal cut across it.*

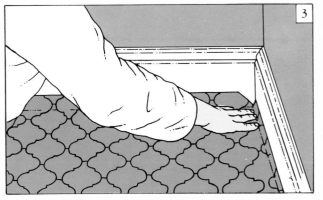

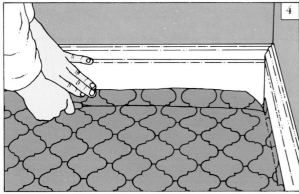

3 & 4 *Press the sheet back into the angle so the tongues on each side lie up against the skirting board. Then use a sharp knife held at a 45° angle to trim the tongues and let the sheet lie flat.*

COPING WITH EXTERNAL CORNERS

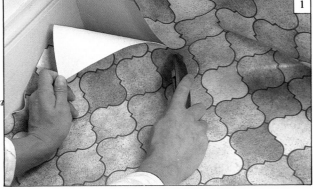

1 & 2 *At external corners, make a diagonal cut downwards from the edge of the sheet to allow the tongues on each side to lap up the skirting board. Don't cut too far. Then roughly trim away excess material.*

3 & 4 *Extend the diagonal cut slightly if necessary to improve the fit of the corner point, then press the tongues down into the angles and trim them neatly to fit the profile of the skirting boards (as for internal angles).*

USING TEMPLATES

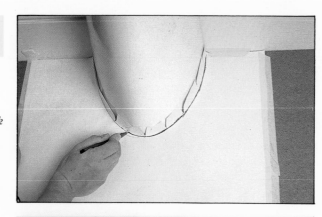

1 *Use a paper template to mark and cut vinyl round awkwardly-shaped obstacles. Cut out the shape roughly and make scissor cuts all round so the tongues can be bent up for accurate marking.*

2 *Snip off the tongues along the pencil line. Then tape the template to the vinyl and transfer the outline of the obstacle on to its rear surface (this is easier than working on the pattern side).*

3 *Use a sharp knife to cut carefully round the marked outline. Make sure that the sheet is resting on scrap material or a hardboard underlay, not on sheet vinyl that has already been laid.*

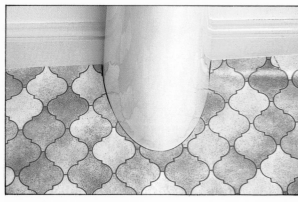

4 *Offer the cut sheet up to the obstacle and make any slight adjustments that may be needed. Then trim the excess material from the wall edge behind it to complete the job.*

to trim within the alcove to achieve a perfect fit no matter how out of square the corner may be. Having made the freeing cut and laid the vinyl flat, you can trim off the bulk of the obvious waste to make the final fitting easier.

Incidentally, don't be daunted by complex shapes such as a hearth, fire surround or chimney breast and alcove combination. Simply make a freeing cut for each external corner as you come to it. As for really complex shapes such as the foot of a WC, at this stage merely make a straight cut from the edge of the vinyl to the point where you judge the front of the pedestal will come, cut out a hole of about the right size in approximately the right place (erring on the side of making it markedly too small). This should allow you to come close enough to laying the vinyl flat around the obstacle for you to make a series of freeing cuts in the vinyl turning up its sides.

You are now in a position to trim the vinyl accurately to fit, and there are two ways in which this can be done. The first applies to the thinner, more flexible vinyls. All you do is push the vinyl into the angle between the floor and the wall, using a block of softwood, so that the edge of the block leaves a sharp crease where the two surfaces meet. You can then simply trim along the crease with a sharp knife, guiding the blade with a straightedge to ensure a neat cut finish. In other words, in essence, it's just a scaled-up version of the technique used to trim wallpaper.

For thicker vinyls, though, you have to use a technique called 'scribing' to mark the line along which you must cut. Assuming a uniform 50mm (2in) trim allowance, lay the vinyl flat on the floor with its edge butted up against the wall. Now, starting in one corner of the room, press a 50mm (2in) wide block of wood against the wall, press a pencil against that, and run the two together down the length of the wall so that the pencil draws a line at a constant 50mm (2in) from the wall's surface. Cut along this line and, when you push the new edge up to the wall, you should find that it fits perfectly, no matter how uneven the line of the wall may be.

Unfortunately, this technique cannot be used to trim round obstacles such as pipes and WCs. What you must do instead is make a paper template. Take a sheet of paper large enough to surround the obstacle while keeping one edge on the edge of the vinyl. In it cut an oversize hole, fit it around the obstacle, and tape it into place making sure the paper still lines up with the vinyl's edge. Next, use your scribing block and pencil to scribe round the obstacle in order to produce an oversize replica of its outline on the paper, then pull both vinyl and paper template clear and lay them out flat on the floor. All you do now is repeat the scribing procedure, this time running the scribing block around the inside of the line drawn on the paper to produce an actual size outline on the vinyl. Cut along this line, and you should be left with the vinyl a perfect fit.

Now what about coping with joins? What you must aim for is a perfect pattern match and a perfect butt joint between lengths, and there is a trick to it. Position the second piece of vinyl so that it overlaps the first, and adjust its

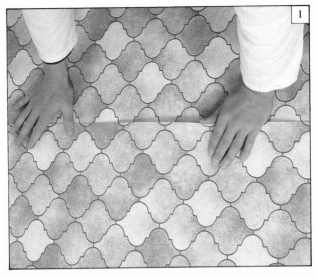

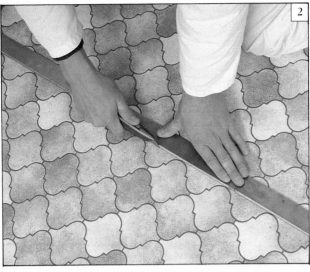

SEAMS AND THRESHOLDS

1 & 2 *To form perfect seams between lengths, overlap the edges slightly and align the pattern carefully. Then lay a steel straightedge along the centre of the overlap and cut cleanly through both layers.*

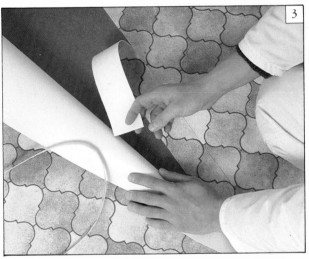

3 & 4 *Discard the offcut strip from the upper layer; then lift this and peel away the offcut from the layer underneath. Position a strip of double-sided adhesive tape underneath the seam and press the cut edges firmly down on to it.*

5 & 6 *Secure the edges of the lengths by bedding double-sided tape all round the perimeter of the room. Finish off at doorways with special threshold strips, nailed into position.*

position until the patterns match perfectly. Now, with the aid of a straightedge, cut along the line of the intended join, carrying the blade through the double thickness of vinyl. Having removed the waste from both vinyl layers, you should be left with a perfect join.

To complete the floor, all that now remains is to do a little sticking to hold the vinyl firmly in place. Now this isn't absolutely essential – vinyl can be loose-laid – but it is definitely advisable. In the vast majority of cases there is no need to stick it down over the entire floor. Merely fixing a strip about 300mm (12in) wide around the perimeter of each sheet (and especially the edge where it joins another sheet) is generally adequate. So, just peel back the edge of the sheet, spread a layer of flooring adhesive on to the floor with a notched spreader (follow the vinyl manufacturer's recommendations on which adhesive to use), and press the edge into place, smoothing it out with a cloth in the direction of the walls and taking care not to trap bubbles of air.

The exception to this rule is where the vinyl flooring is expected to endure a lot of foot traffic, as in a busy hallway, for example. Here it is best to glue the flooring in place across the entire floor. To do this, fold back the vinyl to leave just over half of the floor exposed, and cover this half with adhesive. Carefully roll the vinyl back into place, smoothing it out as you go so as not to trap any air, then fold back the vinyl on the other half of the floor and repeat the process to stick that down. Finally, working from the centre of the floor out towards the edges, drag something smooth, soft, and heavy over the surface of the vinyl to remove any remaining air bubbles, and at the same time bed it firmly into place. One of the best things to use for this job is a thick plastic refuse bag filled with sand or earth. Place a wad of sacking between it and the floor to avoid scratching the surface. Better still, place the bag inside an old sack – plastic bags have a nasty habit of splitting when you least expect it.

If you do decide to stick the vinyl down, whether just

Ceramic tiles are a popular choice for kitchen floors because they are immensely hard-wearing and easy to keep clean. Note the use of a delicate green wood stain on the cupboard fronts to emphasize the colour of the tiles themselves.

around the edges or across the entire floor – and it will help the flooring wear better – there is just one last point to bear in mind. Once the new flooring has been in normal use for a few days, it will start to spread, and with adhesive holding it in place around the edges, that means it will start to lift off the floor in the centre of each sheet. To prevent this, allow the newly trimmed vinyl to settle in for a week or so before sticking it down. It is also worth checking the fit around the edges of the room at that stage. Although a certain amount of expansion can be accommodated by slipping the edges of the vinyl into the gap between skirting board and floor, in severe cases it may be necessary to retrim the flooring slightly.

With the flooring neatly trimmed and glued in place, just one more job remains. That is to give some protection to raw edge of the vinyl left vulnerable in any doorways. A simple wooden or metal threshold strip is all that is required. Fix it firmly to cover the edge using screws or nails.

Vinyl floor tiles provide a durable and hygienic surface that's ideal for busy traffic areas. Here small black squares at the tile intersections give a cool, formal look to the room.

Laying foam-backed carpet

Carpet laying is one of those jobs where, although you are unlikely to make any really major errors at your first attempt, you will probably find that a really neat, professional finish eludes you. The fact is it requires the sort of skill that only comes with practice. For this reason, if you are not a particularly 'handy' person, or if you are buying a very expensive carpet, it is generally best to leave the job to an expert – though don't put too much faith in the 'free fitting' schemes operated by many carpet suppliers. But where you are getting a relatively inexpensive foam-backed carpet for a room where small flaws are likely to go unnoticed – a bedroom, for example – then you may as well have a go. Who knows, you may turn out to be very good at it.

There are four main ways to tackle the job. You can loose-lay the carpet, tack it in place, use double-sided tape or stretch it and use wood or metal gripper strip (a special type is used for foam-backed carpet) to hold it in place around the edges of the room. Of these, the last is undoubtedly the most popular, so let's see how it's done.

Start by fixing the gripper strip right round the perimeter of the room, nailing it in place (using masonry pins on a concrete floor) with its teeth pointing at the wall. Leave a gap roughly equal to the thickness of the carpet between gripper strip and skirting board. Any cutting to length necessary is easily done with a hacksaw.

The next step is to cover the floor with underlay. This is not strictly necessary with foam-backed carpet, but it is worthwhile. It makes the floor warmer and more comfortable, and, just as important, stops the carpet's foam-backing sticking to the floor in heavy traffic areas. Simply roll the underlay out across the floor, smooth it down, and trim it to fit within the inner edges of the gripper strip. To stop it riding up in use, tape together any joins, and fix it in place at one end with carpet tacks or double sided sticky tape.

Now for the carpet. Having unrolled it, manoeuvre it roughly into position, if possible with the pile direction facing the room's main door and with one machine-finished edge lying along a straight, uninterrupted wall. Now begin fixing it to the gripper strip along this wall, starting in the centre and working out towards the corner, stretching the carpet reasonably taut as you go. That done, pull the carpet taut across the room, and hook it on to the gripper strip along the opposite wall, again starting in the centre and working out towards the corner. To complete this first stage of the fitting, stretch the carpet in the other direction, fixing it first along one side wall, then along the other. You should now check that the carpet is lying perfectly flat and that it has been stretched evenly in all directions. If it is wrong, re-stretch the appropriate sections as necessary, working out from the centre of the room so you can refix the edge on the gripper strip.

This stretching is important. It not only leaves the carpet lying flat, but also helps improve its ability to withstand wear and tear. You will find it easiest to do using a special tool called a knee kicker – widely available from tool hire shops. But take care not to overstretch the carpet, nor to

LAYING CARPETS

1 & 2 *Start by fixing carpet gripper strips all round the edge of the room set in from the skirting board by about 6mm (¼in). Then cut the underlay so it will lie within the gripper strips.*

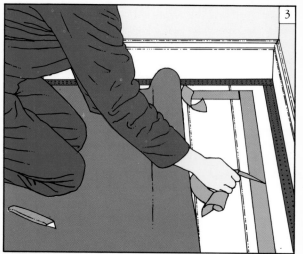

3 & 4 *Secure the underlay to the floor surface with strips of double-sided adhesive tape to stop it creeping while the carpet is laid. Press the underlay down firmly*

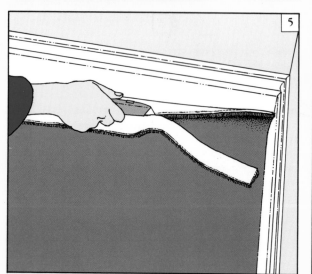

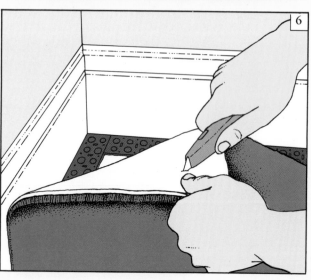

5 & 6 *Lay the carpet out roughly in position, and trim off most of the excess material all round the room. Then press the carpet down into internal corners, lift it away and make a diagonal cut across the corner to allow the tongues to lap up against the skirting board.*

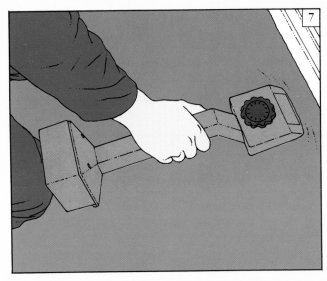

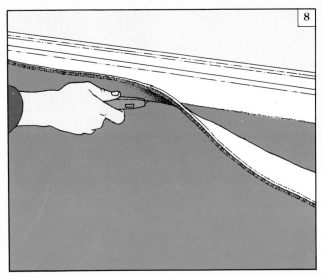

7 & 8 *Before trimming the edges to fit exactly, hook the carpet on to the gripper strips at one side of the room and use a hired knee kicker to tension the carpet across to the other side. Then trim off the excess neatly with the knife held at 45°.*

9 *Finally, fit threshold strips at doorways.*

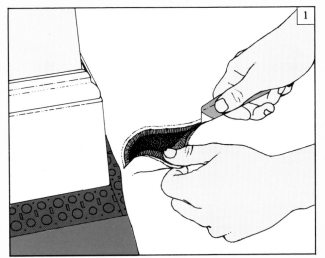

LAYING INTO ALCOVES

1 *Across a chimney breast, allow the carpet to lie up against the face of the chimney breast and make freeing cuts in line with the sides of the breast so the two tongues of carpet can fall back into the recesses.*

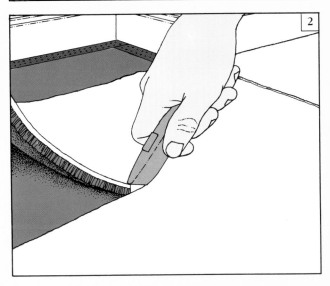

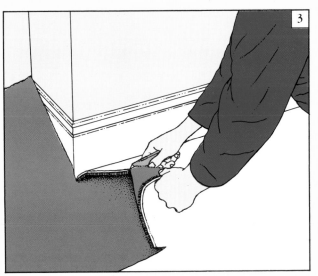

2 & 3 *Trim off the excess material across the face of the chimney breast, then do the same along the rear face of each alcove to complete the fitting.*

stretch it unevenly. That can do more harm than not stretching it at all.

Once you are satisfied with the way the carpet is lying, trim it exactly to size using a sharp knife. Just run the knife blade along the angle between wall and floor, then tuck the trimmed edges neatly out of sight by poking them down in between the skirting board and gripper strip with a bolster chisel or something similar. Finally, trim off the carpet squarely across any doorways, and protect the cut edge with a metal or wooden threshold strip — one with a built-in gripper strip is best.

And what about carpeting around obstacles and awkward corners? The short answer is that you make freeing cuts in just the same way as when laying a sheet vinyl flooring in order to leave the carpet lying flat, then stretch it on to the gripper and trim accurately to fit as described above. The only major problem you are likely to encounter is where the carpet is to be fitted against a rounded or irregular surface — say, with a half-round window bay. You can't buy curved gripper strip. All you can do is cut the gripper strip into short sections, and fix it in place following the curve as closely as possible.

Carpet is by far the most widely used floorcovering in most homes today. The huge range of plain colours and patterns available ensures that you can always find one to suit your colour scheme. Here a neutral colour and a short pile are the perfect foil for the wealth of detail in the decorations and furnishings.

CEILING
IDEAS

In some ways, the ceiling is the Cinderella surface of any room. When thinking about different colour schemes and decor ideas for the room as a whole, it's so easy to find yourself considering the ceiling's decoration as an afterthought – something that deserves no more and no less attention than is needed to keep it looking respectable. To some extent that is understandable. After all, when you enter a room, the ceiling is by no means the first thing you look at – if you look at it at all. But that doesn't mean that the way in which it is treated is of no significance. On the contrary, the ceiling can have an enormous effect on the way people react to the living space beneath.

As we have already seen when looking at the basics of colour scheming, there is the ceiling's height to consider. For whatever reason, the fact is most people associate low ceilings with a sense of cosiness, safety, and intimacy, while high ceilings can conjure up images of grandeur, airiness; even of the inhospitable coldness of distance. And that applies whether the height is real in the physical sense, or purely illusory – a product of the way the surface colour affects our brains.

There is the matter of interest, too. Just because the majority of ceilings are flat, featureless expanses of painted or papered plaster doesn't mean that that approach is necessarily best. After all, ornately decorated ceilings have been around for thousands of years, and for good reason. You don't have to live in the Sistine chapel to benefit from a lively and attractive decorative surface above your head. If you are totally honest about such things, then you have to accept that there are rooms in even the most modern home where you spend a fair amount of time staring at the ceiling – bedrooms and bathrooms are the most obvious example.

And don't forget the more subtle tricks the ceiling decoration can play. There is the effect it can have on the room's lighting, not to mention its ability to generally 'set the scene' – try to imagine an 'olde worlde' cottage without oak beams in the ceiling. So, before settling for one of the usual paint, paper, texture or tile options, look at some of the more exciting and unusual alternatives. Most of them are remarkably simple to achieve.

Since we have already mentioned them, let's start with ceiling beams. For a real taste of yesteryear, you'll find a number of firms now producing replica beams in glass fibre. Cast in moulds taken from genuinely ancient timbers, these are almost uncannily realistic – they even have woodworm holes – yet they are not too expensive, and could hardly be easier to install. Being extremely lightweight, in most cases, the larger beams just snap on to special clips screwed to the existing ceiling, while the smaller members are usually glued in place. Some manufacturers even offer

advice on how to arrange their products to be both architecturally and historically accurate. Having said that, though, it must be said that no amount of antique woodwork (however genuine) will turn a modern suburban 'semi' into a Tudor cottage. This sort of treatment is therefore best reserved for homes that already have a fair measure of olde worlde character and charm.

But some beamed effects do work in more modern looking homes. It's all a matter of choosing obviously modern looking beams, treating them in a modern way, and arranging for the rest of the room's decor to complete the effect. The simplest of these 'modern' beam treatments is to merely fix a series of parallel softwood battens to the ceiling's surface, screwing or nailing them to the existing ceiling joists – running the beams at right-angles to the joists makes this easier. By varying the size of timber used, and the way in which beams and ceiling are coloured, you can exercise considerable control over the finished effect. Even the type of timber used – whether planed or rough sawn – can make a difference.

Alternatively, consider fixing beams well below the level of the existing ceiling, notching their ends into timber wall-plates screwed to opposite walls at the appropriate level. This is essentially the same structure as you would use to support a genuine, clad suspended ceiling, except that you omit to add the cladding. If you paint the ceiling above the beams in a suitably dark colour, the result has just as great an effect on the room's perceived height, yet works out at a fraction of the cost of a full suspended ceiling. As a variation on the idea, consider introducing climbing plants into the arrangement to give it something of the flavour of an outdoor pergola. One tip: support the centres of the beams not with vertical timber hangers, but with lengths of stout galvanised wire twisted around large screw-eyes set into the beams and original ceiling joists. Timber hangers would be visible through the beams and could ruin the effect.

For a pseudo suspended ceiling with an even more outdoor flavour, why not make use of ordinary garden trellis – with or without the addition of suitable indoor climbing plants. This is so light there is really no need to provide it with a supporting timber framework. Instead, merely hang it on lengths of stout wire fixed to the existing ceiling's joists via large screw-eyes. With the trellis painted in a different colour to the ceiling above, the effect can be really very striking.

Remember, too, that there is no need to hang trellis over the entire ceiling area. Experiment with simply hanging a section in the centre of the ceiling to give the surface a split level look. And there is no need to stop at using just a single island of trellis. If you wish, you can dot sections of trellis

FITTING AN ILLUMINATED CEILING

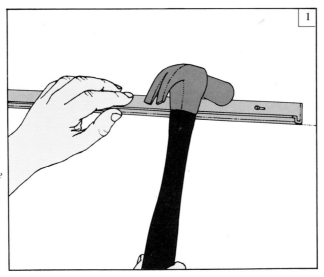

1 & 2 *Decide on the height at which the ceiling is to be fixed, and draw a true horizontal line all round the room at this level. Then nail the perimeter battens to the wall with masonry pins, and position the main cross bearers by resting them on the perimeter battens at the required spacing.*

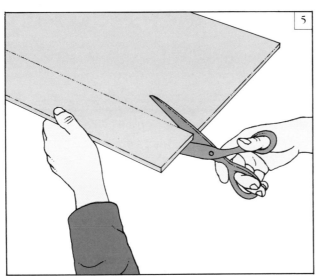

3 & 4 *Next, lay in the short transverse bearers, resting them on the flanges of the main cross bearers — again at the required spacing. With some systems, small clips are used to hold these transverse bearers in position. You can then offer up the whole tiles through the openings in the grid, and drop them into place on the bearer flanges.*

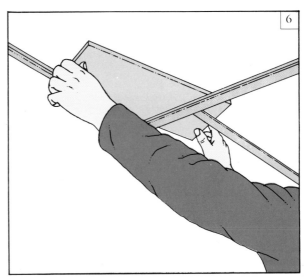

5 & 6 *At the edge of the ceiling, cut narrow filler tiles; you can use scissors on most translucent plastic tiles, but you'll need a sharp knife to cut solid types. Ragged edges will be hidden by the bearer flanges when the pieces are slotted into their final positions.*

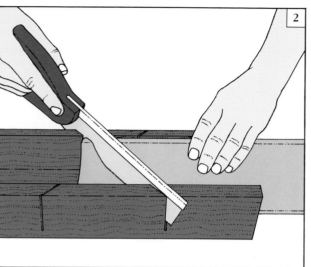

FITTING COVING

1 & 2 *Before starting to fix coving in place, mark a line on the walls to indicate the position of the coving's lower edge and strip wallpaper from the area above it. Then cut a mitre at one end of the first length to be fixed.*

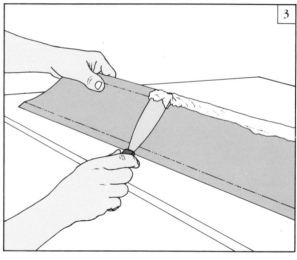

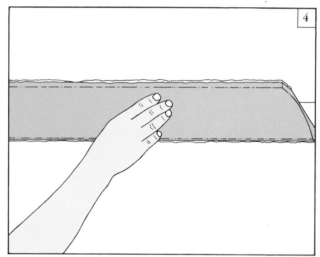

3 & 4 *Butter the coving adhesive onto the rear edges of the length. Then offer the mitred end up to the corner of the room and press it firmly into position. Hold it for a few seconds to allow the adhesive to grip, and if necessary support it with partly-driven masonry pins.*

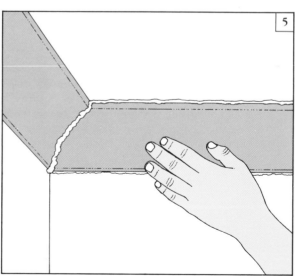

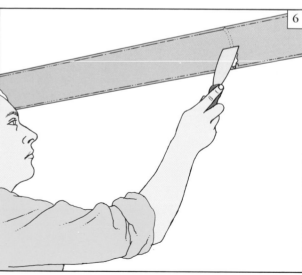

5 & 6 *Complete internal corners by offering up a second length with its mitre cut in the opposite direction. Butter some adhesive onto the mitred end and push the length into position to form a neat join. Add further square-edged lengths as required, and finish off by neatening joins and removing excess adhesive from ceiling and wall surfaces.*

around the room. Come to that, there is no reason why you should limit yourself to using trellis in this way. You can use a solid material such as plasterboard, or tongued and grooved matchboarding if you like. Obviously these heavier materials will need the support of a reasonably substantial timber framework – fixing the panels to stout battens supported entirely by timber hangers screwed to the original ceiling's joists will do in most cases – but the treatment can be made to do more than merely partially alter the ceiling level. Just think of all the possibilities for concealed lighting that it opens up.

There are a number of other variations you might consider, too. For example, having installed the necessary supporting timberwork for a full-scale suspended ceiling you could clad it with timber slats. Bear in mind that they don't have to run in boringly parallel rows. You could clad different areas of the ceiling with battens running in different directions to create a variety of geometric patterns – a basketweave or herringbone design, sequences of concentric mitred squares, concentric diamond patterns, and so on. Even simply running the battens diagonally is worth a try. Carry the diagonal theme a stage further and you could cover the ceiling with dramatic chevrons. And there are dozens of other options.

Another possibility is to fit a different sort of suspended ceiling – what's known as an illuminated ceiling. This consists basically of translucent plastic tiles (available in a variety of colours) supported below the level of the original ceiling on a metal grid (usually aluminium), and the idea is that, by installing fluorescent lighting above this, you illuminate the entire ceiling surface, turning it into a sort of cross between a giant light and a glass roof. If that's a little too much for your taste, then you can tone it down by introducing opaque fibre acoustic tiles into the arrangement. Or you can use opaque tiles throughout, though in this case you may find the result rather too reminiscent of shops, offices and factories.

Whichever type of tile you choose, you will find the system remarkably easy to install. Basically, all you do is screw steel L-shaped bars to the walls at the desired level, and use these to support T-shaped bars spaced a tile width apart which run right across the room – over long runs these may need additional support from vertical hanger bars or wires. The grid is then completed by the addition of shorter T-bars fitted at right angles to the main cross members to create square or rectangular bays ready to receive the tiles. Normally the whole assembly either clips together or else is held in place by its own weight, but different systems vary in detail, so do refer to the normally quite comprehensive instructions supplied by the manufacturer when you buy.

Even simple cornices and covings can make a surprising difference to the look of the ceiling. Available in a variety of styles and materials – wood, plaster, glass fibre, and expanded polystyrene – they are very easy to fix. Timber mouldings are simply pinned in place, while the rest are generally stuck on to the wall with a suitable adhesive. And if you are using mouldings to create a period look, you can

complete the effect with a matching ceiling centre. The majority these days are in expanded polystyrene or glass fibre, and are fixed in exactly the same way as the coving.

Finally, what about using fabric as a ceiling ornament? It's lightness makes it very easy to fix in place, and as well as providing a simple yet effective way of introducing both colour and pattern into the upper reaches of the room, there is no denying that, no matter how inexpensive the fabric you are using, it always gives the room an atmosphere of luxury, if not outright decadence. And of course it's hard to think of a simpler way to lower the ceiling height in order to give the room a more cosy atmosphere; all of which combine to make fabric an excellent choice for bedrooms.

One of the simplest effects to achieve is to take long, fairly narrow strips of light, open weave fabric, and merely drape them across the room in a series of airily billowing parallel stripes, each set slightly apart from its neighbour. If you like, allow the ends of each stripe to hang loosely down the face of the wall. Strips of plain muslin about 450mm (18in) wide are ideal here. If you wish, you can dye them to suit the room's colour scheme. This treatment, incidentally, usually works best in very simply furnished rooms, decorated in light, sunny colours, giving the room something of the feel of an outdoor pavilion.

Alternatively, consider draping shorter lengths of fabric between poles hung from screw eyes driven into the ceiling joists by stout cord. A wider fabric tends to look most effective. Sew deep open hems at each end to receive the poles – decorative curtain poles, lengths of dowel or broomstick, or lengths of bamboo.

Fixing lengths of fabric to the walls at picture rail height or lower and then gathering them all up to a single fixing point in the centre of the ceiling (preferable culminating around a central pendant light) to create a sort of tent, is another popular treatment. It's usually combined with suitable wall hangings, oriental rugs and lots of floor cushions to create sort of Hollywood pastiche of an Arabian harem. But that's up to you.

Do bear in mind that you don't have to carry any of the above treatments across the entire ceiling. Using them over just part of the room can sometimes be equally effective. The ceiling immediately above the bed is an obvious candidate for this sort of partial treatment. For example, you can use either of the first two drape effects to create something of the impression of a four-poster, or you could simply construct the imaginary tent to enclose just the bed.

Whatever you decide, and you can really let your imagination have full rein, there are a few practical points to consider concerning the use of fabric in this sort of situation. First and foremost, think about safety. Since it is not always possible to buy fire-resistant cloth, you should at least make sure that you do all you can to stop a fire starting. In particular, watch the positioning of fabrics in relation to lights. Keep them a safe distance apart. Secondly, although there is nothing to stop you securing fabric to walls and ceilings with a hammer and some tacks, you will undoub-

tedly find a heavy-duty staple gun a lot more convenient. Quite apart from the fact that stapling is quicker and involves less effort, the use of a staple gun will also leave you with one hand free to position the fabric, mould in pleats and tasteful festoons, and so on. Finally, do allow for the fact that fabric drapes are likely to collect quite a lot of dust in a fairly short time. You should therefore at least make sure that the arrangement allows access for cleaning with a vac-

uum cleaner. It is also well worth fixing the fabric with a view to being able to take it down again fairly easily — another plus for the staple gun. It will, after all, need washing from time to time, and there is also the possibility that you might tire of its novelty and fancy a change. Having fixed it in a semi-temporary sort of way, you should be able to remove it without disturbing the rest of the room's decorations.

A heavily-panelled and stained ceiling **above left** *contrasts with pale pine-clad walls.*

A simple tented fabric ceiling **above** *brings a light, airy feel to this dining room.*

FINISHING TOUCHES

Having now looked at all the major decorating materials and the various techniques for applying them, it is worth remembering that a room's decor does not end with paint, paper, and flooring. On the contrary, in many cases it's the details that you put into the room after your decorating equipment is packed away that really make the difference between good decor and a room that is merely proficiently decorated.

Curtains & upholstery

Perhaps the most obvious, and important, of these 'details' is the room's furniture, and soft furnishings. In particular, it is vital that they fit in well with the overall colour scheme.

This doesn't necessarily mean you have to buy new furniture each time you redecorate. Some upholstery fabrics go equally well with a variety of colour combinations. All you need do is select the room's colour scheme accordingly. Even if you feel you really must alter the furniture's colour and pattern, there are cheaper ways to set about it. Wooden and metal items, for example, can be repainted, or stripped and then stained and/or varnished. Upholstered furniture, too, can be given a bright new facelift. Merely adding new cushions will some times do the trick, but for a more drastic change consider transforming them with fitted covers in the furnishing fabric of your choice. So long as the furniture isn't too complex in shape, these are surprisingly easy to make up. Basically all you need is a moderate amount of skill with a sewing machine, and a good, specialist book on the subject to show you the ropes.

Existing curtaining can also be given a facelift if you wish. Often, simply having them cleaned and making all necessary repairs to the tape and linings can work wonders. And if they are in reasonably good condition, and you simply want a change of colour, consider dyeing them. Unpick them to remove the lining, and then follow the instructions on the dye's pack. However, do first check that the fabric is suitable. Some synthetics — pleated Tricel, acrylics, and glass fibre, for example — will not take the dye. Think about replacing old linings and curtain tape, too. In the latter case, you can alter the curtains' appearance considerably at the same time by choosing a new tape that gives a slightly different style of pleating. And if you really have to get new curtains? Have a go at making them up yourself. As with loose covers, there is no shortage of literature on the subject, and so long as you are not too ambitious too soon, there is no reason why you shouldn't do an excellent job.

While you are thinking about curtains, don't forget that the curtain track may also benefit from an overhaul. Clean it up, make sure that it works smoothly, and check that any cording is in good condition. Make sure, too, that it is securely fixed to the wall or ceiling. If necessary, refix the

Curtains and other fabric accessories such as bedspreads and cushions add the finishing touches to a room. Here **left** the colours have been chosen to echo those of the wallcovering. The fabric pelmet has been cleverly extended right round the room to draw the eye downwards from a high ceiling.

Upholstery in a neutral colour is in keeping with the light, airy feel of this room **right**. The piping on the cushions picks up the blue of the carpet, while cane and bamboo shelves and accessories suit the style of the room to perfection.

track, drilling fresh holes and using fresh wallplugs to receive the screws.

However, if you have decided to buy new curtains, it is well worth considering buying new curtain track to go with them. You will probably have to in any case if the new curtains are heavier than the old — the existing track may not take the additional weight. There are several different types on the market, made from either plastic or metal, but your choice really depends on just three basic factors. First, there is the track's strength to consider. Heavy curtains need strong track. Second, do you want a cord operated track, or are you happy to draw the curtains by hand. And finally, where the track will show, does it suit the style of the room. Would curtain poles look better? If they would but you have always chosen track because you want cord operation, consider buying a corded track designed to look like a pole. There are now quite a few on the market.

Having chosen the track, make sure you fix it correctly. It must be absolutely level — check this with a spirit-level — and securely anchored to the wall, ceiling, or window frame, as appropriate. For a wall fixing, use screws and wall-plugs. If drilling the required number of holes proves too tedious, screw and plug a timber batten to the wall, and then fix the track's brackets to that. For a ceiling fixing, drive woodscrews into the joists. If these don't happen to be in the right place, bridge them on the underside of the ceiling with a timber batten, screw the batten to the joists, then screw the curtain track to the batten. If fitting to the window frame, screw directly into the frame if possible. Failing that — and it may be that the frame timbers are too small to accept the brackets — screw them to a batten fixed to the underside of the window reveal using screws and wallplugs. There is one further point to watch. If you are fixing to a batten laid over masonry, make sure the timber is thick enough to accommodate the full length of the track bracket's screws.

Blinds

Naturally, curtains are far from the only option when it comes to decorating windows. In many cases, blinds are not only better looking, but also considerably more practical. In a kitchen or bathroom, for example, most blinds tend to stand up far better to the humid conditions than any curtaining.

There are, of course, a number of different types of blind to choose from. Roller blinds are generally simplest and cheapest. Available in a wide range of sizes, materials and designs, you should have little difficulty in finding ones suitable for virtually every room in the house. Although the majority are sold made to measure, roller blinds are widely sold in kit form, too, though unless the kit allows you to use your own fabric — with the aid of a stiffening spray — this does rather limit your choice of design.

Venetian blinds are another traditional choice, but give you rather greater control over the amount of light entering the room. You can either tilt the slats, or pull the blind up completely out of the way. It's true that the difficulty of

cleaning the slats places a question mark over their use in the kitchen, but elsewhere in the house they can really help give a room a touch of class. Just look at some of the most modern versions aimed at the domestic market. Made to measure in a good range of really striking colours, they are a far cry from the drab 'office grey' venetian blinds you are probably familiar with.

Alternatively, consider vertical louvre blinds. These are almost, but not quite, venetian blinds hung on their sides — the operating mechanism is, in fact, rather different, and they have rather wider slats, generally made of plastic or fabric. You will find these particularly good for very large glazed areas — patio doors being their real forte. Like venetian blinds, they are normally sold made to measure.

For a slightly more decorative effect, consider roman blinds, or one of the really ornate, frilly festoon blinds. The former are drawn up in straight pleats when you pull the cord to open them; the latter are gathered up in billowing swags. Look out, too, for the many other variations on the pleated blind theme — normally made from translucent paper or plastic. And don't forget about roll-up blinds made from split cane.

Simple accessories and smart pleated blinds give this room a cool, uncluttered air **far left**. *The plants provide living highlights to an otherwise neutral colour scheme.*

An all-white colour scheme **above left**, *extended to include the roller blinds as well, calls for simple furnishings — wicker chairs complement it perfectly.*

Cleverly concealed lighting and a slimline venetian blind add to the air of cool, streamlined efficiency in this modern kitchen **left**.

But whatever you choose, do make sure that you fit it properly. To begin with, make sure that the blind is the right size for the window. If you are buying a made-to-measure blind, make sure you measure up accurately in the manner specified by the blind manufacturer. If you are buying off-the-shelf, make sure that the blind is either exactly the right size, or slightly large and capable of being cut down. And do remember that it is not only the width you have to worry about. The length of the blind is also important.

Having got a blind that fits, fixing it is generally just a matter of screwing brackets to either the window frame itself, or to the underside of the window reveal's soffit — with most blinds you can choose whichever is the more convenient. In both cases, make sure that when the blind is hung on its brackets it will be absolutely horizontal. You can easily check this with a spirit level when working out where to drill the holes that take the fixing screws, but watch out if you have decided on a soffit fixing — the window opening may well be out of true. With most blinds, a slight discrepancy shouldn't matter too much, but if the soffit is badly awry, or if you are hanging a blind that might object to being put up on a slope (with a vertical louvre, for example, gravity could cause the blind to open or close of its own volition) you must take steps to correct the fault.

How you do this mainly depends on how many fixings you need to make in the soffit. If it is just a couple, merely insert packing pieces of thin card beneath one of the brackets as you screw it into place to leave it level with its twin. Where several fixings are required, screw a timber batten to the soffit, packing out behind this as necessary to level it, then screw the blind to the batten. Any unsightly gap between batten and soffit can be concealed with caulking or interior filler.

Once the brackets are securely in place, normally all you do is hook the blind on to them, and check to see that it works properly. However, do read the manufacturer's instructions to find out exactly how the blind should be fitted and if there is anything else you have to do in the way of adjustments to make the thing work properly. For example, roller blinds have to be correctly tensioned to run up and down smoothly.

Lighting

The lighting is another important 'detail', and one that is often sadly neglected. The fact is that, in terms of its effect on the decor, there is a lot more to a good lighting scheme than buying pretty light fittings which fit the style and colour scheme of the room. You have to think about the effect on the room of the light provided by those fittings. Will it be attractive? Will you be able to vary the effect to suit the occasion? Will it be practical? Will it be safe? Finding the answers to these questions requires detailed planning, and although the choice of fittings does come into that planning process, it should come at the very end.

Now obviously, learning to design lighting schemes properly, having regard to all of the many factors that must

Lighting should not only illuminate the room and any task being carried out in it, it should also reflect the style of the room and its furnishings. In this ornate bathroom **right** the brass fittings and glass shades are in perfect harmony with the decorations.

The most unusual feature of this room **far left** is the use of fabric for both the walls and the pleated window blind. The floor-to-ceiling mirrors round the fireplace help lighten what could otherwise be an oppressive colour scheme, while the pale upholstery provides a natural focal point.

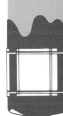

be taken into consideration, could take you years. It would certainly take an entire book to explain how to do it. However, follow a few simple guidelines, and combine them with ideas gleaned from books, magazines, other peoples' houses and so on, and there is no reason why you should not come up with a fairly respectable scheme. Build up to it one step at a time.

Start by thinking about background lighting — lighting that lets you see where you are going. Ceiling mounted fittings and ordinary pendant lights are the usual choice here, and very effective they are, too. But, with the possible exception of a workroom, such as a kitchen, and stairwells where your ability to see where you are going is obviously vital to your safety, don't try using them to light the whole room in one go. The result is at best flatly boring; at worst stark, and altogether very unhomely. Instead, keep this sort of background lighting to a fairly low level. Better still, control the relevant lights with dimmer switches so that you can vary the intensity of background light to meet your needs at the time.

Next, think about what you need in the way of purely practical lighting — lighting that lets you see what you are doing. In the bedroom and living room, for example, do you need reading lights, and if so, how many and where? In the kitchen, does the overhead light really illuminate the working surfaces or would some additional lighting help? Is a separate light needed above the dining table? As far as reading lamps are concerned, the most important thing to decide on when choosing the fittings that will do the job is brightness. Ideally, you should arrive at a compromise. You need a light that's bright enough for you to see with absolute clarity, yet not so bright that the reflected glare off the page quickly tires your eyes.

With more general purpose working lights you must also try to avoid positioning the lamps so that shadows are cast across whatever it is you are doing. For this reason, you may find the overhead light in a kitchen rather unsatisfactory as a working light. Standing at the worktops laid out round the room, you tend to have your back to it, and so are constantly working in your own shadow. A better solution might be to provide both general and working light with downlighters — cylindrical lights mounted into or on to the ceiling so that they illuminate only the area immediately beneath them — arranging them in rows directly above the most used worktops. Alternatively, supplement the background lighting with fluorescent or tungsten strip lights mounted on the undersides of the wall cupboards.

You should also think about what is perhaps best described as the lighting position's permanency. For example, above a workbench, do you want a light that pushes out of the way when you have finished the close work and are moving on to something that requires a little more elbow room? In this sort of situation, consider clip-on spotlights and desk lamps. Elsewhere, spotlight and table lamps of all sorts can be pressed into service. It is also worth thinking about the lighting position's permanency in terms of how often you need it. For instance, you may need a bright work-

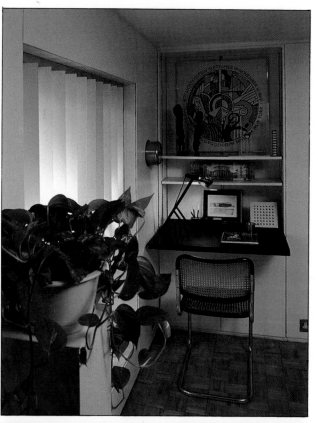

Simplicity in colour scheming is often all that is needed in a perfectly proportioned period room. Here a plain fabric wallcovering **right** *matches the curtains and complements the rich colour of the polished floorboards.*

Black and silver colour highlights **left** *stand out in stark contrast against white walls and a pale parquet floor.*

Shelving can be eye-catching too. Here **left** *an alcove has been fitted with concealed lighting to show off the ornaments within it, and the shelves have been decorated with the same wallpaper as the rest of the room.*

Pale varnished cork provides the perfect backdrop for an unusual collection of treasures, and the effect is matched by the use of handmade trelliswork in the partition leading to the entrance hall.

and dramatic shadows; lights that break the room up into cosy, well defined areas, and so on. The possibilities are almost endless here, and there is no shortage of hardware on the market designed to create purely decorative lighting effects. There are ordinary wall lights designed to make a contribution to the background lighting. There are wall lights, wall washers, and spotlights that allow you to transform the look of plain walls by flooding them with light. There are uplighters and downlighters, designed respectively to throw a pool of light on to the ceiling and floor. And there are straightforward table lamps and floor lamps which, thanks to the beauty of their shades, can act almost as lit sculptures as well as performing any number of the lighting functions already mentioned.

Having worked out the basic elements of the room's lighting scheme, try to imagine how they will work together in concert, in all the various combinations made possible by turning some lights off while leaving others on. The greater your ability to conduct the lighting like an orchestra in order to transform the mood and appearance of the room, the better. Which, of course, raises the subject of controls. In general, it's a case of the more the merrier. But don't just restrict yourself to straightforward on/off switches. Consider two-way switching arrangements that allow you to control the same lights from two or more different parts of the room or house. Think about dimmer switches that give you the ability to fine tune the parts of your lighting orchestra, increasing its versatility still further. There are also a great many specialized switches that may be of use — remote control switches, and security timer switches, for example.

And what about safety? The most important point is to make sure that if the new lighting scheme involves making any alterations to your home's wiring (and it almost certainly will) they are carried out by a qualified electrician. Secondly, when choosing lights and switches for the bathroom, make sure they are safe, or the electrician simply won't fit them. Basically, if you stick to lights specifically designed for bathrooms, have them permanently wired in (you cannot have plugs and power sockets in bathrooms), and control them using a cord-operated pull switch, you should be alright, though there are obviously a number of more detailed rules in the electrical regulations. And finally, do remember what we said earlier about lighting staircases. To reduce the risk of people tripping, these must be adequately lit, preferably in such a way that the treads of the staircases are made still more obvious by the shadows they cast. Do take care, though, if you are using spotlights or other fittings with exposed bulbs to do the job. If these are positioned where people using the stairs might be dazzled, they could be as dangerous as having no lights at all.

ing light in order to operate the stereo or video recorder, but for most of the time, that light will be sitting around doing nothing. An easily adjustable spotlight could be the answer. When not needed as a working light its versatile beam can be directed elsewhere to play some other role in the lighting scheme.

The next step is to consider lights whose purpose is partly practical and partly decorative. These are lights used to highlight particular objects or collections of objects — lights pinpointing your favourite picture, or illuminating a collection of ornaments on a shelf. In many cases, spotlights are again a good choice for this sort of job, but there are other possibilities. Shelf and cabinet lighting for example, could be provided by small tungsten or fluorescent strip lights partially concealed by being mounted on the undersides of the shelves. Strip lights can also be used to illuminate pictures on the wall, and in fact you will find wall mounted lights specially designed for the purpose.

Finally, taking into account the effect of all of the above types of lighting on the room, think about installing lights that have a purely decorative value — lights that highlight certain features within the room, lights that cast interesting

Hardware

To complete the transformation of your rooms, give some thought to the hardware detailing.

The doors, for example, might well benefit from some new door furniture — door furniture more in keeping with

Bare brick and natural timber **above** *frame this fireplace attractively, allowing the enamelled cast iron stove and brightly polished steel fender to catch the eye.*

The strong colours in the curtains are complemented by the painted spiral staircase **above right**. *The unusual fish mural gives an illusion of descending into deep water.*

the new decor. There is an enormous variety to choose from here with knobs, handles finger plates, escutcheon plates, kick plates, key hole covers, lavatory latches, name plates and much more besides widely available in materials as diverse as gold plate and porcelain — though for those without a bottomless bank account, brass, aluminium, steel and plastic are the normal choices – and in styles ranging from ornate reproduction period pieces to modern fittings so sleek and brightly coloured as to be almost futuristic. Take a wander round a good specialist hardware store to get a taste of what's on offer. Walking into one of the better outlets is like entering an Aladdin's cave for interior designers.

The room's windows can also be improved with new catches and window stays. But don't forget the security aspect when choosing. In the average house a window is to a burglar what the front door is to you, so make sure that all windows on the ground floor, together with any on the upper storeys that can be reached by climbing extensions, drainpipes, and so on, are fitted with good quality window locks of some sort. Lockable stays, cockspur handles, and catches are best for the windows you use most frequently.

Elsewhere less convenient security devices such as dual screws (which literally screw the window to the frame) are more economical.

External doors also need good security. Although the majority can be adequately protected by a reasonable lock and a good bolt at top and bottom, the door by which you normally come and go (the 'front door') needs something more sophisticated – you cannot bolt it shut from the outside. Consider a good cylinder rim lock backed up by a mortise lock and a door chain as the bare minimum.

Door and window furniture isn't the only type of hardware you should be thinking about. In the hall and bathroom, think about adding bright new coat hooks. In the bathroom and kitchen, consider changing the taps to give baths, basins, and sinks a brand new look. Lavatories and bathrooms also give you the opportunity to introduce a great deal more hardware that is not only practical, but also helps add interest to the decor. There are towel rails, toilet roll holders, toothbrush holders, medicine cabinets, shaver sockets, soap dishes and more besides. Again, look round a good specialist hardware store, department store or 'designer' store to see what's on offer.

GLOSSARY

Acoustic tiles
Made either of porous mineral fibre or perforated metal trays with glass backing, they provide an efficient sound-proofing layer.

All-surface paints
Resin-based paints for use on any interior surface.

Architrave
Moulded decorative frame surrounding a window or door.

Artex
Trade name for the most widely known textured finish for walls and ceilings. It is sold in powder form for mixing with water.

Base colour
Foundation or background colour of a design. Sometimes referred to as the 'ground colour'.

Beading
A narrow, decorative edging strip.

Bevel
Literally a slanting edge, as in the shape of a chisel blade.

Brick tiles
Wafer-thin pieces of brick fired in the same way as real bricks. They can be bedded in mortar or tile adhesive.

Butt joint
A joint where the two edges touch but do not overlap.

Carpet squares
Pieces of carpet with finished edges, made in rectangular, round and oval shapes.

Carpet tiles
Small sections of carpet which are a cross between wall-to-wall carpets and tile flooring. Most are laid loose.

Chalkline
A chalk-coated piece of string which is pulled taut across a surface and then snapped to leave an accurate guide line.

Chamfer
An acute edge or corner smoothed to a 45 degree angle.

Cladding
Generic term for any type of profiled wooden board suitable for interior and exterior walls as a decorative finish.

Cornice and coving
A cornice is an ornamental moulding fixed in the angle between a room wall and ceiling. Coving is just a simple curve linking the two surfaces. Both were traditionally formed in situ, but now are almost always pre-fabricated.

Countersink
To expand the outer edge of a previously drilled hole into a cone shape so that a screw-head can be sunk below the surface.

Crossing off (see Laying off)

Cutting in
Applying paint into an angle or onto a narrow surface such as a glazing bar.

Dado rail
A rail fixed to the lower half of the wall above the skirting-board.

Distemper
Method of painting on plaster or chalk, using colours mixed with egg yolk or size.

Dowel
Metal or wooden pins used to secure and strengthen a joint.

Downlighters
Recessed spotlights in the ceiling that cast light downwards.

Dragging
A special paint effect achieved by dragging a dry brush over wet paint.

Eggshell paint
The term used to describe oil-based paints that dry to a matt-like finish.

Emulsion paint
A mixture of pigments and binders suspended as an emulsion in water. After the paint is applied, the water in it evaporates and the binders coalesce as a continuous surface film.

Expanded polystyrene
A lightweight decorating material produced in a wide range of surface effects and sold mainly as tiles.

Flush
The term used to describe two perfectly level adjacent surfaces.

Friezes and borders
A frieze is a horizontal band of decoration (usually printed wallpaper) hung round a room just below the junction between wall and ceiling. A border is similar and is used to form decorative surrounds on a wall or ceiling. Both are sold in rolls.

Gloss paint
The traditional paint for woodwork and metal, it is made from synthetic resins that are hard-wearing and resistant to yellowing. When the paint is applied it dries partly by evaporation and partly by a chemical reaction to form a hard, continuous film.

Galvanized
Zinc-coated metal which resists rusting.

Glue size
Thinned adhesive used to seal walls and ceilings prior to wallpapering.

Grasscloth
A luxury wallcovering consisting of strands of natural grasses bound lightly into a mat on a paper backing.

Grouting
A waterproof 'mortar' used to fill the joints between ceramic and mosaic tiles.

Gypsum
Calcium sulphate used to make plaster.

Gypsum-board
A form of plasterboard.

Hessian
A popular, paper-backed, coarse fabric wallcovering.

Illuminated ceiling
A suspended ceiling consisting of a geometric framework of lightweight battens, fixed below an existing ceiling, which carry translucent panels lit from above, usually by fluorescent lights.

Jute
A coarse fabric wallcovering, a little like hessian and hung in the same way.

Key
The process of roughening a surface to improve adhesion before painting or plastering.

Lacquer
A type of paint used mainly on metal; clear lacquer prevents metals such as copper and brass from tarnishing. Lacquer dries by evaporation only, leaving a hard but brittle surface film. It is best applied with a spray gun.

Lagging
The insulating material used to cover tanks and pipes to prevent heat escaping.

Laminates
Plastic laminates are made by bonding together layers of resin-impregnated paper to form a sheet. The topmost layer is clear, and protects the layer beneath which carries the design.

Laying off
The uniform direction of finishing brushstrokes as well as the application of them; with most types of paint it should be done towards the light.

Lining paper
Plain paper used on walls and ceilings to provide a uniform, even surface on which other wallcoverings can be hung. It is particularly suitable for cracked, uneven surfaces or those already decorated with gloss paint.

Marbling
A decorative effect created with a brush or crushed newspaper on wet paint.

Matchboarding (see Tongued-and-grooved boards)

Metallic tiles
Small hollow-backed wall tiles, available in a variety of shiny or matt metallic finishes. They are often over-printed with patterns.

Mitre
Cutting the ends of two lengths of wood at a 45 degree angle so that they form a right angle when joined together.

Mortise
A hole in a door framework designed to house the tongue of a lock.

Mosaics
Small pieces of ceramic tile in square, round or interlocking geometric shapes, mounted on a net backing for use on walls and floors.

Moulding
A decorative strip made from a shaped length of wood.

Novamura
An innovative wallcovering made from foamed polyethylene (polythene) and printed with a wide range of patterns and designs. No paper is involved in its manufacture.

Panelling
Wood or man-made boards used to decorate walls and ceilings.

Parquet
Floorcovering of small hardwood pieces or blocks laid in a pattern such as herringbone or basketweave. Originally laid block by block, parquet is now sold in panels with several blocks stuck together, sanded down and sealed.

Plasterboard
A sheet of plaster covered on either side with stiff paper. One side of the board is finished and can be used without further treatment.

Plastic laminate (see Laminates)

Polythene wallcovering (see Novamura)

Polyurethane varnish
A special varnish for wood and board materials, made with polyurethane resins which form a harder, more durable surface film than traditional oil varnishes.

Primer
Paint used to seal and key a surface before the application of an undercoat.

Pumice
A light, porous volcanic rock used for polishing and scrubbing shiny surfaces.

Quarry tiles
Unglazed ceramic floor tiles made chiefly in red, brown and buff shades with a pleasant rustic look. They are usually laid in a mortar bed and the surface is sealed or polished.

Ragging
A three-dimensional paint effect achieved by passing a crumpled rag over wet paint.

Relief wallcovering
A wallcovering with a three-dimensional surface, regularly or randomly patterned, and designed to be over-painted.

Rendering
The coat of plaster covering a brick or stone wall.

Retarder
A colourless gel agent mixed with some water-based paints to retard their drying time by inhibiting evaporation.

Satin paints
Resin- or water-based (emulsion) paints that dry to a film with a surface sheen resembling satin.

Screed
A floor-levelling layer of cement-based material.

Screed bead
A wire mesh strip, straight or angled, used to strengthen corners before plastering or to hide holes in plaster walls.

Scrim
A strong, woven material used to hide plasterboard joins.

Scumbling
A variant of stippling.

Self-adhesive plastic film
A printed plastic sheet material used as a wallcovering. It is coated on the back with adhesive and protected with a backing paper that is removed just before use.

Shiplap
Type of wall cladding, consisting of profiled wooden boards fitted horizontally so that the lower edge of one board overlaps the upper edge of the board below.

Silk paint
Resin- or water-based (emulsion) paint that dries to a silky finish. Also called satin paint.

Silk wallcovering
Luxury wallcovering of fine silk in a variety of colours bonded to a paper backing.

Spattering
Spraying paints in different colours onto wet paint to create a multi-coloured look.

Sponging
Applying layer after layer of paint with a sponge, usually combining opaque and translucent colours.

Stencils
Thin sheets of paper or card punched with a design that is reproduced on other surfaces by laying on the stencil and applying paint through the cut-out parts.

Stippling
Using a sharp, stiff-bristled brush to create a pattern that resembles fine grit.

Swag
An elaborate treatment for hanging curtains so that the material falls in a series of elegant curves.

Template
A piece of paper or card, cut to a specific shape and used as an outline for cutting the same shape from another material.

Textured emulsion paint
Emulsion paint, usually white, with added fillers that make it thick enough to produce a definite surface texture before it dries.

Textured finishes
Ready-mixed or powder products used to give indoor walls and ceilings a textured surface. The mixture is applied with a brush or spatula and then given a regular or random texture using a variety of techniques before it sets.

Tipping off
Touching the tips of brush bristles on the side of a paint kettle to eject excess paint from them.

Toggle
Small metal screw with wings. The wings open out when pushed through a hole in a partition wall to hold the screw in place.

Tongued-and-grooved boards
Strips of softwood with a tongue machined along one edge and a groove along the other so that adjacent planks interlock.

Transfers
Decorative motifs used to enliven walls or furniture.

Underlay
A layer of strong material laid under a carpet to provide added protection.

Veneer
An external layer of attractive timber applied to a strong wood core.

Wallboards
Man-made boards or panels used to line walls and ceilings. Usually made of thin plywood or hardboard, one side is covered with a decorative finish.

Wallplug
Expandable screw encasement, inserted into a drill hole to help the screw grip. It can be cut to length.

Wash
A thinned coat of colour applied all over a surface, either over another paint or as a mist coat when emulsion is applied to new plaster.

Wet-and-dry
Abrasive paper designed to smooth a surface with alternate applications of lubricated and dry abrasion.

INDEX

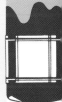

PICTURE CREDITS

Unless otherwise indicated, all photographs are by Rose Jones.

(l—left: r—right: c—centre: t—top: b—bottom)

ICI DULUX — 10/11b (*Walls and ceiling:* English rose, vinyl matt from the Dulux Colour Collections. *Cornice and piping on alcove:* Rose White, vinyl matt from the Dulux Soft Shades of White. *Door, skirting and door surround:* Rose White Gloss. *Piping on door:* Ballet 1041 gloss from the Dulux Matchmaker Range.) 11t (*Walls:* Miranda 1338 vinyl matt from the Dulux Matchmaker range. *Skirting and borders:* Pure Brilliant White, gloss.) 34 (*Walls:* Wheatmeal, vinyl matt from the Dulux Colour Collections. *Ceiling and cornice:* Apricot White, vinyl matt from the Dulux Soft Shades of White range. *Doors:* Sandalwood silthane silk from the Dulux Colour Collections. *Door surrounds & skirting:* Apricot White, gloss from the Dulux Soft Shades of White range.) 36 (*Walls:* Soft Peach, vinyl matt from the Dulux Colour Collections. *Ceiling:* Apricot White, vinyl matt, from the Dulux Soft Shades of White range. *Woodwork:* Apricot White, gloss. *Cornice:* Sandalwood, silthane silk, from the Dulux Colour Collections. *Fireplace:* Marbling effect, Crumpet 1171, Whisper 1563, Chantilly 1120 in silthane silk from the Dulux Matchmaker range.) 37 (*Ceiling, cornice, dado & skirting:* Pure Brilliant White, vinyl matt. *Walls above dado:* Bolero 1067, vinyl matt from the Dulux Matchmaker range. *Walls below dado:* Morello 1349, vinyl matt from the Dulux Matchmaker range. *Stencil:* Argosy 1026, vinyl matt from the Dulux Matchmaker range.)

Elizabeth Whiting and Associates — 6 Michael Dunne. 10/11t M Dunne. 11br Spike Powell. 12 M Dunne. 13t Michael Nicholson, br S Powell, bl Jerry Tubby. 14t M Dunne, b Clive Helm. 15 Graham Henderson. 17tl C Helm, tc M Dunne, tr J Tubby, cl C Helm, cr Steve Colby, bl M Nicholson, c Tom Leighton, r M Dunne. 18 Tim Street-Porter. 19t S Powell, b T Leighton. 23tl HOME IMPROVEMENT, c M Nicholson, r T Street-Porter, cl Julian Nieman, c T Street-Porter, r Neil Lorimer, bl Friedhelm Thomas, c T Street-Porter, r M Dunne. 24 J Tubby. 25tr J Tubby, l S Powell, cl S Powell, bl S Powell, br T Street-Porter. 29tl M Dunne, tc Richard Davies, tr N Lorimer, cl J Tubby, C M Dunne, R T Street-Porter, r M Dunne. 31tl M Dunne, c M Dunne, R N Lorimer, cl M Dunne, c N Lorimer, r N Lorimer, bl Jon Bouchier, c N Lorimer, r N Lorimer. 32tl M Dunne, tr M Nicholson, bl David Cripps, br T Street-Porter. 35 M Dunne. 38t M Dunne, b Gary Chowanetz. 39 M Dunne. 40r C Helm, l T Street-Porter. 62 t & b T Leighton. 97l M Dunne, tr M Nicholson, b M Nicholson. 122 Dennis Stone. 123tl C Helm, tr Eigenhuis, b T Street-Porter, 124l & r S Powell. 141b T Street-Porter. 150 M Dunne. 159 G Chowanetz. 164 C Helm. 165 J Tubby. 168 J Tubby. 174l M Nicholson, r C Helm. 176 M Nicholson. 177 T Leighton. 178 M Nicholson. 179t S Colby, b C Helm. 180 M Dunne. 181 S Powell. 182t M Nicholson, b C Helm. 183 J Bouchier. 184 EWA. 185l J Tubby, r M Nicholson.

ACKNOWLEDGEMENTS

Paul Wharton
David Hammond
Franchi, London
Homebase, Croydon
Hodkin & Jones, London
Andersons, London
ICI Dulux